"Dr. Stuart Dauermann knows what every turtle knows: if you want to get anywhere in life you have to stick your neck out. This he does, in his extremely insightful and provocative new book. . . . Long live the Dauermanns of the world who stick their necks out. Long live the Dauermanns of the world who appreciate the Jewish shell and who are doggedly determined to stay at home in it—over and against the protestations of younger reptiles who don't happen to have a protective, 3,500-year-old home to dwell in. Lastly, long live all who, with Dauermann, want to explore what does really mean to be a 'Jewish' believer in Yeshua/Jesus? Those who don't agree with his answers 100 percent will still agree that he's asking the right questions, and that his answers are serious forces to be reckoned with both now and in the days ahead."

    —JEFFREY L. SEIF, University Distinguished Professor of Bible and Jewish
        Studies, Kings University

Converging Destinies

Converging Destinies

Jews, Christians, and the Mission of God

STUART DAUERMANN

FOREWORD BY CALVIN L. SMITH

CASCADE *Books* · Eugene, Oregon

CONVERGING DESTINIES
Jews, Christians, and the Mission of God

Copyright © 2017 Stuart Dauermann. All rights reserved. Except for brief quotations in critical publications or reviews, no part of this book may be reproduced in any manner without prior written permission from the publisher. Write: Permissions, Wipf and Stock Publishers, 199 W. 8th Ave., Suite 3, Eugene, OR 97401.

Cascade Books
An Imprint of Wipf and Stock Publishers
199 W. 8th Ave., Suite 3
Eugene, OR 97401

www.wipfandstock.com

PAPERBACK ISBN: 978-1-62564-614-9
HARDCOVER ISBN: 978-1-4982-8547-6
EBOOK ISBN: 978-1-4982-4464-0

Cataloguing-in-Publication data:

Names: Dauermann, Stuart.

Title: Converging destinies : Jews, Christians, and the mission of God. / Stuart Dauermann.

Description: Eugene, OR: Cascade Books, 2016 | Includes bibliographical references and indexes.

Identifiers: ISBN 978-1-62564-614-9 (paperback) | ISBN 978-1-4982-8547-6 (hardcover) | ISBN 978-1-4982-4464-0 (ebook)

Subjects: LCSH: 1. Israel—Biblical teaching. | 2. Interfaith relations. | 3. Election (Theology)—Biblical teaching. | 4. Title.

Classification: BS2417.J4 D50 2017 (print) | BS2417 (ebook)

Manufactured in the U.S.A.   MARCH 13, 2017

Chapter 7, "What Is the Gospel We Should Be Commending to All Israel?" is
adapted from a paper delivered October 2007 at the Borough Park Symposium,
Brooklyn, New York, and published in Stuart Dauermann, John Fischer, et al., *The
Borough Park Papers Symposium I: The Gospel and the Jewish People* (Clarksville,
MD: Messianic Jewish Publishers), 2012. Used with permission.

Material from Alan Brill, *Judaism and Other Religions* (London: Palgrave-Macmil-
lan, 2010, 2014) in chapter 3, "Jewish Missiological Perspectives and the Christian
Other," is used with permission.

Dedicated to Sholem Asch, of blessed memory, who paid such a high price for speaking of the converging destines of Jews, Christians, and the mission of God.

Contents

Foreword

by Calvin L. Smith

SEVERAL YEARS AGO A dispensational colleague and I were chatting about the future hope of Israel. During the conversation I mentioned briefly several of the challenges—not least identity issues—facing Jewish believers in Jesus in the present within the wider church. His immediate response was that God's dealings with Israel are reserved for the eschatological era and in the current dispensation Jewish people are like anyone else within the body of Christ, having no distinct identity as a people within the church. He supported this opinion by referring to the first part of the Apostle Paul's famous statement in Galatians 3:28, "There is neither Jew nor Gentile."

I pointed out that Paul also goes on to say in the same verse, "there is neither male nor female." Yet in his other writings he discusses the separate roles of men and women within the Christian family and church body in a manner that clearly indicates the apostle *did* believe in separate male/female identities. Thus, I suggested Paul was not stating that in Christ there is no longer any such thing as Jewish or Gentile identity, just as he was not saying there is no longer a differentiation between the sexes, and Paul was making a slightly different point to that being argued. As my colleague paused for a moment to reconsider his proof-text, I went on to ask why, in a culturally diverse church in which we celebrate African, Asian, Latin American, Roma, or other expressions of faith in Jesus, Jewish identity in Jesus seems somehow to be unique in that for many it should not be celebrated at all, and indeed subsumed within a broader Christian identity.

What is significant here is that someone from a strongly dispensational background, which traditionally supports the view that God retains a plan and future hope for Israel and strongly challenges supersessionism, had not reflected upon Jewish identity in Jesus in the present. Of course, many dispensationalists do *not* think this way (there are many who do celebrate distinctly Jewish expressions of the faith). But my point is, if a champion of Israel and the Jewish people had assumed there was no distinct Jewish identity within the church, it indicates an even wider skepticism among less Israel-enthusiastic Christians.

The fact is, many Christians, among them some of the staunchest Christian Zionists and nonsupersessionists, have given little thought to the matter of the identity of Jewish believers in Jesus within a predominantly Gentile church. Indeed, although raised by parents who taught me from a young age how the Scriptures teach that God has not finished with Israel, it was not until I engaged at some length with supersessionism and in the process came into contact with Messianic believers and thought in a more meaningful way, that I fully began to appreciate the importance of this issue.

It is not just that Jewish believers should, like other groups, have the freedom to worship and practice their faith in Yeshua in a particular cultural manner. The issue runs much deeper than that. For example, God called Israel to serve as his salvific vehicle through which comes our Jewish Messiah. The early church was wholly Jewish, while today's Messianic body (which Paul refers to as the "remnant") represents the continuation of Old Testament Israel. Indeed, they are not only Jewish in an Old Testament sense, but also, according to the Apostle Paul, even more so, theologically speaking, in Christ (Rom 2:9). Why, then, should the wider church expect Messianic believers to hide or subsume their historic and distinct identity as Jewish believers in Jesus?

Meanwhile, Old Testament "Jewishness" involved communal religious observance involving the entire congregation of Israel. Yet does today's church welcome Jewish believers to the extent that it makes room for such communal observance? Some Christians dismiss the issue of Torah observance, too often limiting discussion to a one-dimensional soteriological approach focusing on how the sacrificial Mosaic laws are superseded by Christ's work on the cross. Yet such an approach fails to engage with why some Jewish believers in Jesus are deeply committed to Torah observance (or aspects of it) for other than soteriological reasons based on calling, covenant, and love for God. At the very least Paul seems to suggest that it is eminently proper for some Jewish people who come to a saving knowledge of Yeshua HaMashiach to continue in their communal observances as Jews (1 Cor 7:18).

To summarize, is it reasonable for some Jewish believers to continue to live a life of communal religious observance? And if so, how does this ecclesially work out within a predominantly Gentile church to which Jewish believers belong? What bearing do these issues have on Jewish and Gentile Christian identity and the relationship of both groups one to another? The fact is, although that conversation has been taking place within the

Messianic community for a couple or three decades, within the wider Gentile church it is barely just beginning.

Increasingly the modern Messianic movement is moving beyond a simple expression of Jewish faith in Jesus to a sophisticated engagement with the theological ramifications of what it means to be both Jewish and a believer in Yeshua. It involves a range of issues, for example, grappling with one's relationship to and engagement with a church that has a long history of anti-Judaism at best, and triumphalist punitive supersessionism that has often degenerated into anti-Semitism at worst or how one shares one's faith with Jewish family members suspicious of this long-standing animosity expressed towards the root of the Christian church. Crucial, too, are questions about if and how one engages in an authentic expression of Jewish worship, praxis, and community within a Gentile context. Then there is how all this feeds in to a wider understanding of the canonical narrative, the purposes of God, and the vehicle he has chosen for his plan for humanity. There are those who maintain the concept of a rupture in God's eternal plan, with Israel ditched and replaced part way through the canonical narrative. But arguably much more persuasive (exegetically and theologically) is the concept of continuity beyond the Old Testament to incorporate Israel and the church in God's eternal plan. In short, the issues are not just about identity, worship, praxis, and Jewish-Gentile relationships, but major theological themes that run through the canonical Bible.

Scholarly studies exploring these and related issues are scarce, but a body of literature is slowly emerging (a notable example being Mark Kizer's *Post-Missionary Messianic Judaism*). This is where Stuart Dauermann's invaluable *Converging Destinies* comes in. In this excellent, thoughtful, and sophisticated volume, Dauermann provides readers with a compelling theological treatment of these and related issues. Reading the first chapter alone, one is struck by his intimate involvement at the highest levels with the modern Messianic movement from its infancy through to the present day. Dauermann has also played a key role in shaping the movement's direction and much of its thought. Not only that, he has contributed substantially to practice and worship. Earning a PhD at Fuller Theological Seminary, he also studied music and, in a quest for an authentic Jewish expression of Christian worship, composed some of the early movement's music so widely known today. It is this intimate involvement with the Messianic movement at so many levels throughout most of its modern period that makes Dauermann so highly qualified to write a scholarly work in this important field.

Converging Destinies offers readers a carefully thought-out, systematic, and well-argued approach to these and other related issues. I do not say that I agree *in toto* with Dr. Dauermann's position, although I have a great deal of sympathy for much of what he writes. But that is neither here nor there. What is essential here is that his contribution represents a systematic, thought-out, theologically sophisticated, and absolutely essential part of this much-needed conversation. As such, it represents absolutely must-read material for both Messianic believers grappling with identity and ecclesiological issues as well as a wider Gentile church that needs to begin considering deeply how it responds and relates to the Messianic movement.

In short, this book adds substantially to the limited (but growing) scholarly literature on these issues, and anyone interested in this area simply cannot afford to ignore it. The author's approach is deep and extensive yet interesting and enlightening, thought-provoking yet gentle, to the point, yet sensitive, theologically sophisticated yet wholly practical. I trust you will enjoy reading it and feel all the more enlightened for having done so.

Acknowledgements

LOOKING BACK, AND LOOKING around me, I see so many people to whom I am indebted, whose influence combines to make me who I am and this work what it is. First are my parents, of blessed memory, Herman Dauermann (Chaim ben Yitzchak) and Mary Donato Dauermann (Miriam bat Avraham v'Sarah), who, despite my mother's Orthodox conversion, together with their families, taught me firsthand that the Jewish and Christian worlds more often collide than converge.

There were many mentors along the way. Moishe Rosen, of blessed memory, helped me to converge my faith in Yeshua with a professional trajectory to enrich the Jewish and Christian worlds. And Rachmiel Frydland, also of blessed memory, modeled the sweetness of religious Jewish life and the depth of Jewish piety with a weightiness that rests upon me still.

Arthur Glasser, again of blessed memory, took an interest in me when I was at a mid-life turning point, inviting me to pursue my mid-career MA and PhD in Intercultural Studies just when the invitation was most needed. It was the generosity of Bob and Susan Chenoweth that made this education possible, for which I am forever in their debt.

In addition to Arthur Glasser, my teachers Charles Van Engen, Bobby Clinton, Dan Shaw, and Charles Kraft, of the Fuller Seminary School of Intercultural Studies, shaped me toward who I now am, while leaving plenty of room for me to find my own way—no mean achievement. My colleagues in Hashivenu, the think tank we established in the 1990s, bear special note, for iron has indeed sharpened iron, and we are all better for the association: Ellen Goldsmith, Mark Kinzer, Paul Saal, Rich Nichol, Michael Schiffman, and formerly, Bob Chenoweth.

On the technical side of things, I thank editor Susan Carlson Wood for applying her unerring skills and pastoral touch in helping bring this work to press. Without her, nothing would have been finished.

In addition to these, special friendships sustained me, of whom I name here Randy Northrup, and most of all, my faithful and inspiring wife,

Naomi, and our children, Chaim, Jonathan, and Abigail, who believed in me even when I had trouble doing so.

To all of these and more, unending thanks.

Prologue

A Missiological Biography

FOR TWO MILLENNIA, THE Jewish and Christian communities have defined themselves in contradistinction to each other. But especially since the Shoah and the promulgation of the Vatican II Document *Nostra Aetate* in 1965, both communities have felt compelled to rethink their partisan stance and rhetoric. But "all beginnings are hard."[1] Despite changing times and various influences, Jews and Christians still tend to deal with each other the way porcupines make love: very carefully. This is especially so for community leaders and official bodies.

For fifty years I have found myself manning the intersection between the Christian and Jewish worlds, a participant observer among professionals struggling either to hold the line on old paradigms, or to stretch and redraw boundaries. This book will examine some of these paradigms, and factors contributing to or retarding change. It will suggest a new perspective and paradigm of intercommunal relationship characterized by a proleptic openness to divine reassurance and rebuke. This is based on the conviction that whenever God speaks to his people, his word is always a mixture of such reassurance and rebuke. So shall it be for us now. This paradigm summons both communities to humility and mutual vulnerability under the authority of Scripture and the Divine Presence toward discovering and together serving a new eschatological synergy between two communities historically at odds, but destined in the end for renewal and reconciliation.

To best understand who I am and how and why I came to write this book, two factors need to be kept in mind. First, this is something of a missiological biography. It visits the diverse paradigms of other-group assessment and engagement that I have encountered, employed, or shaped as a Jew among Christians, and a Messianic Jew among Jews. Second, some may

---

1. Midrash Mechilta, Parshat Yitro.

1

choose to label me and my views as "marginal." If so, please go ahead. I accept the characterization. This is my world. Welcome to it![2]

BORN AND RAISED ON THE MARGINS

A useful definition of *marginal* is "one that is considered to be at a lower or outer limit, as of social acceptability."[3] Throughout this volume we will be discovering how aptly this definition applies to how various proponents and "camps" have regarded one another.

I come by my marginality honestly. My father Chaim (or as he was to be known in America, Herman), was the only son of an Orthodox Jewish immigrant family. He "came over on the boat" in third-class steerage, passing through Ellis Island in November of 1912 along with his mother, Shifra, and sister, Raizel, to join his father, Yitzchak, who had come over almost four years earlier. Like other Jews, the Dauermann family knew they were judged marginal long before they left Austria-Hungary to pass under the shadow of Miss Liberty's torch. Even after arriving in "The Goldeneh Medina" ("The Golden Land," the United States) the sense of being "at a lower or outer limit, as of social acceptability" remained a Jewish fact of life. As my father entered the job market at sixteen, some want ads specified "Jews need not apply." To his dying day, this brilliant and perfectionistic accountant would say that he would have gotten further in the corporate culture in which he worked but for the fact that he was a Jew. And as in most matters, he was more likely right than not. Despite a lifelong hunger for acceptance, he lived a life on the margins, "considered to be at a lower or outer limit, as of social acceptability."

It was in the workplace that Herman met Mary, an olive-skinned beauty, one of six children of a Sicilian immigrant family. Mary converted, becoming "Miriam, daughter of Abraham and Sarah," and they married five years before the birth of a daughter, Judith, and twelve years before I came along. We were Conservative Jews, an American modification of the hard-right Orthodoxy of my father's upbringing. His family remained Orthodox, and after the death of his father, every year Chaim had the honor of leading the family seder in Borough Park, where I spent every Shabbat in my youth, except for summers in the Catskills, where we all lived in the same house.

Nearly fifty years after they met and married, I sat in the hearse with my mom on the day we buried Dad. It was then that she told me what she

---

2. Marginality has its upside. Paul Pierson of the Fuller Seminary School of Intercultural Studies has long taught that religious renewal always comes from the margins.

3. Free Online Dictionary, http://www.thefreedictionary.com/marginality.

had never dared say while he was alive: "I never felt accepted by his family." A few years ago I asked my oldest cousin David, son of my father's sister and favorite grandchild to his mother, "Is it true? Did they not accept my mother?" "Oh sure," he said. "We called her Herman's *narishkeit* [foolishness or triviality]." Like Dad, Mom read the social landscape rightly. And like him, she lived a life of marginality.

Let none stand in harsh judgment over my father's family. In Europe, they had for many centuries learned their lessons well: Jews were the most marginalized of people, and for nearly two thousand years, have returned the compliment, regarding Gentiles, even converts like my mother to be "at a lower or outer limit as of acceptability." One can hardly blame immigrant Orthodox Jews for regarding as "other" those who locked them out of the workplace—and their relatives in railway cars. And my father, the only Jew to marry into my mother's family, was treated as an honored guest, as Mary's husband, Herman, but still, an import.

MY PERSONAL MARGINALITY: EXILE AND RETURN

And then there's me. One of my iconic memories is a mental snapshot taken in Livingston Manor, New York, on Old Route 17 in the Catskill Mountains, the northern end and thus the buckle of the Borscht Belt, in that house on Old Route 17 where my family and my aunt's family, including my grandmother, lived together each summer.

About 150 yards up the road was Congregation Agudas Achim, the Orthodox shul where I attended every Shabbat with my cousins. In this picture, it is 1957 and I am a month or so away from my Bar Mitzvah. It is morning. I have come through the screen door off the porch into my cousins' living room where they are praying the morning liturgy in Hebrew, at warp speed. I pick up an aged *siddur* (prayer book). Of course I have some acquaintance with it, having attended Hebrew School in Brooklyn at the local Conservative synagogue. But I am no Yeshiva boy like my cousins. If you look you can see me standing back watching them *shuckling*, shifting their weight from foot to foot in spiritual fervor. You can see cousin David pointing out to me where they are in my *siddur*. You can see that it soon becomes clear to me that their train is traveling just too fast for me to climb aboard. I try for a while, and then retreat, out the screen door, onto the porch, back into the margins.

Marginality, exile, and return is my continuing story, that of my family and people, and of the Messianic Jewish movement of which I have been a part.[4] And marginality is also the criterion by which both the church and the synagogue have habitually assessed each other. However, what if those assessments are wrong? What if Israel, the church, and even the fledgling Messianic Jewish movement are all essential to the progress of God's mission? And what if this essentiality is meant to become more evident as we approach a consummation where Israel and the church are destined to converge? And to paraphrase Rabbi Hillel, "If then, what about now?"

Martin Buber spoke of exile and radical marginality in these words: "Everyone must come out of his exile in his own way."[5] While he was speaking of one's exile from God, since none of us gives birth to himself or buries himself, the process of return is also one of returning to one's people. All of us are on a journey, gravitating toward a center not always clearly defined, coming out of exile in our own way.[6]

SEEKING THE CENTER

From earliest childhood, I had a Jewish drive and an intellectual curiosity, a homing instinct to Jewish identity. The first birthday gift I remember asking for, when I was about ten years old, was a Hebrew-English dictionary. My parents were delighted and surprised, and I can remember my father driving us down to the Hebrew Publishing Company on Delancey Street to pick up the volume.

The years since have been a saga of various ways God has been guiding me by means of this inner homing beacon, guiding me not simply back to himself, which is the standard evangelical concern, nor simply back to myself, which is the standard postmodern concern, but also guiding me back to the Jewish people as the locus of my selfhood. Finding oneself and finding God in a deeper way includes finding that people of whom one is a part. At least that is the way it is for me.[7] And determining one's social place

---

4. It is likely that many reading this imagine themselves not to be marginal at all. It is just Stuart Dauermann and his crowd who have the problem. But look around you. Chances are, you are only the center of your own universe, no one else's! To them you are marginal, as they are to you!

5. This was Buber's offhand remark during a lecture at Columbia University in response to a question by Joseph Campbell. See Campbell, *Myths of Light*, 2.

6. I am reminded of Abram, whom God called to leave his father's house and his country of origin to go to a land that God would afterward show him . . . but not yet. Journeying onward, but not entirely clear where one is going. Is this not true of the human condition?

7. In a lovely passage in the Tanach (2 Kgs 4), the prophet Elisha has a conversation with a woman of Shunem. Upon inquiring what he might do for her in reciprocity

also involves assessing and reassessing the otherness of the other. I cannot know who I am without knowing and rightly assessing the us-ness of us, the me-ness of myself, the otherness of others, and the you-ness of you.

And as we shall see in this volume, the progress of the mission of God, what God is up to in the world, necessarily involves Israel and the church coming out from the marginality to which each has consigned the other so as to discover and to serve converging destinies in the mission of God.

Like the migrations of the Jewish people throughout time, my journey to God, to a deeper sense of myself, and both away from and back toward my people, has at times taken me through foreign territory. To see how this is so, let's travel for a moment back to the Catskills.

LIFE AT THE INTERSECTION: DEFINING, DEFENDING, AND DEFYING THE MARGINS

In the summer of my fourteenth year, while working as a caddy at a Catskills resort golf course, I was befriended by the band, and my passion for music was kindled. At seventeen I entered Manhattan School of Music, while earning decent money as a musician for catered affairs, saloons, and community dances. In 1962, in the second half of my second year there, I was invited to a Bible study in the cafeteria being conducted by a shy student from Michigan involved with a group called InterVarsity Christian Fellowship. Within seven weeks of joining that study I had become convinced of the truth of the Bible, the gravitas of Yeshua (Jesus), and my need to draw nearer to the Holy One. I experienced a transformational spiritual infusion, and sensed myself very definitely closer to the Center of all centers.

So began my meanderings through various missiological paradigms, assessing by new criteria the relationship between Christians and Jews and their respective roles in the mission of God, all against the background of seeking to discern just what God is up to in the world—his mission.

The Hebrew Christian Paradigm

In the early 1960s, Jewish believers in Yeshua usually called themselves either Hebrew Christians or Jewish Christians. Most found themselves in

---

for her kindness to him, she responds that she is already doing well by saying "I dwell among my own people." So it is that one cannot do well when estranged from one's people: fullness of blessing includes being with those from whom one comes, and the Bible even speaks of a good death as being "gathered to one's people" (see Gen 25:8, 17; 35:29: 49:33; Num 20:24, 26; Deut 32:50).

Christian fundamentalist circles, where others often called them "completed Jews," a rather odious term since it is predicated on the categorization of all other Jews as "incomplete." *Oy!* The few Jews I knew who believed in Yeshua viewed themselves to be people with a Jewish past living as Christians in the present.[8] We gave too little thought to the Jewish future, and failed to invest in our own Jewish present. As good Hebrew Christians we went to church, and I cannot remember us ever discussing whether we should live religious Jewish lives, loyal to the imperatives of Torah.

Early on, one of the people at the church I attended told me there was a meeting for Hebrew Christians that met there one Thursday night each month, a group called the Hebrew Christian Alliance. I never went. I knew I was a Jew, and was certainly not ashamed to be such. But I was already becoming socialized into thinking it inappropriate to claim an identity distinct from others who believed in Jesus. Misconstruing the intent of Scripture, I didn't want to rebuild the middle wall of partition that I knew was mentioned in the Bible somewhere. It was only later that I realized that although we Jews are no better than others, we are different, and that this is a difference that needs to be honored.

In those years I was still a student at Manhattan School of Music, on my way to a masters degree in music education, and becoming a public school music teacher. I was also busy avidly sharing with other Jews what I had found to be true. As I was entering my master's program, I became more conscious of a certain gravitation to spending my life more consistently in such spiritual sharing. I felt a certain imperative to investigate how I might spend more of my time and more of my life sharing with other Jews what I had discovered. Following this imperative resulted in my helping to design a new paradigm of identity and engagement for Jewish believers in Yeshua.

The Jews for Jesus Paradigm

In 1966 or 1967 I sought out the only agency I knew to be engaged in proclaiming the good news of Yeshua to Jews, the American Board of Missions to the Jews, on 72nd Street in Manhattan. There I met their director of missionary training, Martin Meyer "Moishe" Rosen. He conducted services every Sunday afternoon at 3:00 PM in a meeting place redesigned to look

---

8. Of course the Six-Day War roused some of us to a deeper sense of urgency about Jewish communal survival. And since all of us were treated as "special" because we were Jews who had come to believe in Jesus, of course none of us forgot we were Jews, nor did we wish to. But we lacked the theological grid and context to integrate Jewish life into Yeshua faith. That would come years later, as this narrative will demonstrate.

like a synagogue. (How tell-tale it is that these services for Jewish people were conducted on a Sunday. How much this says about how churchy was the thinking at the time). I had visited there before the remodeling as well, when it had been a shabby storefront with folding chairs and fly-specked pictures of Jerusalem on the walls. The remodeling was sorely needed and well done. However, even so, as soon as people at their services opened their mouths to sing, I knew that had a problem: their music was totally *goyishe* (foreign, alien). On the one hand they redesigned their décor to underscore the Jewishness of the message and the milieu. On the other hand, the music was what I termed "pure Nebraska." But at that time, there was no alternative. There simply was no Jewish sounding music available anywhere for Jewish believers in Yeshua to use in their gatherings.

Moishe Rosen suggested that rather than complain, I should try to write songs for these services, since, after all, I was in music school. I laughed at the idea. Writing music was something I only did for school assignments. However, I already had extensive experience with Jewish music idioms from my professional career, so I sat down at a piano, with a pencil and staff paper to see what I could do. And so it was that I became the father of Messianic Music, the first to write in the genre.[9] These were the earliest days of the birthing of Jews for Jesus, and I was part of the birthing team. At its inception, those of us who called ourselves Jews for Jesus were seeking new approaches to communicating the message about Yeshua in ways that the Jewish community might relate to.[10]

Our paradigm was different. While Hebrew Christians claimed a Jewish past and lived a Christian present, Jews for Jesus began to claim Jewish identity as a frontal aspect of our *present* identity: "We *are* Jews and we *are* for Jesus." As the group moved to California, our guys even began wearing *kippot* (traditional Jewish skull caps), and some began to use their Hebrew names rather than their English names in daily life. These measures were

9. Eventually, six or seven albums were released featuring mostly my music, and a Jews for Jesus music team (the Liberated Wailing Wall) performed my music around the world for about thirty-five years.

10. In the late 1960s, Sidney Lawrence, director of the Jewish Community Relations Bureau in Kansas City, Kansas, addressed a group of people working in missions to the Jews, the Fellowship of Christian Testimonies to the Jews (FCTJ), who had asked him to address them on "The Image of Jewish Missions in the Jewish Community." He summarized his message in two words: *chutzpah* and *narishkeit. Chutzpah* (effrontery, gall) because these religious functionaries and the nerve to imagine they even *had* an image in the Jewish community, and *narishkeit* (foolishness, triviality) because that is all that could or would be said of them in the Jewish world. Everyone in the audience was insulted and defensive. All except Moishe Rosen who had the good sense to know that Sidney Lawrence was right: what these professionals were doing was largely irrelevant and unnoticed in the larger Jewish world. He set about to change that.

all advances over the Hebrew Christian paradigm, and in their day were regarded as taking a bold and controversial stance before the wider Jewish and Christian worlds. Old-style mission functionaries from the American Board of Missions to the Jews from which Jews for Jesus formally separated in October of 1973 regarded all of this to be silly at best, and ecclesiologically deviant at worst.

In the earliest days of Jews for Jesus, the Jewish community was still trying to figure out where to place us in their hierarchy of reality. Perhaps at our earliest stages, they thought us young Jewish kids going through a fad of some sort. In the eclectic, hippie-fied atmosphere of early 1970s northern California, we were even invited to participate in a Jewish Community Fair in Marin County. But when the Jews for Jesus workshop drew more attendees than any other, the Northern California Board of Rabbis closed ranks and forbade any Jewish agency from giving us a platform. Still, at that time, the boundaries took time to coalesce. Susan Perlman and I both attended a local Marin County Conservative synagogue where Jacob Milgrom, of blessed memory, was rabbi. Susan had actually joined the shul, but was asked to leave after the cantor refused to do High Holy Day Services with her there. Joel Brooks, Northern California Director of the American Jewish Congress, tried to keep some of us connected to Jewish community and Jewish life. I remember going with another Jew for Jesus to a Jewish consciousness-raising session he held at a home in Marin County in the early 1970s.

Of course, the boundaries hardened rather rapidly, and as in the Israeli-Palestinian issue of today, each side had their own version of what territories were disputed, and who was invading whom. The Jewish community decided that they had to treat the Jews for Jesus as a seductive "other." And for Jews for Jesus, the Jewish community was reduced to being nothing much more than our target audience, with church people being our supportive friends and adoptive family. I have a name for this process. I call it "themification"—we were quickly classed as "them" by the wider Jewish community, and the wider Jewish community was quickly becoming "them" to us. I regard this to be a tragic loss for both sides. But considering the patterns of thought and action available at that time, the then current paradigms, the separation was inevitable. With few exceptions, all family members of Jews for Jesus thought us confused or worse, and of course, to us they were "unsaved Jews" who had not seen the light, and who might hinder our walk with God if we were not careful.

Those of us in Jews for Jesus insisted we had as much of a claim to Jewish identity as other Jews did: "I was born a Jew and I will die a Jew" was for us a well-worn phrase. But as someone said years later of our music group, the Liberated Wailing Wall, "These people are capitalizing on their Jewishness without investing in it." There was no growing edge to our Jewishness, nor did we think it strange that this was so. We were people with a Jewish past, a Jewish persona, but little or no Jewish present or future.

I now regard it as fair to portray my first forty-four years as a journey from a marginalized family of origin to a marginalized and marginalizing organization—we Jews for Jesus were at best on the margins of the Jewish community regardless of what we claimed. We wanted to hold on to our Jewish identities, but were generally barred from association. And sadly, we did not encourage each other to grow as Jews. We simply treated our Jewishness as a given. Moishe Rosen was a tactical genius whose vision of reality dominated the landscape of the organization. He was also a workaholic who expected everyone in the group to view the work as primary, and a cynic who viewed all other priorities as most likely self-serving distractions. Accordingly, he assumed that anyone seeking to embrace Jewish life more fully after coming to believe in Yeshua was more likely than not taking a naïve or prideful detour from the real work, the hard work that needed doing, which was always and only evangelism. I don't know if this is how it is in Jews for Jesus today. It is most certainly the way it was when I was involved.[11] Our greatest popularity was with fundamentalists, conservative Christians, and those whom others might term "sectarian," people who took exception to the way things were commonly conceived and done.

But other paradigms remained to be discovered and employed. Enter the Messianic Jewish congregational movement.

The Messianic Jewish Congregational Paradigm: Part One

One may argue about whether movements shape their times, or whether times shape movements, but none should deny that both Jews for Jesus and the Messianic Jewish congregational movement were shaped by their times. Mark Kinzer singles out three factors: "a social movement (i.e., the youth counterculture), a cultural trend (i.e., ethnic self-assertion and pride), and a political-military event (i.e., the Six-Day War)."[12]

To these I would add two more. The first is the Jesus Movement, a late 1960s and 1970s religious revival centered especially in California, but with national and international impact. This revival especially took hold in the

11. I have come a long way since then, and view deeper engagement with Jewish community and covenantal living as a necessary marker of authentic engagement when Jews claim Yeshua-faith. I view authentic engagement with Messiah and authentic engagement with Torah living to be inseparable. But more of that later.

12. Kinzer, *Postmissionary Messianic Judaism*, 286.

counterculture. A significant percentage of those hippies who were putting their "hand in the hand of the Man from Galilee" were Jews.[13] This was the reason that Moishe Rosen moved to the San Francisco Bay area in 1970, to tap into the creativity of this burgeoning counterculture, and to help Jewish hippies who had come to Yeshua-faith integrate their faith in Yeshua with their Jewish identities. Because he was always a man with a message, Moishe was especially keen to tap into new modalities of ideological communication being employed by such young people.

The final formative factor shaping the times and the ethos of these movements was Hal Lindsey's 1970 best seller, *The Late Great Planet Earth*. Lindsey's book was a publishing supernova, the absolutely right book for the right time, integrating Vietnam War–fed apocalypticism, the founding of the modern State of Israel, and the recent Six-Day War into an easily grasped and literalist dispensational approach to biblical prophecy. Surely tens of thousands of Jews touched by the Jesus Revolution were propelled toward Yeshua-faith through reading it.[14]

It is not only the times that make movements, and movements that make the times: it is also people, among them Martin and Joanna Chernoff, and later their sons David and Joel, who engineered the transformation of the old Hebrew Christian Alliance into the Messianic Jewish Alliance which continues to be a center of the family's influence some forty years later. The elder Chernoffs and other leaders in the Messianic Jewish congregational movement were missionaries going through a paradigm shift, and some shifted slowly and in stages if at all. In the early 1970s I remember being a passenger in a car with Jerome and Mildred Fleischer, missionaries serving with the American Board of Missions to the Jews, as Jerry ranted about the unacceptability of Messianic Jewish congregations. He was a die-hard Hebrew Christian who believed the only right place for a Jewish believer in Jesus was in a church. Despite having his heels well dug in, and perhaps in deference to the principle, "If you can't beat them, join them," he eventually became an active proponent of Messianic Jewish congregations, for many years leading one in Daly City, California, and his daughter Ruth remains to this day a Messianic Jewish congregational leader in Great Britain.

13. The metaphor of putting one's hand in the hand of the Man from Galilee is borrowed from a popular 1971 song by Canadian composer Gene MacLelland, recorded by Anne Murray, Elvis Presley, and others.

14. Susan Perlman reports on a 1983 survey of Jewish believers in Yeshua conducted by Beverly Jamison and Mitch Glaser that found that Lindsey's book was, next to the Bible, the most influential book in Jews coming to faith in Yeshua during that period ("Eschatology and Mission").

Like Jerry and Mildred Fleischer, virtually all of the leaders in the early Messianic Jewish congregational movement had their roots in Christian churches and Hebrew Christian missions, trained in Christian Bible schools and seminaries. While they were changing with the times, they brought past assumptions with them. In varying degrees, their congregations treated Jewish life and artifacts as evangelistically savvy and culturally appropriate. However, none embraced Jewish life as a current covenantal mandate. Like their Hebrew Christian forbears, they treated "the religion of the rabbis" and the rabbinical establishment with suspicion if not hostility. In the earliest days of the congregational movement, the closest they could come to practicing Judaism was to naively claim that they were advocating "biblical Judaism," and to this day one hears some people in and around the movement speaking of keeping "biblically kosher." Behind such terms is reflexive distancing from the Oral Law and "the religion of the rabbis," and certain self-congratulation over being "biblical" rather than simply traditional. This is Protestantism on a bagel. For both the Jews for Jesus organization and the Messianic Jewish congregational movement engagement with Jewish tradition was at most a matter of superficial nostalgia, intermarriage was a prevalent occurrence, and one looked in vain for any growing edge in Jewish covenantal living. Born in a countercultural milieu, the movement was at its inception axiomatically counter-traditional.

However, Jews for Jesus and the Messianic Jewish congregational movement differed in this respect. While the congregational movement sought to enfold its members into Messianic Congregations rather than in churches, Moishe Rosen and the Jews for Jesus took pride in placing their staff and converts in "Bible-believing churches." This latter arrangement was almost certainly for the purpose of reassuring the mailing list of conservative and fundamentalist Christians that underneath it all, the Jews for Jesus were bonafide Christians worthy of the missionary dollar.

The Hashivenu Paradigm

In 1989, I resigned from Jews for Jesus to come to Fuller Seminary and pursue a mid-life MA and PhD in intercultural studies. God bless my wife, Naomi, she never once winced about my resigning a well-paid job to move to Los Angeles, jobless with three children and a wife. Off we went, and at the invitation of a friend who had formerly been with Jews for Jesus, we became members of Ahavat Zion Messianic Synagogue.

After my first year at the school I was invited to teach a course, "The Jewish Prayer Book From a Missiological Perspective." It was to become the crucible in which I began forging principles and migrating toward an entirely new paradigm. With one or two exceptions, all of my students were Jews for Jesus staff members and their spouses. During that two-week intensive, every Jews for Jesus staff member and spouse in attendance was flipped from their former opposition to agreement with my insistence that we must speak to Jewish people from within Jewish life, not from outside it or as critics of "the religion of the rabbis." But what at that time was a pragmatic concern (the best way to talk to Jews about Yeshua) would later mature into a theological conviction, that it is incumbent upon Jews who believe in Yeshua to live communally covenantal Jewish lives. Papers written while working on my MA helped me work through various aspects of the paradigm, and in my dissertation research I explored the role of the rabbi, showing its relationship to and derivation from the roles of priests and Levites in First and Second Temple Judaism. I knew that if the Messianic Movement was to be a truly Jewish movement, its leaders would have to be rabbis in some meaningful sense, and not simply pastors or missionaries with switched labels. I also knew that this was a movement with a high degree of "biblical anxiety," a need to have new insights validated from Scripture.

In December of 1991 I became rabbi at Ahavat Zion Synagogue. In the early 1990s I sensed what I perceived to be a divine call to found Hashivenu, selecting a small core of board members who, with one exception, remain board members today. We sensed an inchoate commonality that cried out to be defined. Our enterprise was constructed on the premise that renewal for the Messianic Jewish Movement would not come through galloping off into some hitherto unforeseen future but would involve moving forward through connecting with our Jewish past: "Renew our Days as of Old." Our mission statement was, and remains, "Toward a mature Messianic Judaism."

Sometime in 1994 or 1995 we gathered together in the living room of Cindy Kuttler, a lawyer friend who helped craft our incorporation papers. In a two-day meeting, we sought to make our commonality specific, drafting the Core Values of Hashivenu, which have stood the test of time. For me, the first five of these principles especially address the issue of Jewish community, and the paradigm shift I and others made from being Yeshua believers who simply laid claim to an individualistic Jewish identity, people with Jewish past who fail to invest in the Jewish present or communal continuity, isolated from the wider Jewish world, to Jews who know ourselves to be returning exiles, returning to our true selves by returning to our people and our ways of holy living.

These are the first five core values of Hashivenu:

1. Messianic Judaism is a Judaism, and not a cosmetically altered "Jewish-style" version of what is extant in the wider Christian community.

2. God's particular relationship with Israel is expressed in the Torah, God's unique covenant with the Jewish people.

3. Yeshua is the fullness of Torah.

4. The Jewish people are "us" not "them."

5. The richness of the Rabbinic tradition is a valuable part of our heritage as Jewish people.[15]

This of course represents a seismic shift from former paradigms. Gone is the "themification" of the Jewish community, gone is the axiomatic suspicion and even hostility toward the religion of the rabbis and the rabbis of the tradition, gone is the utilization of Jewish sancta as devices to make a point or to attract a following. Present is an identification with the Jewish community as our primary community of reference.

Behind such a reconfigured view lies some profound paradigm/worldview shifts in how the boundaries between the Jewish and Christian worlds are to be conceived and which ones, if any, are to be maintained. This requires that we step back and reassess the relationship between Israel, the church, and the mission of God, embracing a certain vision of the consummation, of the complementary and synergistic roles of the Israel and the nations, and thus the church and the Jewish people, to determine implications for how to view what God is up to in the world and its implications for how each community is to be related to and cooperate with the other and to the work we are called to do.

The Messianic Congregational Paradigm: Part Two

As a think tank with a discrete and consistent view of the Messianic Jewish reality and of a desired future, Hashivenu has spurred the founding of a number of institutions informed by its ethos. Among these is the Messianic Jewish Theological Institute, an educational entity servicing the Union of Messianic Jewish Congregations.[16] This online school offers programs for rabbinical training and a masters degree in Jewish studies, in service to "a mature Messianic Judaism." Teachers and staff hold advanced degrees, and all involved take scholarship and Jewish life seriously. Another development

15. These core values may be found online at http://www.hashivenu.org/index.php?option=com_content&view=section&layout=blog&id=6&Itemid=54.

16. See www.MJTI.org and www.MJTI.edu.

from the Hashivenu stream is the Messianic Jewish Rabbinical Council (MJRC), a professional association of rabbis (currently all ordained within the Union of Messianic Jewish Congregations, but in the future, likely to include others who conform to our standards). This group researches and establishes halachic guidelines while processing all manner of issues intrinsic to the functioning of a professional rabbinate serving "a mature Messianic Judaism." This has included developing standards and procedures for conversion to Messianic Judaism of those few and select people from among the other nations who demonstrate a mature commitment both to Jewish covenantal life and Yeshua the Messiah. The members of the MJRC do not take these matters lightly, nor do they treat Jewish status like a commodity to be merchandized about. But having a conversion process is a measure of how seriously they take the covenantal and communal nature of Jewish identity. This is the antithesis of the individualism that formerly prevailed. All members of the MJRC are ordained rabbis, some of them PhDs from some of the finest schools in areas such as Near Eastern languages and civilizations, Rabbinics, intercultural studies, and related fields.

Hashivenu has signficantly impacted the wider Messianic Jewish world as well, although its views are resisted by some. The Messianic Jewish movement is a diverse phenomenon, and there are a variety of associations including the basically charismatic/Pentecostal IAMCS (International Association of Messianic Congregations and Synagogues) under the auspices of the Messianic Jewish Alliance (MJAA) which has long used the catchphrase "God's end time Jewish revival."[17] Another congregational association is the older and more diverse Union of Messianic Jewish Congregations (UMJC) which includes Pentecostal/Charismatic-style congregations as well as the more Jewish traditional Hashivenu-influenced congregations. Some UMJC congregations have few if any Jews. A small fundamentalist group, The Association of Messianic Congregations, was established in 2003 perpetuating Hebrew Christian theological views. Their founding documents state, "The Association of Messianic Congregations exists to strengthen Messianic Congregations by providing resources, teaching and fellowship that promote Biblical values, proclaims personal faith in Yeshua as the one Atonement for all humanity, and encourages worship through the diversity of Jewish expressions of faith."[18]

On the whole, the Messianic Jewish movement has attracted more Gentiles than Jews, some of them seeking to assist in "Raising Up Jewish

---

17. The MJAA is now termed MJAAROI, "The Messianic Jewish Alliance for the Redemption of Israel."

18. http://www.messianicassociation.org/membership.htm.

Congregations for Yeshua in the Household of Israel" (a UMJC motto), while some others seem enamored of what they view to be an elite religion, Messianic Judaism. Leaders in both the UMJC and IAMCS seek to discourage such naïve views, but they persist nonetheless, at least in some quarters. Within the UMJC, congregations influenced by Hashivenu, the MJTI, and the MJRC value and cultivate majority Jewish demographics with services and governmental structures quite analogous to what one encounters in the wider Jewish community.

To its credit, and in large measure due to the influence of Hashivenu, the Union of Messianic Jewish Congregations (UMJC) has sought to standardize the rhetoric and practice of its member congregations. In 2002, a basic and expanded definition statement of Messianic Judaism was ratified by the delegates of the UMJC, and was again ratified in an edited and expanded form in 2005. It is readily apparent that this paradigm differs markedly from the Hebrew Christian and Jews for Jesus approaches.

Basic Statement

The Union of Messianic Jewish Congregations (UMJC) envisions Messianic Judaism as a movement of Jewish congregations and groups committed to Yeshua the Messiah that embrace the covenantal responsibility of Jewish life and identity rooted in Torah, expressed in tradition, and renewed and applied in the context of the New Covenant. Messianic Jewish groups may also include those from non-Jewish backgrounds who have a confirmed call to participate fully in the life and destiny of the Jewish people. We are committed to embodying this definition in our constituent congregations and in our shared institutions.

Expanded Statement

Jewish life is life in a concrete, historical community. Thus, Messianic Jewish groups must be fully part of the Jewish people, sharing its history and its covenantal responsibility as a people chosen by God. At the same time, faith in Yeshua also has a crucial communal dimension. This faith unites the Messianic Jewish community and the Christian Church, which is the assembly of the faithful from the nations who are joined to Israel through the Messiah. Together the Messianic Jewish community and the Christian Church constitute the *ekklesia*, the one Body of Messiah, a community of Jews and Gentiles who in their ongoing distinction and mutual blessing anticipate the shalom of the world to come.

For a Messianic Jewish group (1) to fulfill the covenantal responsibility incumbent upon all Jews, (2) to bear witness to Yeshua within the people of Israel, and (3) to serve as an authentic and effective representative of the Jewish people within the body of Messiah, it must place a priority on integration with the wider Jewish world, while sustaining a vital corporate relationship with the Christian Church.

In the Messianic Jewish way of life, we seek to fulfill Israel's covenantal responsibility embodied in the Torah within a New Covenant context. Messianic Jewish halakhah is rooted in Scripture (Tanakh and the New Covenant writings), which is of unique sanctity and authority. It also draws upon Jewish tradition, especially those practices and concepts that have won near-universal acceptance by devout Jews through the centuries. Furthermore, as is common within Judaism, Messianic Judaism recognizes that halakhah is and must be dynamic, involving the application of the Torah to a wide variety of changing situations and circumstances.

Messianic Judaism embraces the fullness of New Covenant realities available through Yeshua, and seeks to express them in forms drawn from Jewish experience and accessible to Jewish people.[19]

Clearly this vision for Messianic Judaism and Messianic Jewish congregations diverges dramatically from the Hebrew Christian model that persisted until the 1960s.[20] New paradigms have exerted their influence even among those who do not fully subscribe to them. Clearly, by stretching the boundaries of former definitions, Hashivenu has been instrumental in helping redefine the center. However, it is one thing to ratify a statement and quite another to live it out. This UMJC Definitional Statement represents an aspiration not yet fully realized. While pursued and honored by some, in practice there are those who neglect and resist its implementation, paying it only lip service. It is my conviction that the leadership of the Union, including myself as then chairman of the theology committee, failed to understand, implement, and maintain the necessary insights of change dynamics

---

19. UMJC Theology Committee (of which I was then chairman), Definition Statement, ratified by delegate vote July 20, 2005, online at http://www.umjc.org/home-main menu-1/global-vision-mainmenu-42/13-vision/225-defining-messianic-judaism.

20. Hebrew Christians are Jewish believers in Jesus who generally see themselves to be rooted in the church world, and encourage the Jews whom they win to their faith to affiliate with "Bible-believing churches," and with the Christian world as their primary community of reference. They tend to see themselves as Christians of the Jewish kind, rather than as Jews of the Yeshua kind.

theory. Because of an institutional deference to an organizational metaphor of seeing the UMJC as "a big tent" harboring a diversity of viewpoints, the leadership of the Union has not, in my view, been sufficiently consistent or aggressive in enforcing adherence to this Definitional Statement and its implications among its member congregations.

THE NATURE AND STRUCTURE OF THIS BOOK

Although this confession may dismay some readers, I need to say at the outset that this book is not so much about providing answers as it is about raising questions and suggesting directions deserving exploration. The various paradigms for understanding the nature and mission of God's people Israel, the nature and mission of God's people the church and the relationship of each to the other and of both to the mission of God, can be compared to tectonic plates that have not yet reached their place of stasis. The shifting of paradigms and the process of reaching a comprehensive and adequate understanding is ongoing. Meanwhile, "we see through a glass darkly" (1 Cor 13:12).

Discussing the shifting of missiological paradigms, David Bosch explains these shifts in interaction with the thought of Thomas Kuhn, Paul Heibert, Thomas Torrance, and others. He reminds us that a new paradigm "takes decades, sometimes even centuries, to develop distinctive contours. The new paradigm is therefore still emerging and it is, as yet, not clear which shape it will eventually adopt."[21]

Bosch's words precisely describe where I locate this book in the current discussion of missiological theory concerning the roles, relationships, and responsibilities of Israel and the church in the mission of God. We are living in time when a new paradigm is still being incubated, with its final shape as yet unknown. The tectonic plates of relationship between Christians and Jews are still shifting, have not yet reached stasis, with occasional groanings and earthquakes reminding us of unresolved tensions some prefer to ignore. We are living in an untidy time, and as vexing as this might be to those who like their theological beds with tightly tucked in corners, this is how things are. We must all come to terms with Bosch's reminder that "a time of a paradigm shift is a time of deep uncertainty."[22]

I attempt to help clarify the pathway out of this uncertainty by assessing where we started, where we are now, and how we got here, while summarizing how others assess both our location and direction. I have in

21. Bosch, *Transforming Mission*, 349.
22. Ibid.

mind four audiences: leaders and laity in the church, rabbis and members of the Messianic Jewish congregational movement, leaders and workers in the Jewish missions community, and leaders, rabbis, and laity of the wider Jewish world. I am not presuming to tell any of these communities what to think, and in varying degrees some may consider me to be a meddling or disqualified voice. Still I offer these thoughts because I must. I feel as though the Holy One will be pleased as I use my hammer and chisel to reshape a massive boulder (my writing task), prior to casting it into the pool of missiological and interreligious debate (my publishing task), making waves and ripples that will go in their direction with results as yet unforeseen.

It helps to see this book as informed by three questions which name its three foci. Part one is one chapter long, and addresses the question, *What is our starting point?* The answer to this question is "God's Everlasting Love for Israel" without which there is no hope for anyone or for the cosmos itself. There us no traction for any of us unless we begin here and find the ground solid beneath our feet. In this chapter I discuss supersessionism, and examine as a case in point supersessionist assumptions underlying the writings of N.T. Wright. I summarize how Douglas Harink refutes them, standing instead for Israel's continuing election. I call my readers to likewise stand for the legitimacy of a postsupersessionist missiology, one not predicated on the expiration of Israel's elect status.

Part two addresses the question, *Where have we been?* Chapter 2, "Do You See What I See? Western Christian Theologizing as a Skewed Tradition" is a protest against how the Western theological tradition has turned the Son of David into the Son of Man without a country, the people of Israel into God's ex-wife, and the multi-ethnic consummation into a disembodied Neoplatonic eternal contemplation of the Divine perfections. As an alternative, I advocate for a new creation eschatology, as ably articulated by Craig Blaising and the same N.T. Wright. Chapter 3 turns to the Jewish community examining "Jewish Missiological Perspectives and the Christian Other." It is especially meant to inform Christian readers who are unfamiliar with Jewish community perspectives on God's mission, and that of Israel and the church. The chapter especially highlights the prescient creative contributions of Sholem Asch, Irving (Yiztchak) Greenberg, and David Novak, all Jews, while comparing these to the views of a non-Jew, Father Lev Gillet.

Part three (chapters 4–9) addresses the question, *Where are we going?* It begins with chapter 4, "The Mission of God and the Mission of Protestant Churches in Relation to That of Israel," which summarizes in some detail the nature and evolution of Christian discussion about the Jews and the Jewish State in the World Council of Churches (WCC), the Lausanne Consultation/Committee for World Evangelization (LCWE). Chapter 5, "The

Mission of God and the Mission of the Roman Catholic Church in Relation to That of Israel," summarizes discussion of these matters has evolved in the Roman Catholic context. These two chapters are especially intended for academics, professional clergy, and other readers who prefer to see perceptions validated by documentation.

With chapter 6, "Paths and Detours on the Journey toward Synerjoy," we answer the question, *Where are we going?* In this brief sixth chapter, I use broad strokes to briefly sketch six models of how the Christian and Jewish communities have learned to regard themselves and each other, especially with respect to the mission of God, what God is up to in the world. I label these models Divergent, Intersecting, Parallel, Merging, Overlapping, and Complementarian. To these I add a seventh which I commend, the Converging Destinies Model, which I also term *the Converging Model.*

Chapter 7, "What Is the Gospel We Should Be Commending to All Israel?" is an edited expansion of an address originally delivered at broad-based meeting of professionals engaged in promoting the message of Yeshua among Jewish people, both from the missions world and the Messianic Jewish congregational context. However, it is also applicable to Christian leaders and I expect will come as a surprise to Jewish readers. I seek here to demonstrate how the Christian gospel as normally conceived and preached is a bad news message rightly rejected by thinking Jews. I contrast this standard approach with apostolic missional motivations, and then outline what the gospel should look like if it is to be true to the broader context of the Bible and received as "good news to Zion" (Isa 52:7), "good news of great joy that will be for all the people [of Israel]" (Luke 2:10).

Chapter 8, "Bilaterial Ecclesiology and Postsupersessionist Missiology as Inseparable Jewels," is both an appreciation and critique of how Mark Kinzer articulates his bilaterial ecclesiology paradigm, which I term "Kinzer's jewel." That paradigm underlies much of my own thought. However, I argue in this chapter that Kinzer's jewel is flawed because it lacks a robust companion missiological paradigm, which I outline. To change the metaphor, seeing these two paradigms as conjoined twins helps us grasp how neither a bilateral ecclesiology nor a converging destinies missiology can survive without the other.

In chapter 9, "Seeds, Weeds, and Walking the High Wire: The Role of the Messianic Jewish Remnant," instead of addressing the Jewish missions world, I address the Messianic Jewish congregational context. I focus on the proper role of the Messianic Jewish Movement with respect to the destiny and mission of wider Israel.

PART ONE

What Is Our Starting Point?

1

God's Everlasting Love for Israel

SURROUNDED BY ROLLING FARMLAND, looking like some harmless recreational campground, Auschwitz waits. We arrive only to be swallowed up by the silence. Shuffling along, instinctively quiet, mirroring in life the ringing silence of death, we listen to bored tour guides regurgitating rehearsed explanations decrying "what Nazi Germans did on Polish soil." But such learned scripts fail to drown out the sound of the silence sobbing about absence, millions of voices gone in a moment, and myriads of descendants of the holy seed of Israel forever unborn. Even on this sunny day, the darkness overwhelms us, while the silence screams, there, at the edge of that foul maw that swallowed the holy nation, the royal priesthood, God's treasured possession.

Horrified, we strain our ears for sounds of life, and our eyes for light, *any light* to lead us away from this infernal vestibule. A voice pierces primordial night: "Let there be light." Darkness flees before unquenchable brightness: the voice of God on the lips of man.

Auschwitz opened a new intercommunal dialogue for Jews and Christians, like endless caverns suddenly unearthed, aflood with the light brought by spelunkers from above. Having stood together at the brink of extinction, one community as victim, the other as bystander, each knows that after the Shoah, further silence only increases the darkness.[1] Light-giving words must be spoken, united with deeds. The "never again" carved by Christians

---

1. Leon Klenicki teaches how Auschwitz calls for intercommunal *teshuvah* (repentance) by both Jews and Christians, that "*Teshuvah* means to recall that history has changed human existence after the diabolic reality of Auschwitz. We are summoned after total evil to be together in, and toward, God" ("On Christianity," 82.)

and Jews is the only fitting monument to the six million. It requires the hammer and chisel of words spoken in communal self-examination and courageous, determined dialogue. Like a hammer pinging on the anvil of a bright new morning, it is only such living voices that can drown out the silence of the dead.

A phoenix arising from crematoria ash, the modern State of Israel gave Jews a new voice in the council of nations, while repudiating two millennia of Christian assumptions. Facing unprecedented horror on the one hand, and ecstatic fulfillment on the other, both communities cry out, "Surely the LORD is in this place; and I did not know it" (Gen 28:16). Suspecting that God is breaking through the confines of comfortable provincialisms, like the congenitally deaf with cochlear implants now learning to hear for the first time, each community struggles to discern and interpret the voice of God as he speaks through the "foreign lips and strange tongue" of the other (Isa 28:11; cf. 1 Cor 14:21).[2]

But how do we discern the way out of an abyss where even God was given up for dead? And what is the right response to dry bones resurrected, realizing a prophetic hope sustained in prayer, marinated in blood, awash with the tears of two thousand years? Is it even possible to discover what God is up to in the world, and the roles he has assigned to Israel and the church at a time when graves split asunder?

Increasingly, Jews and Christians are realizing that we must find answers to these questions, and must do it together. It is as if the Holy One has given to each community half of a treasure map indecipherable apart from the piece held by the other. Unless Jews and Christians can come together and form a respectful, trusting, and communicative partnership, the map will continue to remain obscure and its treasure buried, inaccessible to all.

Before she can partner with Israel and rightly interpret the treasure map of the purposes of God, the church must first hear as if for the first time God's word concerning Israel's enduring election, for she can neither accompany nor learn from her Jewish partner apart from this radically transformative hearing. In its early youth, the church became blind and deaf to

2. Reformed theologian David Holwerda comments, "The Holocaust and the establishment of the State of Israel have had a radical impact on the shape of the questions in the ongoing debate about Jesus and Israel. Jewish voices, silenced for centuries, demand to be heard. The Christian church should not be unaware of these voices and should reflect on how it speaks about the relationship of Jesus and Israel and what it claims concerning that relationship" (Holwerda, *Jesus and Israel*, x-xi). But surely the church must go beyond simply "not being unaware" of these "Jewish voices." If the Holocaust did not chasten the church, nothing will, and a chastened church must be prepared to hear the voice of God from the lips of Israel, or else remain theologically autistic.

these things. It is time to be healed, and the first signs of healing are already among us.

Mark's gospel portrays the leadership of Israel and the church as each in process, blind and seemingly unable to comprehend the truth about themselves, each other, and the mission of God. The text provides both diagnosis and cure.[3] In Mark 8:22–26, Jesus heals a blind man, not suddenly, but in stages. After first putting saliva in his eyes, and laying hands on him, Jesus asks, "Do you see anything?" Looking upward, the man reports, "I see men; but they look like trees, walking." Jesus lays hands upon him again, and it is only then that "he looked intently and was restored, and saw everything clearly."

At its birth, the church was already touched by Yeshua. And propelled by the convulsive impetus of the Shoah and the founding of the modern State of Israel, churches and theologians are reaching conclusions, issuing statements, and adopting policies denouncing anti-Semitism and anti-Judaism, affirming the continuing election of the Jewish people. Yet, some view these developments with suspicion, dismissing such theologians as trendy post-Holocaust theological revisionists, as if theology must never be revised, even if it is known to have undergirded genocidal horrors. Even in those circles where such revisions are officially embraced, a paradigm shift is one thing, a shift in practice, quite another. It is hard for the church to see things differently, after two thousand years of skewed perceptions. It is harder for her to detect and uproot habits and reflexes shaped by millennia of supersessionist triumphalism.

The church needs a second touch if it would see herself, Israel, and Messiah as they really are, instead of in the distorted manner to which she has become accustomed. Indeed, both church and synagogue must learn to doubt their misperceptions as just so many walking trees, seeking a second touch from God bringing them into a new partnership. God has decreed that neither community can enter into the consummation of all things apart from forming this respectful, attentive, and communicative alliance. The first sign of their healing will be when church and synagogue see one another differently than before.

---

3. Richard Peace opens our eyes to the blindness of the apostles and the long healing process God puts them through in *Conversion in the New Testament*. Here, Peace defends his thesis that the Gospel of Mark is a study in the slow and cyclical conversion of the apostles, which process he contrasts with the crisis conversion of Paul of Tarsus. Peace challenges us to recognize that not all conversions are sudden turns of 180 degrees. For many, perhaps most of us, the turning is gradual, in stages, and involves regressions and recommitments along the way.

This chapter highlights what Israel remembers and the church forgets, that the people of Israel are eternally beloved. The church needs to learn this lesson, review it constantly, and explore its implications deeply. Israel is destined to be her senior partner in the consummation of the mission of God. The idea of Israel being the church's senior partner will be quite jarring and even offensive for many Christians, but far less jarring and offensive than when Jews continue to endure the cacophony of the church's claim to be the new Israel—words that seek to unmake the "let there be light" of Israel's creation.

As a lesson for us all to consider, here I will speak of how Israel's election persists despite supersessionist arguments to the contrary, such as those of N.T. Wright, a man worthy of great respect, but wrong on this issue.

THE NATURE AND GROUNDS OF ISRAEL'S ELECTION

Because he roots his views in the text of Scripture, Orthodox Jewish theologian Michael Wyschogrod is widely read and appreciated by many Christians. But not all can digest what he says in passages like this. Many reflexively recoil:

> The people of Israel pursues its course in history in the faith that it is the people of God. Because God loved Abraham, he chose him and his seed as the people of his Covenant. Because this people is a human family with all the frailties and failings of humankind, the people of Israel has never ceased to prove unworthy of its election, rebelling against the mission laid upon it by God, more often than is seemly to say. God, in his infinite mercy, nevertheless continues to love this people above all others. To it, he has given his name so that he is known to all the families of the earth as the God of Israel.[4]

Such unequivocal, stirring words, warmly resonant for most Jews, meet a far different reaction from many Christians who react with caveats, reservations, and categorical denials. Joel S. Kaminsky attributes this reflexive dismissal to two legacies. The first is the Christian West's post-Enlightenment preference for the universal over the particular, assuming ultimate truth to lie always beyond and above the particulars of human experience and perception. The second is the historical and theological legacy of supersessionism.[5]

4. Wyschogrod, "Israel, the Church and Election," 182.
5. Kaminsky, *Yet I Loved Jacob*, 1–6.

A Particularist Election

Will Herberg nicely summarizes the West's aversion to particularist election.

> A truly rational and universal God, it is maintained, could not
> do anything so arbitrary as to "choose" one particular group out
> of mankind as a whole. . . . God is the God of all alike, and,
> therefore, cannot make distinctions between nations and peo-
> ples. To this is added the moral argument that the doctrine of
> "chosenness" is little better than crude ethnocentrism, in which
> a particular group regards itself as the center of the universe and
> develops doctrines that will flatter its pride and minister to its
> glory.[6]

Many reading Herberg's characterization are apt to respond, "Amen!"
Such a commitment to universality and rejection of particularism is reflexive in the Western theological and philosophical tradition. However, that
this idea has a long beard does not guarantee its wisdom, and the Jewish
world would no more forsake their confidence in God's election than would
the church posit its own abandonment by Christ.

Where does this aversion to particularism come from? Kaminsky
credits Baruch Spinoza and Immanuel Kant with steering the West toward
the universal. Spinoza taught that the social and political organization of the
Jewish people was chosen, but not the people themselves, thus gutting the
doctrine of election. Kant stressed that Christianity is a religion of universal ethical principles known and validated through reason alone, and thus
superior to any sort of particularist tribalism. But Kaminsky is surely right
when he characterizes and critiques the Christian tradition for reflexively
assuming "the truest and best parts of the Bible are those that correlate most
closely with a certain idea of universalism (but, to the contrary), this universalism is an Enlightenment ideal that is more indebted to Kant than to
anything in either the Hebrew Bible or the New Testament."[7] Like carefully
watching a stage magician to catch him in his craft of misdirected attention,
we would do well to remember that whenever universality is being extolled,
the Jewish people are being shoved down some hidden trap door.[8]

Despite Christendom's philosophical tradition of universality, Judaism remains stubbornly particularist about Israel's unique and enduring

6. Will Herberg, quoted in Kaminsky, *Yet I Have Loved Jacob*, 1.

7. Kaminsky, *Yet I Have Loved Jacob*, 5.

8. When referring to the Jewish people, theologically considered, David Holwerda uses the term "Jewish Israel" as distinct from "Israel" which he takes to mean the
church. I reserve the term "Israel" for the Jewish people, and find the term "Jewish
Israel" a tautology like "canine dogs" or "two-legged bipeds."

election. This is one of those intersections where Christendom and Judaism collide.

Israel's particularist convictions are founded on a wide base, and variously defended. For Israel, even the Creation account serves as evidence. Commenting on the first verse of Genesis, Rashi (Rabbi Shlomo Yitzhaqi, 1040–1105) suggests that the reason the Bible begins with the Creation account rather than with Israel at Sinai is so that Israel could have an answer for those who denied to them the right to the land of Canaan. He argues that the entire world belongs to the Creator God, who distributed portions of it in accordance with his plan. Just as he exercised his authority in granting the Land of Canaan to the seven nations of Canaan, so he exercised that authority in granting the Holy Land to Israel. Christian missiologists tend instead to focus on chapters 1–11 of Genesis as setting up the background for God's blessing to "all the families of the earth." But the question of focus is crucial: Is Israel loved as a means to an end, or is she loved for her own sake? Christopher Wright brings the issue to a head, when he writes:

> The election of Israel and the promise of land are . . . to be set in the context of God's ultimate purpose for the salvation of humanity and the recreation of all the earth; they were not ends in themselves, but means to a greater end. God's commitment to Israel therefore needs to be seen as derivative from his commitment to humanity, not prior to it or separable from it. Election indeed involves use of particular means, but for a universal goal.[9]

This sets off alarm bells for Jews, and contrasts sharply with Wyschogrod's perspective. One must listen carefully to this question and ponder it deeply: Does God freely love Israel as who she is, or does he love her rather as a means to a greater, even if noble and universal end? Much hangs on how one answers. Make no mistake here: one answer shuts the door to supersessionism, while the other opens it wide.

Israel understands her election as a consequence of God's free and merciful choice.[10] From the outset, the very shape of the biblical narrative underscores Israel's continuing election. For David Novak, the Creation narrative highlights God's free, self-motivated choosing. We are not told why God created, nor of his thoughts prior to Creation. The sacred text contrasts Abraham's election with that of Noah. In the case of Noah, even before his election, his righteousness commended him in his generation. Not so with

---

9. Wright, *A Christian Approach*, 1.

10. Paul the Apostle echoes these tones in Romans 9 where he postulates God's freedom and mercy as the foundation of Israel's election.

Abraham, whose righteous standing is subsequent to his election.[11] Finally, Torah does not tell us why God chose the people of Israel, nor indeed why he chose any people at all.[12] Instead, we are told that the God who chose to bring Creation into being, and who chose Abram, in this choosing elected his descendants after him, apart from human deserving.

Joel S. Kaminsky explores how the shape of the canonical narrative, especially in Genesis, foreshadows and probes issues arising from Israel's enduring national election. He examines the story of Cain and Abel as the first of four Genesis stories where God counterintuitively prefers the younger to the elder. This aspect of the shape of the narrative establishes how God's choices are from the beginning mysterious, and not for the sake of the elect alone; the non-elect are also blessed, but must learn to not resent the elect who are God's chosen means of blessing to all. The lesson still merits learning, and from afar casts light upon controversies surrounding Pauline texts and Christian assumptions.

Kaminsky next focuses on the story of Ishmael and Isaac, Hagar and Sarah, a case in point of patriarchal family/sibling rivalry stories where human agency may impede but cannot ultimately thwart divine intent. In Ishmael, we see writ large the blessedness of the non-elect, who are blessed along with the elect and because of the blessedness of the elect. But we must not miss that although God blesses Ishmael too, his covenant is through Isaac, apart from human deserving. In the story of Jacob and Esau, Kaminsky further explores the ambiguities inherent in God's election, especially the question of whether human choices, even devious ones, are necessary or expeditious for the progress of the *missio dei*. If you are getting the impression that election is a core issue underlying the shaping of the text, you are getting the point.

Examining the saga of Joseph, Kaminsky explores the suffering of the elect, who are tested, and, if they will endure the test, purified by their suffering, through which they have the opportunity to glorify God. Israel's theologizing demonstrates that the Holy One who leads us in righteous paths for his name's sake often takes us through the valley of the shadow of death. This theme of righteous suffering for the sanctification of God's name, prominent in Scripture and in Jewish theologizing, underscores for us how we must not misconstrue Israel's failures and suffering as *prima facie* evidence that her election is either terminable or terminated.

Wyschogrod lays out for us the nature and persistence of this election:

---

11. Novak, *The Election of Israel*, 115.

12. See Exod 19:5; Deut 7:6–8, 10:14.

This election (of Israel) is that of the seed of Abraham. A descendant of Abraham, Isaac, and Jacob is a Jew irrespective of
what he believes or how virtuous he is. . . . Nowhere does the
Bible tell us why Abraham rather than someone else was chosen.
The implication is that God chooses whom he wishes and that
he owes no accounting to anyone for his choices.

Israel's election is therefore a carnal election. . . . If it was
his decision to make Abraham his beloved servant and the descendants of Abraham his beloved people, then it is for man to
accept God's will with obedience.[13]

If Wyschogrod is correct, then in this twenty-first century of its existence,
the church will have to learn to stammer such strange syllables. Otherwise,
she cannot walk with the people of Israel, nor can she truly walk with God.

Jean-Marie Cardinal Lustiger makes this point clearly, speaking of the
church's election as enfolded *within* that of Israel: "God chooses, among
all the pagan nations, sons and daughters who, through faith in Christ . . .
henceforth share in Israel's Election, grace and mission . . . (and) through
and with the crucified and living Messiah . . . share in the filial adoption
promised to Israel."[14] Notice his careful language: the church shares in Israel's (prior) filial adoption. There is no language of usurpation here. Not only
can the church not walk as the people of God apart from Israel's election:
without Israel's enduring election, the church cannot *be* the people of God.

Far from being embarrassed or apologetic on the matter, the biblical text highlights the arbitrariness of Israel's election: "It was not because
you were more in number than any other people that the Lord set his love
upon you and chose you, for you were the fewest of all peoples; but it is
because the Lord loves you, and is keeping the oath which he swore to your
fathers" (Deut 7:7–8). Later, Paul will confirm this thrust, highlighting that
Jacob was elected instead of the older Esau "though they were not yet born
and had done nothing either good or bad, in order that God's purpose of
election might continue" (Rom 9:10–11). Again highlighting the counter-
intuitiveness of God's election, Paul will show how even in their stance as
opponents to the gospel of God, Israel remains beloved for the sake of the fathers, because the gifts and calling of God are irrevocable (Rom 11:28–29).[15]

13. Wyschogrod, *The Body of Faith*, 176.

14. Lustiger, *The Promise*, 95.

15. Against such a background, it is remarkable that the Reformed (Calvin-
ist) stream of Christianity has historically been at the forefront of supersessionism,
postulating the cessation of Israel's elect status. You would think that the wing of
Christendom that most stresses sovereign election would have the least problem with
Israel's continuing election. However, such is not the case. For a thorough treatment

Markus Barth blows away the fog that often clings to these issues. His words on the matter are a worthy template for our own, exhibiting a clarity of thought that somehow eludes many:

> It is God's prerogative to decide who is God's people. This people is constituted by God's choice and promise alone; it is sustained by his faithfulness and power, judged by his righteousness, pardoned by his mercy, and made complete for his honor. Its characteristics and identity, therefore, are not determined by the inclusive or exclusive self-consciousness of either Jews or Christians, except perhaps by the recognition common to both—that each of them is utterly unworthy to belong to this people.[16]

While it is difficult to disagree with Markus Barth here, many in the church have their heels dug in. This is due in part to a culturally inculcated preference for the universal over the particular.

A Personal Election

Jonathan Sacks reminds us that Christendom's reflexive preference for the universal over the particular is traceable to Plato's postulate that the world of Forms is the realm of truth rather than the illusory and limited shadow-reality of the world of appearances. Following Plato, Western civilization remains prone to accept as a given that truth becomes purer, clearer, and more universal as we move up the ladder of abstraction. Subconsciously, we believe that the more general and comprehensive a statement the more likely it is to be true for all. Sacks calls us to reconsider and repudiate these assumptions, insisting that the God of the Hebrew Bible is not a Platonic Being, loving a generalized, abstract humanity. God is a particularist, loving particular people and people groups in a particular way.

Things could hardly be otherwise, because, by its very nature, love makes choices of one as over against possible others. As Wyschogrod insists, God is not, nor can he be, generally loving. No less than in human relationships, the Divine Being loves by choosing *this* beloved over other rivals for his affections.

Israel's election is not some theological datum, but a personal reality for God, and a familial reality for Jews. In the 1990s I spoke by invitation

---

of Reformed supersessionism, anti-Judaism, and anti-Semitism by a committed Reformed scholar, see Horner, *Future Israel*. Horner traces supersessionism and its anti-Judaic, anti-Semitic spawn back to the Patristic period, and especially to Augustine, whose views became formative of the Western theological tradition.

16. Barth, *The People of God*, 44.

to a chapel at Reformed Bible College, Grand Rapids, Michigan. It was a simple devotional talk on Genesis 15, the Covenant Between the Pieces. Afterwards, one of the professors indicated how struck he had been by the different worldview assumptions evident in my presentation. He summed up his insight, saying, "We Calvinists have God so locked up in his attributes that we have destroyed his freedom." What a statement! But it is not simply God's freedom that is chained by our theological constructs: it is his person-hood. When we make God the uppermost figure on our ladder of abstrac-tion, we depersonalize him and make love impossible. Election is but a term for God's free and loving choice. Love is only possible between persons: and God personally loves Israel above all the families of the earth.[17] When the church finds this objectionable she shows herself to be descended from the older brother in the Parable of the Prodigal Son.

This love is a family matter for Jews. One way we know that God so tends and cares for Israel is the eye-to-eye contact we have with other Jews sitting across the Passover table every year. At such times we viscerally and communally know that we are that people whom God delivered from Egyptian bondage, that family of Abraham to whom God demonstrates his faithfulness, and each of us can say with certainty, "It is because of what the Lord did for me in the Exodus that I am here today." Each Passover we expe-rience the reality that Israel is God's carnal anchor in the midst of time, just as God is Israel's spiritual anchor in the midst of eternity, the one who loves her with an everlasting love that will not let her go.[18] This consciousness of election is especially reinforced in the Jewish liturgical tradition, where praying Jews repeatedly affirm how our security and that of our people is based on God's faithfulness, and not our own, grounded in promises made to our ancestors. In this, Jews understand Romans 11:28–29 more deeply than some Christians.

All of this is crucial for the church because this differentiated, par-ticularistic, personal, and familial love is the scandalous hope upon which all else depends. God's differentiated love for Israel is the foundation from which he reaches out and embraces all other nations. Yet, while also blessed and loved, these nations remain "other" than Israel. Paul speaks of this "oth-er" relationship as adoption, and by reminding us that Gentiles remain wild

17. See Amos 3:2, as well as Exod 19:5,6; Deut 7:6, 10:15, 26:18, 32:9; Ps 147:19; and Isa 63:19.

18. Wyschogrod sees the Jews as "the abode of the divine presence in the world. It is the carnal anchor that God has sunk into the soil of creation" (*The Body of Faith*, 256). As such, Jewish survival and fulfillment of its communal mission is important not simply to the Jews, but to the entire world—for God has chosen to make himself one with this people, and to join his name to theirs.

olive shoots even when grafted into Israel's olive tree, while even Jews who do not believe in Yeshua remain ever and always natural branches. God's election is particularist and differentiated, expressed in enduring covenants and promises, and the seed of Jacob always retains a unique status.

A Promised and Covenanted Election

Kaminsky helpfully defines covenants as "formalizations of promises made to Israel's ancestors as well as of Israel's self understanding that they are God's chosen people."[19] The promissory, covenantal texts affirming Israel's covenantal relationship with God are so numerous as to be numbing in the recounting. Some theologians and exegetes draw sharp and absolute distinctions between conditional and unconditional covenants, emphasizing the Abrahamic as unconditional, and the Mosaic as conditional. Usually, the Christian line of argument holds that the Mosaic covenant is no longer in force, because broken or because predesigned for eventual obsolescence, having now been replaced by the Newer Covenant, while the Abrahamic covenant, at least some aspects of it, endures for the Jewish people. Jewish commentators would of course argue for the enduring validity of both, and even some Christian commentators and theologians view such contrasts between conditional and unconditional covenants to be overdrawn.

How Contingent Are These Covenants?

Without doubt Israel's covenant relationship with God includes obligations. Long before Israel arrives at Sinai, the patriarchal narrative indicates that such a structured faithfulness is implicit in the covenant with Abraham (Gen 18:17–20, 26:5). Yet, God's faithful love of Israel is secured entirely by divine intent, unmotivated by any factors outside of God's self, being both prior to and apart from Israel's performance.

Jon Levenson reminds us, "for all the language of choice that characterizes covenant texts, the Hebrew Bible never regards the choice to decline covenant as legitimate. The fact that a choice is given does not make the alternative good or even acceptable, as the proponent of a purely contractual ethic might wish."[20] The seed of Jacob is effectually and irrevocably called

---

19. Kaminsky, *Yet I Loved Jacob,* 84.

20. Levenson, *Creation and the Persistence of Evil,* 141. For an excellent, though slightly dated, survey of Jewish attitudes toward covenant, see Dorff, "The Meaning of Covenant." Also of value is Kravitz, "The Covenant in Jewish Tradition."

and expected to obey,"[21] and "there is no autonomous ground from which we can choose one specific thing or another and to which we can always safely return. God is sovereign over both the self and the other, the individual person and collective society."[22]

God has chosen Israel. This is certain. This is secure. For this reason, collectively and individually, Israel must strive to live up to the implications of that choosing. And the church must make peace with God's choice, even at the expense of some pet convictions and sibling rivalry.

How Bilateral Is the Covenant?

I addressed the issue of the bilateral character of this covenant relationship in a prior publication.[23]

> God places an opportunity before the children of Israel: if they will obey him fully and keep his covenant, then out of all nations they will be his treasured possession. Although it is a mistake to reduce the Sinai event to a Divine-human *quid pro quo*, it is yet

---

21. This foundation of grace in the freedom of God is mirrored in the apostolic writings which speaks of those "who were born, not of blood nor of the will of the flesh nor of the will of man, but of God" (John 1:12), and of Paul's strong theologizing in Romans 9:16, where he states that this chosenness, this election, "depends not upon man's will or exertion, but upon God's mercy."

22. Novak, *The Election of Israel*, 143. I prefer Novak's emphasis on divine sovereignty to that of other commentators who stress the conditionality of the covenant, and thus the parity of the covenant partners. For example, Umberto Cassuto refers to Exodus 19:3 and the verses following as a proposal "that Israel should make a covenant and be chosen as 'a people of special possession' on condition that they accept certain obligations. . . . The proposal envisages a bilateral covenant giving Israel an exalted position among the nations in lieu of acceptance of a special discipline" (*Commentary on the Book of Exodus*, 227).

Midrashic sources side with Novak over Cassuto, pointing out that at the time of the making of the covenant God suspended the mountain over the head of Israel and, more like the Godfather than the Father God, gave Israel an offer they couldn't refuse (TB Shabbat 88a in Epstein, ed., *The Babylonian Talmud*). Other commentators divide over the issue of the conditionality of the Sinai covenant, with some toward the right on this issue, stressing its bilateral nature (Durham, *Exodus*, 260; Ellison, *Exodus*, 99; Goldingay, *Theological Diversity and the Authority of the Old Testament*, 66), and others more toward the left, perhaps seeing a resemblance to or elements of the vassal treaty form, but being unwilling to press the parallel too hard, or even denying the parallel altogether (see Childs, *The Book of Exodus*, 342; Fretheim, *Exodus*, 208–9). Among those denying the bilateral nature of the covenant is James Philip Hyatt, who does not see the Ancient Near Eastern covenant form evident in this material at all, with the resultant absence of any note of reciprocity and conditionality.

23. Dauermann, *The Rabbi as a Surrogate Priest*, 22–23.

altogether proper that God, being God, should stipulate how his people should behave so as to honor their relationship with him. Nahum Sarna expresses this plainly: "Israel is chosen to enter into a special and unique relationship with God. This bond imposes obligations and responsibilities."[24] He rightly emphasizes how God is the initiating covenant partner who chooses Israel for a special and unique relationship with himself. Obligations and responsibilities come with the territory, in view of who the Suzerain is, and what he has done for lowly Israel. John Durham strikes a nice balance as he discusses the Lord's expectations regarding Israel's response. He suggests it will not be a forced response, nor a choice between obedience and disobedience, but rather an offer from the Holy One indicating what an appropriate response would be if Israel were to so choose. "If Israel chooses to make an appropriate response, it is to pay the most careful attention to his instruction concerning what is expected of them and then to 'keep,' that is, abide by, the terms of this covenant."[25]

Terence Fretheim takes a surprising and iconoclastic approach. He avers that Israel is *not* elected at Sinai, but earlier. In fact, "there is no 'election' of Israel in the book of Exodus; election is assumed. The covenant at Sinai does *not* establish relationship between Israel and God. Rather, the Sinai covenant is a specific covenant within the context of the Abrahamic covenant."[26] Although his language is shocking and hyperbolic, I think Fretheim is right. The covenant at Sinai involves the structuring and deepening of a relationship already begun with Abraham. And this is a relationship with the seed of the patriarchs and matriarchs of Israel throughout and beyond time.

AVOIDING AND VOIDING ISRAEL'S ELECTION

Repelled by this reality, and entrenched in a Neoplatonic post-Enlightenment worldview, the church has historically theologized around and away from Israel's election, relegating her to being God's ex-wife, and installing the church as God's new and everlasting beloved. The name for this alleged divine divorce and remarriage is supersessionism, which Kendall Soulen identifies under three species.[27]

24. Sarna, *Exodus*, 103. .
25. Durham, *Exodus*, 262.
26. Fretheim, *Exodus*, 208–9.
27. Soulen, *The God of Israel and Christian Theology*, 29–32.

Punitive supersessionism teaches that God has rejected the Jews because of their rejection of Christ. The catastrophes of AD 70 and AD 135 were the political expressions and evidentiary proof of God's abandonment of faithless Israel, which had first rejected the holy one and his Christ. Therefore, God has turned his back on Israel and embraced the church in their stead.

Economic supersessionism is more subtle, its fecund spores sown widely across church history. It argues that the entire economy or dispensation of Israel from Sinai to Christ was always designed by God to be only a temporary symbol or type of an eternal spiritual religion to be revealed by Christ and embodied in Christianity. The nationalist, ethnic, physical, defining features of Judaism are all, like the entire story of Old Testament Israel, only a preparatory carnal symbol, divinely intended to pass away with the coming of the anti-type, the church. Modern Jews and Judaism are but the remembrance of things past.

Structural supersessionism is more subtle still, involving the habit of reading Scripture with the distinctly Jewish elements merely window dressing and background to "the real story" in the foreground, a story that can be summarized as creation, fall, incarnation, consummation. Israel *per se* is not really even in the *main* story of the Bible. In such a narrative construal, Israel is useful to but not really essential to the real story. This, it seems to me, is the background to the Western tradition of speaking of "the Jewish problem." Christendom only asks "What are we going to do with the Jews?" because it has written them out of the script.

Supersessionism in its varied forms is not like some sort of passing infection of Christ's body. It is more like a garish tattoo the church has worn for so long that she no longer notices it. And like such a tattoo, as the church becomes aware of it, she is beginning to ask herself, "What ever got into me that I had this done?" Yes, the tattoo *can* be removed, although faint traces will always remain. But removing it will take awareness, decisiveness, and protracted effort.

Especially since the Shoah and the founding of the modern State of Israel, varied voices are challenging supersessionism, calling for the removal of the tattoo, seeking to exorcise Plato's ghost. Jewish and Christian scholars, confident that the Bible is better understood as telling an entirely different story than that construed by supersessionism, are agreeing that Israel's elect status is the enduring foundation for everything else, indispensable to his consummating purposes for Israel, the church, and the world.[28]

---

28. For an insider's critique of Reformed supersessionism and its historical legacy, see Horner, *Future Israel*.

Such irrevocable love toward Israel—later to be extended to the church from among the nations—is the riverbed underlying the predetermined converging destines of both communities. These two historical communities, hushed and humbled, are destined to rejoin each other, profoundly aware that they cannot claim for themselves Divine mercies they deny to each other, since these mercies proceed from One who owes no one any explanation for his choices, "for from him, of him and to him are all things." In this matter, we do well to remember what Lesslie Newbigin says so well: "God's electing grace, his choosing of some to be bearers of his salvation to all, is a matter for awe and wonder and thankfulness. . . . His grace is free and sovereign, and there is no place for an exclusive claim on his grace, a claim by which others are excluded."[29]

Although we cannot explore and critique supersessionism extensively here, we would do well to develop a nuanced sense of its texture through examining the writings of one of supersessionism's ablest proponents, N.T. Wright.

N.T. Wright's Challenge to God's Everlasting Love for Israel

N.T. Wright is unabashedly a supersessionist: "Paul explicitly and consciously transfers blessings from Israel according to the flesh to the Messiah, and thence to the church. . . . Gal. 2–4 argues precisely that the worldwide believing church is the true family of Abraham, and that those who remain as 'Israel according to the flesh' are in fact the theological descendants of Hagar and Ishmael, with no title to the promises."[30] This is supersessionism in the raw.

Following Barth, Wright collapses all of Israel's destiny and identity into Christ. While Paul and the Jews of his day expected that Israel would return from exile and pagan Rome be driven from the Land as a consequence of Israel's suffering, Wright contends that it was the suffering of *Messiah* that brought this to pass. For Wright, "Israel's destiny had been *summed up* and *achieved* in Jesus the Messiah."[31] Within such a scenario, ethnic, national Israel simply drops out, and Jesus himself (and with him, the church) becomes the new Israel. Wright's construal could hardly be more supersessionistic, or more negative in its implications:

29. Newbigin, *The Gospel in a Pluralist Society*.

30. Wright, "The Messiah and the People of God," 193, cf. 135–40, 194–97. See also *The Climax of the Covenant*, 237, 250; and "Jerusalem in the New Testament," 53–77.

31. Wright, *What Saint Paul Really Said*, 37.

[Where] she was called, that is, Israel as a whole has failed; Israel's representative, the Messiah, Jesus has succeeded. . . . He was
the true, representative Israelite. . . . Israel's true fulfillment is
now to be found in Jesus Christ and the Spirit. Israel rejected the
call of Jesus, and now rejects the apostolic message about Jesus,
because it challenges that which has become her all-consuming
interest: her relentless pursuit of national, ethnic and territorial
identity.[32]

Most Jews would join me in characterizing this statement as nasty. And I
say this as an admirer of Wright, but not of his supersessionism. You could
scarcely devise a more negative portrayal of the Jewish people. But it gets
worse.

I was astonished to discover Wright using as simple description a
metaphor I have used hyperbolically in my attempt to describe the hubris
of supersessionism. He says this: "The covenant always envisioned a worldwide family; Israel, clinging to her own special status as covenant bearer, has
betrayed the purpose for which that covenant was made. *It is as though the
postman were to imagine that all the letters in the bag were for him.*"[33] Wright
seems to neither notice nor care how insulting it is to reduce God's everlastingly beloved firstborn to the status of being a postman for the church. For
Wright, Israel was chosen for a missional purpose with respect to the nations. Since she failed to accomplish her task, God has made other arrange-
ments. In such a construct, in Douglas Harink's stark words, "*God himself
does not remain loyal to the actual Jewish people.*"[34]

Douglas Harink's Able Refutation of Wright's Supersessionism

Point by point Harink summarizes and refutes arguments in which Wright
alleges that his supersessionism is but the mirror of Paul's. He does this by
identifying and toppling three pillars upon which Wright's argument rests.

Wright's first pillar alleges that the Older Testament portrays Israel's
election as being merely instrumental against the background of a creation,
fall, incarnation, redemption, consummation narrative construal. Wright
argues that Abraham is called specifically to "deal with the problem of
Adam. This theme . . . is central to (e.g.) Isaiah 40–55, and is visible also in

---

32. Ibid., 84.

33. Ibid., 108, emphasis added.

34. Harink, *Paul Among the Postliberals*, 159.

the final redaction of the Pentateuch. Both, clearly, are passages on which Paul drew heavily."[35]

Harink demonstrates, to the contrary, how the very texts Wright chooses from Isaiah 40–55 and from portions of Deuteronomy, actually refute Wright's contentions. Scripture portrays Adam as background and preparation for the story of Abraham and his descendants, which is central in the biblical narrative. Even comparing the amount of space devoted to each demonstrates this. The story of Abraham presented in the Torah "is not a story of *redemption* for the nations, but of the *election and creation* of a people. The story of Abram and Sarai is another stage in God's work of creation. And in the Isaiah passages which Wright invokes, the Creator rules over the nations for the sake of Israel whom he has chosen.[36]

> In text after text the exilic prophets affirm the great love and fidelity between God and Israel. YHWH is bound to his people with a powerful bond of love. It is this love that drives him to seek out and redeem his people from bondage; it is this love that gives the prophet the confidence to declare comfort to God's people.
>
> It is difficult to see in the entire text of Isaiah 40–55 where Wright could derive the notion that Israel exists only to serve a role, purpose, function, or mission, which if it failed in it, would result in God simply abandoning one people for another, otherwise constituted. Rather, much more to the point, and to the very point at the center of Paul's claim in Romans 9–11, if *God* fails to finally redeem his people, Israel in the flesh, then there is no reason at all to find comfort in the prophet's words. Then this "God" might as well be abandoned. If Jews today await a final deliverance, one which (from a Christian theological perspective) has already been inaugurated in Jesus Christ, then they stand firmly on the sure words of the Law (Genesis, Exodus, Deuteronomy) and the Prophets (Isaiah). And there is no reason to believe that Paul thought differently.[37]

There is a vast difference between Israel being chosen for the sake of the nations, and the nations being blessed because of Israel. In Paul's words, the nations are blessed by becoming joined to the commonwealth of Israel.

Two leitmotifs emerging from the call of Abram persist throughout Scripture, one which Israel must hear, and the other which the church must hear. Israel must hear that its blessing is not for itself alone, but also for the

35. Wright, "Romans and the Theology of Paul."

36. Harink, *Paul Among the Postliberals,* 161–63.

37. Ibid., 166–68.

sake of the nations. The church must hear that its blessing is contingent on that of Israel, that it is not blessed for itself alone, but because of Israel's blessedness and chosenness. Those who would object that the church is blessed, not because of Israel, but because of Christ, misread the identity of the One in whom they are blessed, whose role is first "to raise up the tribes of Jacob and to restore the preserved of Israel," and also to be "a light to the nations, that [God's] salvation may reach to the end of the earth" (Isa 49:6, see Luke 2:32). The church has forgotten what Pilate remembered: Jesus of Nazareth is still the King of the Jews, and the living guarantor of Israel's blessed final destiny.

The second pillar of Wright's argument is the claim that Paul represents the Jewish story to be essentially about Israel's "failure" to fulfill its mission, its rejection of the gospel, and about God instead pursuing Plan B, through Christ and the church. By this construal, Israel failed to bring in the apocalyptic blessings anticipated in Scripture: the temple was not rebuilt, Messiah had not yet come to reign, pagans were still in ascendancy over the seed of Jacob in the Holy Land, the nations were not coming up to Jerusalem to learn Torah, and Israel itself remained deeply compromised and sinful. Before coming to faith in Yeshua, Paul lived and worked to hasten the fulfillment of all of this. For Wright, Paul's conversion was from being a pre-Messiah Jew to a post-Messiah Jew, and the climax of the story was different than had been anticipated. Messiah had not come at the end of time, but in the middle of time, and it was not Israel that had been vindicated, but the Messiah himself.

Wright says God has therefore redefined Israel, "and all forms of Judaism that do not recognize this and conform are at best out of date, and at worst, dangerous compromises and parodies."[38] He views Paul as engaged in an ongoing critique of Israel for its failure to achieve her God-given tasks. The resurrected Christ himself proves that failure, as he absorbs in himself, in transmuted form, Israel's eschatological destiny and identity. Meanwhile, discarded Christ-rejecting Israel pursues its preoccupation with "relentless pursuit of national, ethnic and territorial identity." Israel is now driven by blood and soil, Nazis out of time.[39] Their only hope is conversion to Christianity.

For Wright, Paul did not abandon Judaism for something else, but rather found and sought to establish the "true Judaism," with all other forms of Judaism being false.[40] His mission is to bring a threefold "Jewish story"

---

38. Quoted in Harink, *Paul Among the Postliberals*, 156.

39. Wright, *What Paul Really Said*, 84, 156–57.

40. Ibid., 157.

and worldview to the Gentiles, one focusing on monotheism, election, and eschatology.

Wright contends the purpose of the Covenant in the Hebrew Bible and some subsequent writings was to address and save the world. "The call of Abraham was designed to undo the sin of Adam."[41] Jews without Christ are now effectively pagans. The covenant blessings were through, but apparently not to, the Jews. Therefore, Paul's message is "Jewish" but is not a good news message about the Jews. In fact, the coming of Christ is bad news for Jews as a whole, because all Israel has been put on notice that their election has expired and can only be renewed through faith in Christ. With the coming of Christ, Israel took a giant leap backward, correctable for *individuals* only through Yeshua-faith. The nation as a whole has undergone incalculable loss. And while Paul is loyal to a redefined Judaism, Harink says the for Wright, "*God himself* does not remain loyal to the actual Jewish *people*."[42]

Wright's protestations that his position is not anti-Judaic are not convincing. If all Judaism and its adherents after Christ are parodies and compromises of Christianity (true Judaism), standing on the same ground as paganism, can a Christian approach to Judaism and Jews ever be anything other than a full-orbed supersessionism at best and never far from anti-Judaism or anti-Semitism at worst?

Properly alarmed and outraged, Harink rises to the defense both of Israel and of Paul, again turning Scripture back upon Wright. Wright bases his allegations of Israel's "failure" on Romans chapters 9–11. He postulates that Romans 9 is all about Israel's rebellion, failure, and judgment by God: that she has become a "vessel of wrath fit for destruction." He even postulates Paul's use of the golden calf incident as a template, which frame of reference Harink can neither understand nor find in Romans 9–11.

Harink instead asks where in Romans 9 Paul indicates that his theme is how God will deal with evil? Is the theme not rather God's faithfulness to Israel, and that the hardening of Israel is God's doing? Israel's hardening is for the purpose of God's glorification, as in case of Pharaoh. God has hardened and not condemned and it is he who makes vessels of wrath suited to destruction for his own purposes.

Paul's announced and defended conviction is that the word of God has not failed (9:6). In a remarkable rhetorical tour de force Paul writes the entire passage from 9:6 to 9:27 using nearly twenty active verbs depicting God's action, but using only a few verbs, all passive, with respect to humanity. He thus makes the point absolutely clear, namely that the current

41. Harink, *Paul Among the Postliberals*, 158, quoting Wright.

42. Ibid., 159.

"plight" of Israel after the flesh is entirely the result of God's decisions. Thus Lloyd Gaston rightly asks:

> How is it that people can say that chapter 9 deals with the unbelief of Israel when it is never mentioned, and all human activity, whether doing or believing, whether Jewish or Gentile, is expressly excluded from consideration?
>
> [Is it not true that Romans 9 is about] God's dealings with Israel, namely that God will remain faithful to Israel, despite the fact that the Gentiles [the non-Israel nations] now seem to be receiving God's mercy while Israel does not? Further, [is it not true that] Paul insists that the current condition of Israel's "hardening" is entirely God's doing, Israel's actions and moral conditioning . . . do not enter the picture at all. . . . [Paul notes], with reference to Jacob and Esau, that's God's purpose was declared to Rebecca "before they had been born or had done anything good or bad" (9:11). God's choosing "the younger," Jacob, is not injustice on God's part precisely because the issue is not about moral success or failure [as to who is more deserving, remains deserving, or not] but about God's mercy and hardening, enacted not with respect to a moral condition, but strictly with respect to a divine purpose that must be accomplished.[43]

It seems that Wright and Harink are reading two different books, both named Paul's Epistle to the Romans. It also appears that Harink does better listening to the text than does Wright, whose supersessionist assumptions condition what he hears. For Harink's Paul, the hardening of Israel is not a judgment from God, but is rather for the sake of the nations. Although cast aside for the time being in the role of an enemy of the gospel, Israel is to be restored. Through it all, she remains "beloved for the sake of the fathers."

Wright's third pillar is his contention that Paul employs a linear covenant-historical narrative in a structural supersessionist manner. He holds that Paul sees Israel's history as one of planned obsolescence, leading to the coming of Christ who succeeds where Israel failed, calling forth a new Israel on a new basis, and letting the old one fall away. Contradicting him, Harink demonstrates how the coming of Christ is a consummating apocalyptic in-breaking rather than a surprise twist to a story ending differently than expected.

The covenant-historical narrative Wright imagines sees Israel as always failing, and this saga lurking behind every Pauline context. True to his instrumentalist presuppositions, Wright's Israel is called for the sake of

---

43. Ibid, 169–70, in part quoting Lloyd Gaston.

redeeming the world. Because Israel failed, God's purpose for her within creation is now being accomplished in Christ, with Israel's own chosenness terminated. Behind the master narrative of historical development, as construed by Wright, lies a metanarrative of creation, fall, functional covenant with Israel, incarnation (wherein the covenant with Israel is cancelled), the church as the new Israel, and consummation.

Harink will have none of this because the text does not support it. First, Paul does not portray such a linear soap opera in even a single text. He mentions Old Testament figures not as links in a historical drama but as prototypes for today, as evidences of God's faithfulness to Israel in the past, and so, in the present and future. Wright sees the Exodus story behind every Pauline bush, while Harink's Paul doesn't recount the story of the Exodus as a continuing story line, mentioning it but once. He speaks only of the present, using the past as a template.

Furthermore, Harink reminds us how Romans 8:31–39 leads directly into Romans 9–11. God will not allow his elect people to be separated from his love in Messiah Yeshua, the Lord. There is no bailing out on "failing Israel," no switch to some Plan B focused instead upon the church. Harink's Paul does not conceive of Jesus as the recapitulation of Israel's story, now subsumed in himself. This Paul speaks of Israel not to chronicle her decline, but to highlight God's actions toward and through her. Harink reminds us that Christ is not the terminus of a historical narrative. Rather, his inbreaking apocalypse encloses the entire cosmos, church, and Israel, within itself, bringing all things to fruition.

Harink supplies a nice summational statement about Romans 9–11, well-suited to conclude our considerations:

> Throughout the sustained argument of Romans 9–11 Paul has kept a single thesis in view. God may harden and show mercy, now toward the nations, now toward a portion of Israel, as he wills, each in its season and for a purpose (the revelation of God's glory), but God will never reject his chosen fleshly people or allow them to fail in the race of salvation. If Israel of the flesh "fails" as a whole people, God fails. But fleshly Israel as a people neither has failed in its purpose (despite its unbelief and disobedience, i.e., the state of God's hardening) nor can it fail, since its election, purpose, and destiny reside not in itself (as if they were gifts to be given to God in return for God's ongoing faithfulness or mercy; 11:35), but are hidden in the unreachable decisions and inscrutable ways of God (11:33–35). If that is Paul's claim,

then Wright has given a misleading and quite possibly dangerous reading of Romans 9–11.[44]

"Dangerous," Dr. Harink? Aren't you being a bit hyperbolic? No, not at
all.[45] If we have learned anything from the Shoah, it is that "the teaching
of contempt"[46] laid the tracks upon which railway cars sped multitudes to
showers without soap, and death without mercy. But a far happier journey
awaits Israel and the church, if, as partners, we will help each other to discern and serve the *missio dei*, hastening the consummation of all things.
This can only happen if and as the church repudiates supersessionism's
self-congratulation, speaking words of sincere repentance affirming Israel
as first in God's heart, and because of this, still his means of blessing to those
who will bless and not curse them (Gen 12:3; Nu 23:8; 24:1–9).[47]

44. Ibid., *174*.

45. Barry Horner exposes the moral and ethical consequences of supersessionism
in *Future Israel*. Conscious that many recoil from such an assessment, he writes in his
introduction, "The wrong perception of Israel and the Jews by Christians . . . has produced consequences of horrific proportions during the history of the Christian church
in all its stands. . . . The reader who is disturbed by such a charge is simply asked to hold
back judgment until the following evidence is weighed" (*Future Israel*, xix). Horner's
book, a detailed indictment, leaves no doubt that the church has been guilty as charged.

46. This phrase, now intrinsic to Christian and Jewish dialogue about the Shoah,
comes from Jules Isaac's book of the same name, *The Teaching of Contempt*.

47. R. Kendall Soulen contends that blessing through the other is God's preferred
modus operandi, while emphasizing the unique and crucial role of Israel. He refers to
this as "the economy of mutual blessing." "As attested by the Scriptures, God's work as
Consummator engages the human family in a historically decisive way in God's election
of Israel as a blessing to the nations. The resulting distinction and mutual dependence
of Israel and the nations is the fundamental form of the economy of consummation
through which God initiates, sustains, and ultimately fulfills the one human family's
destiny for life with God. So conceived, God's economy of consummation is essentially
constituted as an economy of mutual blessing between those who are and who remain
different" (Soulen, *The God of Israel and Christian Theology*, 133).

PART TWO

Where Have We Been?

2

Do You See What I See?

Western Christian Theologizing as a Skewed Tradition

IF YOU DON'T WANT to be considered a danger to yourself and to society, it is probably best you refrain from throwing a book across the main reading room of your local seminary library. Some years ago, I had to practice just such restraint while reading the words of an evangelical icon. But first some background.

In Acts, chapter 1, we read of the apostles meeting for forty days with the resurrected Messiah, who spent that time giving them proof that he had indeed conquered death, and speaking to them about the kingdom of God. Acts 1:6–8 reports one of the questions they asked him, and how he answered:

> So when they had come together, they asked him, "Lord, will you at this time restore the kingdom to Israel?" He said to them, "It is not for you to know times or seasons which the Father has fixed by his own authority. But you shall receive power when the Holy Spirit has come upon you; and you shall be my witnesses in Jerusalem and in all Judea and Sama'ria and to the end of the earth."

John R. W. Stott comments on the text:

> The mistake they made was to misunderstand both the nature of the kingdom and the relation between the kingdom and the Spirit. Their question must have filled Jesus with dismay. Were

47

they still so lacking in perception? As Calvin commented, "There are as many errors in this question as words."[1]

I have looked carefully at this text and have been unable to find any evidence of Yeshua's dismay, not even in the Greek. I invite you to search as well, but I am certain you will reach the same conclusion. If Yeshua's dismay is not in the text, then where is it? It is in Reverend Stott's theological system! Sitting in Calvin's saddle, and riding into the text on the steed of the Western theological tradition, in one hermeneutical ambush, Stott chastises the apostles for their immature Jewish expectations, and reads into the words of Jesus a dismay that "must" have been his because Stott's theological tradition says so.

I had a good handhold on Stott's book at that point, and just restrained myself from throwing a theological discus.

This systemic aversion to a Jewish perspective on New Covenant truth troubled me and every other Jew I knew at Fuller Seminary. We all agreed that the Christian theological tradition habitually views God's dealings with the descendants of Jacob as merely instrumental, a temporary means to an enduring end. In Christian imagining, the Jewish people are too often simply a preparation for God's work with the church. Such theologizing positions the Jews as the Parcel Post People of God, who deliver the package of salvation to the church, only to then recede from view.[2] We Jews are then the stagehands of salvation whose only role is to move the furniture and scenery out onto the stage of holy history so the real show involving the church can begin. In such a theological theater, even the Jewish apostles have to be careful not to ask irrelevant questions.

In his seminal work, *The God of Israel and Christian Theology*, R. Kendall Soulen names this disenfranchisement of the Jewish people. He terms it "economic supersessionism," whereby "the ultimate obsolescence of carnal Israel is an essential feature of God's one overarching economy of redemption for the world. . . . [Thus] Israel is transient not because it happens to be sinful but because Israel's essential role in the economy of redemption is to prepare for salvation in its spiritual and universal form."[3] Under such a schema, the standard Christian conception of God's program in history is

1. Stott, *The Message of Acts*, 41.

2. As mentioned earlier, although I thought the metaphor was exaggerated and mine alone, I later found this telling statement by N. T. Wright: "The covenant always envisioned a worldwide family; Israel, clinging to her own special status as covenant bearer, has betrayed the purpose for which that covenant was made. *It is as though the postman were to imagine that all the letters in the bag were for him.*" (*What Saint Paul Really Said,* 108, emphasis added.)

3. Soulen, *The God of Israel and Christian Theology*, 29.

creation, fall, incarnation, consummation. The Jewish people are a temporary expedient, background players in a great, overarching drama, in which
the foreground is the church. Economic supersessionism "logically entails
the ontological, historical, and moral obsolescence of Israel's existence after
Christ."[4] This is a dire scenario, to which most honest Christians, steeped in
supersessionist assumptions, would simply say, "Of course! Isn't that what
the Bible teaches?" My response: "May it never be!"

In convincing detail, Soulen chronicles and parses how Christian
supersessionism minimizes and distorts God's dealings with the Jews. His
concern is to sound the alarm that such disenfranchisement not only robs
the Jews of their God-given place in God's economy, but also robs the church
of the only God she can rightly name. "If it is true that the gospel about
Jesus is credible only as predicated of the God of Israel, then the integrity of
Christian theology . . . depends upon bringing traditional forms of Christian thought into a further degree of congruence with the God of Israel."[5]
Apart from this congruence, "Christianity . . . embodies what is in effect an
incomplete conversion toward the living God, the God of Abraham, Isaac
and Jacob."[6] Only the God of Israel is the true and living God. When the
church forgets this, or when the church posits God's abandonment of Israel,
they have no faithful, true, and living God to claim as their own. If this God
could abandon Israel, can the church be far behind?

In the remainder of this chapter I indicate three areas where, like Soulen, I find much Christian theologizing to be incompletely converted, taking
as my point of departure Yeshua's conversation with the woman at the well,
as related in the fourth chapter of John's gospel.

WHEN I READ MOST CHRISTIAN THEOLOGY I SEE ANOTHER JESUS THAN I SEE IN SCRIPTURE

In John, chapter 4, Yeshua identifies himself as a Jew when he says to the
woman at the well, "We worship what we know for salvation is from the
Jews." Similarly, the woman identifies him as a Jew when she asks, "How is
it that you, a Jew, ask a drink of me, a Samaritan woman, since Jews have no
dealings with Samaritans?"

The average Christian would freely admit that Jesus was a Jew. However, this admission is usually little more than lip service. In its artworks,
imaginings, and rhetoric, Christendom sees Jesus as the generic Christ, the

---

4. Ibid., 30.

5. Ibid., xi.

6. Ibid., x.

cosmic Savior, the Man for Others, the Metaphysical Hero—but not as the ultimate descendant of "Jacob our ancestor who gave us this well" (John 4:12), not as the Son of David, not as fully, and as to his human nature, solely, totally, truly, and permanently a Jew.

In an address at the November 2000 Annual Meeting of the Evangelical Theological Society, Craig Blaising addressed this issue squarely. He pointed out how none of the great creeds and confessions of the church make any reference to the Jewish identity and Davidic lineage of Jesus, even though Scripture takes pains to do so, as in Romans 1:6, referencing "The gospel of God which he promised beforehand through his prophets in the holy Scriptures, concerning his Son, who was born of a descendant of David according to the flesh," and 2 Timothy 2:8, "Remember Jesus Christ, risen from the dead, descendant of David, according to my gospel."[7]

In view of the unambiguous testimony of Scripture, we would do well to agree with Blaising, "that the incarnation is not just the union of God and humanity; it is the incarnation of the Son of God in the house of David as the Son of covenant promise. From a human standpoint, Jesus is not just a man, or generic man; he is that man—that descendant of David."[8]

Dominican scholar Bernard Dupuy saw this clearly in 1974: "We have to get back to the One who became incarnate as a Jew among the Jews; to the One for whom being a Jew was not some kind of throw-away garment but his very being."[9] That this is a position we have to "get back to" indicates that the church has departed from a proper awareness of the full identity of Jesus, the Son of David. The main burden of this chapter is to identify this departure, and to urge a return to the truth about who Yeshua is. Once we regain a proper sense of who he is, the Jewish people come out of the shadows, no mere stage hands, but rather, key actors in the continuing drama of God's redemptive purpose.

In his conversation with the Samaritan woman, Yeshua is quite direct on this matter. In effect he says this: "You Samaritans don't know what you are talking about; we Jews do know what we are talking about because salvation is from the Jews." The blessings that come to the nations come from Jacob's well, the covenant people of Israel, and Jesus, the Son of David and King of the Jews, is the vessel, the bucket, that draws this water that the nations might drink and live.

The church has forgotten this. In implicit assumption, even when not through explicit statement, the Christian theological tradition transforms

---

7. Blaising, "The Future of Israel as a Theological Question," 445.

8. Ibid.

9. Dupuy, "What Meaning Has the Fact that Jesus was Jewish for the Christian?," 74.

Jesus, the Seed of Abraham, the Lion of the Tribe of Judah, the Son of David, and ultimate King of Israel and the nations, into a generic Christ, a cosmic Christ, a metaphysical ahistorical figure. Christendom has made the Son of David into the "Son of Man Without a Country."

All Christians should be terrified by this indictment because no such Christ ever existed—such a faith is a faith in nothing, a theology of thin air, a soteriology of smoke and mirrors. This is what Jacques Derrida calls logocentrism. He contends that Western philosophy and theologizing refer only to words compared with other words, so that the concept of coming ever closer to some objective single "truth" or "meaning" through rational processes is but pompous illusion. For Derrida, all Western philosophical discourse is simply talk—words about words.[10]

Is this what *you* believe? Is this *your* "Christ of faith"? Is Christian theology just holy words about holy words? Is it only talk? Or are the words of Christian confession instead rooted in a solid rather than a metaphysical referent? Is your confession of faith rooted in something substantial, in the incarnate Word made flesh—Jewish flesh—covenant flesh? Are your words of faith grounded in the only true Christ who ever lived, Jesus the Son of David, the root and repository of all the covenants, the one in whom all the promises of God are Yea and Amen?

Jesus of Nazareth never has been nor is he now simply the Lord of the church. He is first the Messiah of Israel, who unambiguously self-identified as a Jew, and was recognized as such by all who knew him. There is no Lord of the church who is not first, last, and always the King of the Jews. He is not simply the cosmic Christ, the Son of Man Without a Country, the generic Savior, but bone of Jewish bone, flesh of Jewish flesh, the Holy One of Israel, and the Seed of David in whom *all* the promises of God are fulfilled—his promises to the church, surely, but first, his promises to Israel.

Again, Dupuy puts it beautifully: "It was in becoming incarnate in the Jewish people that Jesus offered himself as savior to the entire human race. We can acknowledge Jesus only as he appeared to us: as *this* particular Jew,

---

10. Derrida is the father of "deconstruction," which advocates freeing texts from the interpretative traditions attached to them. Osborne comments on the views of Derrida and the deconstructionists: "There is no extratextual referentiality, for texts simply point to other texts (intertextuality) and words point to other words (metaphoricity), not to any external world behind the text. Yet it must be stressed that proponents do not consider deconstruction a negative movement that destroys any possibility of communication. They are not hermeneutical anarchists but seek to free the reader/interpreter from the 'false' constraints of Western thinking and from the search for final meaning in a text. From their viewpoint, they are liberationists!" (Osborne, *The Hermeneutical Spiral,* 383).

this just and suffering servant; it is *thus* that he reveals himself in order to reign over the world."[11]

Do you see what Dupuy saw, and do you see what I see? Do you see a Christian theology that has turned away from the one and only Savior to fashion a Christ of its own choosing? Jeremiah's words to his generation apply just as well to Christendom: instead of embracing the Savior whom God sent into the world of, by, for, and through the Jewish people, instead of drinking at Jacob's well, the church has "hewed out cisterns for themselves, broken cisterns that can hold no water."[12]

WHEN I READ MOST CHRISTIAN THEOLOGY I SEE ANOTHER *EKKLESIA*/ANOTHER PEOPLE OF GOD THAN I SEE IN SCRIPTURE

Correcting the defective gospel of the Christian tradition, which has forgotten the well from which it drinks, Soulen summarizes the gospel in this manner: "The God of Israel has worked in Jesus Christ for the sake of all." The church must remember that the God they claim is the one who is Israel's Faithful One. I would amend his statement to read this way: "The God of Israel has worked in Jesus Christ for the sake of Israel and the nations." This God is faithful not only to the church, but first to Israel. Again, Soulen is helpful here, referring to "the grammar of the Christian story."

> Christians should recover the biblical habit of seeing the world as peopled, not by Christians and Jews, but by Jews and gentiles, by Israel and the nations. I am convinced that one reason Christians have a difficult time "inhabiting" the biblical world is that this important biblical distinction has become strange to them. Christians (who are mostly gentiles) tend to think of the distinction as outmoded, un-Christian, and even dangerous. In other words, they think of the distinction as superseded. In contrast, the Bible, including the Apostolic Witness, presents the distinction as an enduring mark of the one human family, still visible in the church and even in the consummated reign of God.[13]

11. Dupuy, "What Meaning Has the Fact that Jesus was Jewish for the Christian?," 74.

12. Jer 2:13

13. Soulen, "The Grammar of the Christian Story."

It is only when and as we correct the grammar of Christian thinking, speaking, and imagining, that Jesus returns to his rightful identity, and the Jewish people to their rightful place in the purposes of God.

In our text we find the Samaritan woman, Yeshua, and the people of the village all in agreement, identifying Yeshua as the Messiah ["Come see a man who told me all that I ever did! Can this be the Messiah?"] and also as Savior of the world ["We have heard for ourselves and believe that he is the Savior of the world"]. Although related, the terms "Messiah" and "Savior" reflect Messiah's twofold ministry first to the lost sheep of the house of Israel and then to that other fold, the other nations, the Gentiles.

We should not forget that Messiah is first of all the King of Israel. Messiah is not simply the King of all nations, but rather he is the King of Israel and the nations. Once we think of this, we begin to see evidence for it all over the Bible.

He is the one of whom it stands written in Isaiah. "It is too small a thing that you should be my chosen one to raise up the outcasts of Israel. I will also make you a light to the Gentiles, that my salvation may reach to the furthest ends of the earth" (Isa 49:6). He is the one whom Righteous Simeon called "a light for revelation to the Gentiles and the glory of your people Israel." He is the one of whom it was said, "unto you is born this day in the City of David a Savior who is Messiah the Lord." He is the one whose coming is the power of God for salvation to everyone who believes, to the Jew first and also to the Gentile. I fear that too many Christians think of the gospel as the power of God for salvation for the Gentiles, and, in rare and celebrated cases, also for some Jews. Something is wrong here.

Yeshua is the King of Israel. That means he is the one who is the personal guarantee of the fulfillment of God's promises to his covenant nation. It is only as he is first and foremost the King of Israel that he can also be "the Savior of the world" (John 4:42).

We must return to the apostolic understanding of the Jewish people as the foundational people of God. The *ekklesia* presented in Scripture is one in which Gentiles become *co-heirs* with Jews of Jewish promises, not *replacement* heirs who bump the Jews off the stage of salvation history and then redefine both the Christ and his people. It is not the Gentiles instead of the Jews, but the Gentiles because of the Jews and together with the Jews—for the blessings that come to the nations come from the hand of God to the people of Israel and through Israel to the nations.

It is just here that we need to listen to Mark Kinzer concerning the bilateral nature of the *ekklesia*. Providing insights into Paul's teaching in the second chapter of Ephesians concerning the One New Man, Kinzer contends that the *ekklesia* is composed both of Torah-faithful Messianic Jews and people from the other nations. Such Torah-faithful Messianic Jews form the living link whereby the church from among the nations is joined to the Commonwealth of Israel, and serve the church by helping her reconceive of her identity and vocation as rooted in that of Israel.

The One New Man of Ephesians names a unity of two distinct communal realities living together not in uniformity, but rather in love and mutual blessing. These two distinct realities are the Yeshua believers in Israel living as Yeshua's people in Torah-based Jewish piety, and the church from among the nations, serving him in their own contexts, apart from the requirements of Jewish piety. Rather than superseding the Jewish people, the church instead joins with them as part of the Commonwealth of Israel. Only in this way can the "dividing wall of hostility"—which supersessionism maintains—be removed, with Israel and the church living in the peace Yeshua established rather than in competitive enmity.

When the *ekklesia* is understood in this manner, the Jewish people are not merely included—they are foundational. This is a different gospel than the church usually preaches.

THE ECCLESIOLOGY OF THE BORG

Many Christians are uncomfortable with this kind of talk. This is in large measure because Christian thinking leans toward the ecclesiology of the Borg.

The Borg is that planet-sized entity floating through space which has become part of the Star Trek saga. All who become members of the Borg become cyborgs—part machine, part human. In the process of being incorporated, their individuality is dissolved. What they once were is of no importance; their origins are immaterial. All that matters is that they are now part of the Borg, a multi-individual, multi-species organization/organism that functions with maximum efficiency as each part does its work. It is known as "The Collective" and collective consciousness is the name of the game. Whenever the Borg encounters a new civilization, this message is beamed out: "We are the Borg. You will be assimilated. We will add your biological and technological distinctiveness to that of our own. Resistance is futile." And that is exactly what happens. Individuality, ethnicity, origins, all are subsumed under the greater good of absorption and full function within the Borg.

You don't have to read long or hard in Christian theology to discover that the prevailing assumptions about the people of God are more Borg than Bible. Indeed, the ecclesiology of the Borg is the prevailing paradigm.

There is no shortage of evidence for the prevalence of the ecclesiology of the Borg. For example, George Beasley-Murray describes the redeemed community in these terms: "The death of the Lamb of God, coupled with his resurrection, brought to men emancipation from sin's slavery, *that they might become members in the race drawn from all nations, a company of kings and priests to God in the new age.*"[14] In his imagining, all of humanity is destined to be subsumed into a new race: ethnicity is no longer significant. Once you were a Jew, once you were a Swede, once you were a proud Ibo, or Hausa, or Dongo, a Tutsi, a Cubana, a Salvadoreña, once you were a Korean, Japanese, or Chinese. But none of that is important now. Now you are a Christian, and that is all that really matters.

Whether this sits well with other ethnic groups, I cannot say. But these assumptions are most troubling to me as a Jew. If giving up my identity as part of that people whom God chose for himself, to declare his praise (Isa 43:21), that people quarried from the bowels of Abraham our father and the womb of Sarah who bore us (Isa 51:2), is the price of redemption in Christ, and if I really believed what most Christian theologizing says about the Jews, I would either have to be a self-hating Jew to embrace Jesus as Messiah, or I would have to renounce faith in him in order to maintain my allegiance to the Jewish people and our holy covenants. The only way I can be both a Jew and a believer in Jesus is to adopt a hermeneutics of deep suspicion concerning the theological tradition of the West, or what might be called the ecclesiology of the Borg.

WHEN I READ MOST CHRISTIAN THEOLOGY I SEE ANOTHER CONSUMMATION THAN I SEE IN SCRIPTURE

In our text, Yeshua speaks of a time when people would no longer worship God on Mount Gerazim, which the Samaritans favored, nor Jerusalem, the holy site of the Jews. But does this mean that Christianity and Messianic Judaism transcend nationality in the sense of making national identity and origin of no importance? There can be no doubt that Christian theologizing moves in this direction, and examples abound.

In dealing with the question of whether the 144,000 of which Revelation speaks might be Jewish people, Robert H. Mounce dismisses the possibility in a very telling manner.

---

14. Beasley-Murray, *The Book of Revelation*, 127–28, emphasis added.

> A few commentators interpret the 144,000 as a literal reference to the nation Israel. But this interpretation seriously complicates the book of Revelation by bringing in racial distinctions that no longer exist in the NT purview. . . . The Church is the eschatological people of God who have taken up Israel's inheritance.[15]

Here he combines in one paragraph two problematic areas of Christian theologizing, the ecclesiology of the Borg even into the eschaton, a people of God with no racial distinctions, and the assumption that Israel is now off the stage of holy history, with the church having taken her place. This is undistilled supersessionism and it is most certainly the norm.

Yet, considering the Book of Revelation's reverences to God as "King of the nations" and the one to whom "all nations will come" (Rev 15:4), and the one who "ransomed for God saints from every tribe and language and people and nation" (5:9]) the one who will "dwell with them as their God, [and] they will be his peoples" (21:3), I conclude that Mounce's theological presuppositions are controlling his conclusions to the unjust disenfranchisement of Israel. He imagines an undifferentiated humanity of which the Bible never speaks.

Behind Mounce's interpretation and that of almost the entire Western Christian theological tradition stands what Craig Blaising terms "spiritual vision eschatology," which views the eternal state as a timeless intense vision of God, an ever-growing knowledge of him, resulting in ever-cresting adoration. This is eternity as epistemic beatific vision.[16] Spiritual vision eschatology imagines humanity as resurrected individuals rather than as part of creational relational webs, with an ethnic, national, and political past now of no consequence and utterly transcended. In such a scenario, Israel has no place, and supersessionism is enshrined.

Blaising advocates a different eschatological perspective, new creation eschatology. His description bears extensive quotation here:

> New creation eschatology emphasizes the liberation of the cosmos from sin, the bodily resurrection and glorification of the righteous, and the liberation of the cosmos to share in the liberty of the children of God. It does not see the eschaton as simply a continuation of the past, but does emphasize its continuity with the past as seen in the resurrection of the body. New creation

15. Mounce, *The Book of Revelation*, 158.

16. In "Premillennialism," 166–69, Blaising traces the origins of this perspective, and the philosophical presuppositions that undergirded it and shaped for it a hospitable womb for the doctrine within the Medieval church and beyond. He roots this perspective in the writings of Origen of Alexandria, and influential proponents like Augustine of Hippo, and Dionysius the Areopagite.

eschatology does not see the eschaton as a timeless, changeless or essentially visionary epistemic state. It is not eternal in the classic timeless sense but everlasting. New creation eschatology has a place for the earth, the cosmos, for the fullness of created life, but especially for resurrected human life living under the lordship of the resurrected Jesus Christ in fellowship with the Triune God. It would see human life in created wholeness—not as undifferentiated individuals but as differentiated individuals. But neither would it see them as just differentiated individuals, but rather differentiated in ethnic and communal dimensions as well, since these form an essential aspect of our identities. And what will we find here except Israel and the Gentiles who are together blessed by God, living under the lordship of Jesus Christ to the glory of God.[17]

Such an eschatological model restores the Jewishness of Jesus, the covenantal status of Israel, and the grammar of the Christian story, with humanity consisting of Israel and the nations united under the reign of Christ the King of Israel and the nations. The second half of Soulen's *The God of Israel and Christian Theology* names, details, and explores how and why this transformed eschatological horizon transforms everything. He foreshadows his treatment in these words, which help to summarize and validate this chapter's interconnection between what Christian theology has said and should say about Jesus, Israel, the nations, the Consummation, and supersessionism.

Christians should acknowledge that God's history with Israel and the nations is the permanent and enduring medium of God's work as the Consummator of human creation, and therefore it is also the permanent and enduring context of the gospel about Jesus.[18]

SUMMARY

If we are to redirect our path, we must identify where we have gone astray. This is what I have sought to do in this chapter, and recapitulate here.

As I read Christian theology, I see another Jesus than I see in Scripture. The church has transformed Jesus the Seed of Abraham, who is the Lion of the Tribe of Judah, the Son of David and the ultimate King of Israel and the nations into a generic Christ, a cosmic Christ, a metaphysical ahistorical

---

17. Blaising, "The Future of Israel as a Theological Question," 448–50.
18. Soulen, *The God of Israel and Christian Theology*, 110.

figure. Christendom has made the Son of David into the "Son of Man Without a Country." Do you see what I see?

As I read Christian theology, I see another people of God than I see in Scripture. I see the church as the Borg, devouring cultures and assimilating people into a multi-individual entity which presses people toward uniformity—everyone being the same, rather than what the Scripture holds out to us—that unity whereby God is glorified people and people groups remaining different yet living in peace. Do you see what I see?

As I read Christian theology, I see the church arrogating to itself the status of being the New Israel, having succumbed to the arrogance which Paul warned about, a church which has forgotten it is a guest in the Jewish house of salvation, grafted into a Jewish olive tree, coheirs with the Jews who were, are, and evermore shall be the foundational people of God. Do you see what I see?

As I read Christian theology, I see another consummation than I see in Scripture. I see spiritual vision eschatology with its assumption of a dehistoricized, depoliticized, actually dehumanized humanity comprised of countless individuals who now have nothing in common except their redeemed and glorified status and their eternal occupation of transfixed adoration. In contrast to this prevailing paradigm of spiritual-vision eschatology, I see an eternal state in which all of us are fully human, with resurrected bodies and ethnic identities intact, rejoicing not simply as individual nationals but as peoples in the presence of the One True God in all the beauty of cultural and ethnic differentiation. In such a vision of the eternal state we will not be less different but more so. As discrete redeemed peoples, tongues, tribes, and nations, we will be utterly diverse. We will all appreciate, rejoice in, and understand totally the richness of each people's uniqueness. We will be gathered together, united but not uniform—all of us redeemed, all of us glorified, and all of us living in peace and unity. In place of a spiritual vision eschatology and supersessionism predicated on a gospel of non-differentiated uniformity, I see the God of Israel and the church as the author of a gospel of differentiated unity. I see a converging destiny for Israel and the nations. Do you see what I see?

I see the outworking of what Yeshua told the Samaritan woman, that salvation is from the Jews. I see a church drinking living water from the same well as the Samaritan woman, a well the church did not herself dig, a well of living water that is first and foremost Jacob's well. And it still is Jacob's well, "for the gifts and the calling of God are irrevocable" (Rom 11:29).

3

Jewish Missiological Perspectives and the Christian Other

Do Jews proselytize? The usual answer is, "No." But is this so? If, by "proselytize," one means, "Do Jews employ campaigns, or manipulation, or even threats to gather converts," then the negative answer stands. Still, the Jewish community has always received converts, and, increasingly, seeks them. In that sense, Jews do in fact proselytize.[1]

Because proselytism is seeking to bring outsiders into one's religious group as adherents, this necessitates a binary category of us and them, and a contemplation of those deemed "other." This chapter surveys past and contemporary Jewish attitudes, rationales, and theologizing about relationship with and mission (outreach) to the other, more specifically, the Christian other.[2] I hope to inform those for whom this information is new, especially those for whom this information corrects what was formerly believed.

---

1. The etymology of the term illumines the direct relationship between the Hebrew *keruv* and English *proselyte*, or *proselytize*, which come via the Latin proselytus, from the Greek *proselytos*, which in turn represents the second aorist stem of *proserchesthai*, to come from *pros* (toward + *erchesthai*, to come). English retains a form of the term *keruv* in the word *cherub* (pl. *cherubim*) a heavenly being close to the throne of God. This being the case, *keruv* (to draw near) and proselytize may be seen to be very close in meaning, so that the distinction that Jews engage in *keruv* but not in proselytism proves inaccurate in meaning, although not in nuance.

2. Thinking, writing, and speaking of Jews/Judaism and Christians/Christianity as "other" to each respective group is predicated on a "parting of the ways" model fast eroding under the weight and scrutiny of modern scholarship. See Becker and Reed, eds., *The Ways That Never Parted* for a wide range of essays demonstrating the breadth and bona fides of this critique. Also see there for references to a wider range of resources

Having laid this groundwork, the chapter then considers how some Jewish thinkers have imagined the complementarity of Jewish and Christian mission, whether Jews and Christians properly have a mission not only with but also to each other, and how this helps pave the way for the Converging Destinies perspective.

CLASSIC JEWISH BIBLICAL PRECEDENTS FOR PROSELYTIZING

Classical Jewish sources build a rationale for Jewish mission upon the biographies of biblical characters. One the most potent of these arguments is the reminder that Abraham the first Jew was himself a convert,[3] and that Abraham and Sarah were the first *missionaries*. We read how Abram and Sarai and Lot his nephew left Haran, yet not alone but with others, *"v'et hanefesh asher asu b'charan"* ("and the persons/soul(s) they had acquired/made in Haran"). Targum Onkelos translates this as "the souls they brought into the realm of the Torah," and Rashi applies this to the work of conversion, saying that Abram converted the men and Sarai the women. The thirteenth-century French commentator known as the Chizkuni says about this passage, *"kan matchil matan Torah*, the Giving of the Torah starts here," (and not with Moses at Sinai, because according to this text, Abraham was the first person to bring others to the knowledge of Torah and thus of Israel's God).

The tradition extols Ruth as a convert and direct ancestor to King David and therefore of Messiah, also presenting David's son Solomon as a champion of outreach. In the Midrash on Song of Songs, Rabbi Jose ben Halafta says that the reason Solomon had cleaved in love to so many foreign women (1 Kings 11:2) was in order "to convert them and to bring them under the wings of the Shekhinah."[4]

---

on the matter, among them, Schwartz, *Imperialism and Jewish Society from 200 B.C.E. to 640 C.E.*, and Boyarin, *Border Lines*, each seminal works in the field. These sources demonstrate that the historical constructs used to undergird the parting of the ways model are more construct than history. Still, this construct is still regarded as historic and social fact by almost all contemporary Christians and Jews, who indeed regard one another as irretrievably "other." Surely, two thousand years of animosity, persecutions, and defining one's camp in contradistinction to another has galvanized the parting of the ways model, and the otherness it entails.

3. "Converts are beloved; in every way God considers them as part of Israel" (Tankhuma B). "Said Resh Lakish: the convert is dearer than the Jews who stood before Mount Sinai." M. Lekh Lekha, cited by Prager in "Judaism Seeks Converts."

4. *Song of Songs Rabbah* 1:1, 10, cited by Seltzer in "Joining the Jewish People from Biblical to Modern Times," 50. Although early rabbinic sources are inclined to see figures like Rahab and Jethro as proselytes, more recent scholarship sees such figures as

In an argument reminiscent of Christian interpretations of the scattering of the saints as recorded in Acts 8, rabbinic opinion further defended mission to the Gentiles by suggesting that exile of the Jews was itself intended as a means of outreach, stating that "the Holy One, Blessed be He, exiled Israel among the nations in order to increase their numbers with the addition of converts."[5]

Despite rumors to the contrary, engaging in mission, that is, doing outreach, has been regarded from ancient times as a Jewish thing to do, while contextual factors have influenced how widely and in what manner such activities would be pursued.[6]

Examining biblical and classical Jewish texts, Alan Brill[7] holds that while stipulating that Jews were to have no foreign gods and view heathen practices as abominable, foolish, and forbidden, the Older Testament nevertheless assumed that Gentiles might freely worship their gods.[8] He offers as an example Orpah, the Moabite sister in law to Ruth. The scriptural account

---

products of their times: people who had embraced Israel's God while yet maintaining fealty to other gods as well (henotheists). Conservative Jewish scholar Shaye D. Cohen reflects this view when he states "The preexilic portions of the Bible do not have a word for 'convert' because the notion of conversion did not yet exist. Pious pagans like Jethro and Rahab might be so impressed with the power of the God of Israel that they sing his praises, but they do not convert. They poly-theistically recognize Israel's God, affirming his ability to do wonders, but they do not deny the pagan gods. There is only one seeming exception to this pattern (Naaman, the Syrian)." "Conversion to Judaism in Historical Perspective," 34.

5. *T. B. Pesachim* 87b.

6. A wide variety of biblical and rabbinic texts are cited in the literature to underscore the propriety of Jewish missionary activity. One of the older books, more dependable for its quotations from primary documents than for the conclusions drawn from them is Bernard J. Bamberger, *Proselytism in the Talmudic Period*, 13–17; for a knowledgeable and articulate critique of Bamberger's unwarranted conclusions regarding conversion in biblical times see Cohen, "Conversion to Judaism in Historical Perspective"; two presentations from the Reform perspective are Joseph R. Rosenbloom, *Conversion to Judaism*, 28–31, and the older somewhat stodgy and naive treatment in Eichorn, ed., *Conversion to Judaism*, 10–28. Other excellent discussions of the biblical and post-biblical religious statements on the issues of conversion and proselytism include Seltzer, "Joining the Jewish People from Biblical to Modern Times," 50–52, 59; Bokser, "Witness and Mission in Judaism"; Prager, "Judaism Seeks Converts"; and Epstein, "A Religious Argument for Welcoming Converts"

7. I initially encountered his views in Alan Brill, "Judaism and Other Religions." However, in subsequently corresponding with him, I discovered this source contained substantial errors and omissions. I corrected my manuscript to incorporate the more authoritative materials found in Brill, *Judaism and Other Religions*. Much of the material in this chapter concerning the postures Jews have historically taken to the non-Jewish other reflects Brill's material.

8. See Deut 4:19; Mic 4:5.

does not censure her for going back to her people and their gods after the death of her husband instead of traveling on with Naomi and Ruth to join the people and God of Israel.[9] The Talmud says that she and her offspring were rewarded for how she had accompanied Naomi on the way,[10] although other references are not so kind, saying that Orpah lay with a hundred men, and even with a dog the night she departed from Naomi.[11] Goliath of Gath, the giant who fought with David the shepherd boy, is said to have come from this promiscuous series of events.[12]

By the time of the prophets, Jewish discussion of the other is more nuanced. Isaiah's Israel is especially chosen by the God who rules over all the world to make his name known, while Zephaniah and Zechariah envision that day when all peoples will serve Israel's God, "And the Lord will become king over all the earth; on that day the Lord will be one and his name one."[13] Isaiah concurs, looking toward that day when

> The mountain of the house of the Lord shall be established as the highest of the mountains . . . and *all the nations shall flow to it,* and *many peoples* shall come, and say: "Come, let us go up to the mountain of the Lord, to the house of the God of Jacob; that he may teach us his ways and that we may walk in his paths." For out of Zion shall go forth the law, and the word of the Lord from Jerusalem. *He shall judge between the nations, and shall decide for many peoples.*[14]

It is fair to stay that, shaped by the polarizing and precarious context of exile in foreign lands under the domination of pagan rulers, the Talmud and classical Judaism speak negatively of Gentiles and their religion, with the tractate *Avodah Zarah* ("Strange Worship") reserving special disdain for Greco-Roman religion.

Here the focus was on worshipping images, which for Judaism was patently ridiculous. Jews took as axiomatic that idols have eyes that cannot see, ears that cannot ear, mouths that cannot speak, and that they cannot carry others but must be carried. This antipathy to idolatry as transferred to

---

9. Brill, *Other Religions,* 32. However, Jewish tradition is not so generous with Orpah, but stigmatizes her severely for choosing to return to idolatrous Moab rather than to cleave to Naomi and the God of Israel.

10. BT Sotah 42b.

11. Ibid.

12. See Midrash Ruth Rabbah 2:20.

13. Zech 14:9, words spoken at the end of every Jewish service.

14. Isa 2:2–5, a passage quoted in part whenever the Torah is read in a Jewish service.

the Greco-Roman context is recorded nicely in the Apocalypse of Abraham (*ca.* 70-150 CE) where we first read Judaism's stories of Abraham's father being an idol maker, and Abraham's spiritual awakening to the bankruptcy of idolatry.

Rabbinic Judaism further ridicules idolatry by alleging that Peor (of the Baal of Peor) is worshipped by his adherents defecating near him, while Merculis, which may be Mercury, is worshipped through casting stones at his image. What these two assumptions have in common is that the worship of idols is patently ridiculous and false especially but not solely as compared with the nobility of Judaism.[15] It is helpful to remember that Judaism had little interest in why or how images were used by pagans or later by Christians in their worship. On the basis of Torah texts like Deuteronomy 11:16 and Numbers 15:39, Maimonides expounds how Jews are not even to think about pagan idolatry or nurture their own curiosity about pagan worship.[16] This is surely one of the reasons one finds in rabbinic sources no curiosity or opinions expressed about reasons, meanings, or nuances connected with pagan or Christian uses of statues in their worship. Religious Jews were and are generally committed to not even wondering about such matters as a matter of obedience to God.

Citing Ephraim Urbach, Brill comments that by the third century CE Jewish sources made a distinction between statues made for the purpose of worship and those made for aesthetic purposes. The latter were not prohibited.[17]

CLASSICAL JUDAISM AND THE CHRISTIAN OTHER: THREE CATEGORIES

Brill begins his discussion of theological categories with a threefold division: exclusivism, pluralistic universalism, and inclusivism. His book is "the first extended application of these categories to a wide variety of Jewish opinions."[18] Although Brill later subdivides these categories, I find these broader categories sufficient for structuring my present treatment.

15. Cf. Sanhedrin 64a and also Maimonides, *Mishneh Torah* (Hilchot Avodat Kochavim), 3:1–5.

16. Maimonides, *Mishneh Torah* (Hilchot Avodat Kochavim), 2:1-4.

17. Brill, *Other Religions,* 46, and Maimonides, *Mishneh Torah* (Hilchot Avodat Kochavim), 7:6. For more information about exceptions that could be made, see Brill and Maimonides, 7, where distinctions between idolatrous statues and permitted aesthetic ones are meticulously explored.

18. Brill, *Other Religions, 16.*

Exclusivists

Exclusivists view their own community, tradition, and encounter with God to be the only true way, with all other communal traditions and claims being false. Accordingly, Jewish exclusivists view Judaism to be categorically true, and Christianity, along with all non-Judaism religions, categorically false. This is a hard-boundary, naïve-realist, binary, either/or, us/them, insider/outsider perspective, commonly termed "fundamentalist." Such a position, annealed in the fires of exile, formed a protective shell for the Jewish community, insulating it from the threat of contamination by the Christian "other."

Brill offer many examples of whom I choose three as typical of the category. The Kabbalist Isaac Luria questioned whether Gentiles had souls, stressing a kind of demonic dualism wherein the Jewish mission was seen to be redemptive, opposing, and redeeming Gentile impurity. In the sixteenth century, R. Yehudah ben Betzalel Lowe (the Maharal) stressed separation and Jewish particularism, saying Israel and Edom (a cipher for Rome and Christianity) are inverse and opposite—when one is in ascent then the other is in descent. At the beginning, Israel is connected to the nations like a shell around a fruit. At the end, the fruit is separated from the shell completely and Israel is separated from them.[19]

Tzvi Yehudah Kook, spiritual father of the Israeli settler movement, promulgated a firm anti-Palestinian and anti-Christian position, holding Christianity to be an internal Jewish heresy, and affirming that God the creator is certainly not a man, that the Jewish God is alive, the Christian God, dead, with Christianity the refuse of Israel. His was a xenophobic perspective, the epitome of us/them thought and action, and without any ambiguity, exclusivist.[20] Although Kook was a right-wing Orthodox Jew, his attitudes are echoed among many Jews distributed across the Jewish spectrum, who view Christians as irretrievably and antagonistically "other," and Christianity as categorically naïve, superstitious, antithetical to all things Jewish, and

19. Rabbi Judah Loew ben Bezalel, *Sefer Gevurot Hashem*, 23. See also his comments on *TB Sanhedrin 21b*.

20. Tzvi Yehudah Kook, *Judaism and Christianity*, referenced in Brill, *Other Religions*, 162. While Kook is an unyielding and strident hard-line antagonist of Christianity in the name of Jewish preservation, other exclusivists have a softer edge. R. Shabbetai Bass (sixteenth century) critiqued Rashi's hard-line stance, while R. Menachem Mendel Schneersohn, from 1951 to his death June 12, 1994, the seventh Rebbe of Chabad Hasidism, sought to reread hard-line texts, holding that they were no longer applicable because we live in a different time, and that religious Jews should seek to bring Gentiles into conformity with the Seven Laws of Noah, a religious Jewish construct outlining the minimal standards of societal decency.

at its root, hostile to Jewish survival. As in every group, there are hard-line extremists in the Jewish camp, such as Rabbis Yitzhak Shapira and Yosef Elitzur of the West Bank settlement of Yitzhar, in a hotly denounced volume of radical Right rabbinic opinion, *Torat HaMelech*, which could not be more rabid in its polarization against non-Jews and negative characterizations of them. The book holds that "non-Jews are 'uncompassionate by nature' and military attacks on them 'curb their evil inclination,' while babies and children of Israel's enemies may be killed since 'it is clear that they will grow to harm us.'"[21] However, this position is no more typical of Jewish attitudes toward Gentiles, than the behavior of the Klu Klux Klan is typical of all Christians.

Universalistic Pluralists

Universalistic pluralism is at the opposite end of the spectrum. Its adherents hold that no one tradition or community can claim a corner on the truth about God. Unlike exclusivisits, universal pluralists speak to and of members of other traditions using the terms native to the "other," seeing religion as a variety of ways to approach God rather than as a means where one community authoritatively and rightly defines God and his ways in contradistinction to all others. Universalistic pluralists instead hold that God is present and active in a wider world than their own tradition.

One needs always to remember that the Jewish tradition is multivocal. Although there is a tendency for the tradition to reach consensus on most matters, this does not negate the tensions which exist and are valued among the varied voices represented. So it is that one may find harsh voices denying Gentiles even the status of being fully human, but also voices that accord to Gentiles a status, if not equal, then at least parallel to that of Israel. For example, "Whoever recognizes idols has denied the entire Torah; and whoever denies idols has recognized the entire Torah."[22] And Torah is given such a high place that Gentiles who study it elevate their status as high as that of Israel's high priest.[23]

---

21. Estrin, "Rabbinic Text or Call to Terror?"

22. *Sifre,* Deut 54, quoted in Brill, *Other Religions*, 47.

23. "R. Meir said: What is the proof that even a gentile who occupies himself with torah is like a high priest? Scripture says, 'With which if a man occupy himself, he shall live by them' (Lev. 18.5). It does not say, 'A priest, a Levite, an Israelite,' but, 'A man.'" Hence you may infer that even a non-Jew who occupies himself with Torah is like a high priest. *Baba Kamma* 38a quoted in Brill, *Other Religions,* 47.

Brill presents Immanuel of Rome as a classical Jewish universalist. Immanuel studied with one of Dante Aligheri's friends and knew him, and one may detect Dante's influence in his *Tofet veEden*, which may be viewed as Immanuel's imitation of *The Divine Comedy*. Immanuel held that paradise was attainable for those Gentiles who pursued a path of intellectual self-discovery. Like many modern secularists, he held that "those gentiles who come to God through their own intellect are the pious of the nations. . . . It is the names that men attached to God and to human religious understanding that cause war and strife."[24] One will have no problem finding proponents of this viewpoint at any Starbucks!

Some who rooted their universal pluralism in biblical texts rather than philosophy viewed the prophetic expectation to be greater and superior to any particularist communal expression, and held that biblical revelation evolved and matured away from its particularist origins. For example, a third-century rabbinic midrash *Sifrei Devarim* says, "When the Holy One Blessed be He, revealed himself to give the Torah to Israel, he revealed himself not only to Israel but to all the other nations."[25] And the medieval midrash, *Tanna Debai Eliyahu* (9:1), says "The prophet Elijah said: I call heaven and earth to bear witness that anyone—Jew or gentile, man or woman, slave or handmaid—if his deeds are worthy, the Divine Spirit will rest upon him."[26]

Samson Raphael Hirsch (1808–1888) should also be considered a universal pluralist, when he states, "The Torah calls Israel a treasured nation. However, this does not imply, as some have mistakenly assumed, that Israel has a monopoly on God's love and favor. On the contrary, Israel's most cherished ideal is that of the universal brotherhood of mankind."[27] While he bases his position squarely on Scripture, others in the Orthodox Jewish stream root their universal pluralist perspective not so much in philosophy or Scripture, as in history. The Sephardic rabbi, Henry Pereira Mendes (1852–1937), was the first professor of homiletics at Rabbi Isaac Elhanan Theological Seminary in New York (part of Yeshiva Univerity), and also was the first president of the Union of Orthodox Jewish Congregations of America. The following quotation from his address at the 1893 Parliament of Religions articulates a historically informed universalistic pluralist perspective:

24. Brill, *Other Religions,* 109

25. *Sifre Devarim*, piska 343, referenced in Brill, *Other Religions,* 47

26. Referenced in Brill, *Other Religions,* 111.

27. *Nineteen Letters of Ben Uzziel,* 15.

There is a legend that, when Adam and Eve were turned out of Eden or earthly paradise, an angel smashed the gates, and the fragments flying all over the earth are the precious stones. We can carry the legend further. The precious stones were picked up by the various religions and philosophers of the world. Each claimed and claims that its own fragment alone reflects the light of heaven, forgetting the setting and incrustations which time has added. Patience my brother. In God's own time we shall, all of us, fit our fragments together and reconstruct the gates of paradise. There will be an era of reconciliation of all living faiths and systems, the era of all being at-one-ment, or atonement, with God. Through the gates shall all people pass to the foot of God's throne.[28]

This is a remarkable statement, strongly stressing the common origins and common destinies of different religious communities. Although such a statement seems progressive and "politically correct" for many, for others, the position is outrageous. As a case in point, Brill references the turmoil attending the publication of *The Dignity of Difference*, by Jonathan Sacks, at that time Chief Rabbi of the United Kingdom. Statements in his first edition brought the wrath of the British Jewish religious establishment down on Sacks, whose position they considered outrageous and heretical. Sacks had written as follows:

> What we cannot do is place ourselves outside the particularities of language to arrive at a truth, a way of understanding and responding to the world that applies to everyone at all times. . . .
>
> God is universal, religions are particular. Religion is the translation of God into a particular language and thus into the life of a group, a nation, a community of faith. In the course of history, God has spoken to mankind in many languages: through Judaism to Jews, Christianity to Christians, Islam to Muslims. . . . *God is God of all humanity, but no single faith is or should be the faith of all humanity.*[29]

This is clearly the antipode of exclusivism. Antagonists accused Sacks of heresy, and the clamor was so severe and unrelenting that he was forced to revise his text for later editions, while resisting the demand that he remove

28. Mendes, "Orthodox or Historical Judaism," quoted in Brill, *Other Religions,* 125. This metaphor reminds me of a one used in discussions at the Fuller Theological Seminary School of Intercultural Studies, where the various cultures of the world are compared to tiles of a mosaic, with each component contributing a unique and necessary part of a wider picture of God's self-revelation.

29. Sacks, *The Dignity of Difference,* 54–55.

the first edition from the shelves of bookstores where it was already available. Notice the neutered language of his revision:

> God communicates in human language, but there are dimensions of the divine that must forever elude us. As Jews we believe that God has made a covenant with a singular people, but that does not exclude the possibility of other peoples, cultures, and faiths finding their own relationship with God within the shared frame of the Noahide laws.
>
> God is the God of all humanity, but between Babel and the end of days no single faith is the faith of all humanity.[30]

His experience demonstrates that Jewish exclusivism survives, at least in some wings of contemporary Jewry, utterly intolerant of any sort of universal pluralism.[31]

Jewish Inclusivists

The inclusivist acknowledges that there are many communities and faiths, each with its own tradition and truth, but views his own path and perspective as encompassing or perfecting these other truths and paths. The inclusivist uses his own theological language to interpret the religion of the "other."

Twelfth-century Spanish Jewish poet Yehudah HaLevi took an inclusivist stance in his influential apologetic treatise, *The Kuzari*, a series of conversations between a rabbi and the King of the Khazars. Halevi expounds the supreme truth of Judaism and the superiority of revealed religion over philosophical speculation. He sees all religions after the giving of the Law at Sinai as part of the process of all humanity coming toward and into the truth of Judaism. As the truth and primacy of Israel's religion and her God become manifest, "all nations will become one tree, recognizing the common root they had previously scorned."[32] This is pure inclusivism.

Ya'akov Emden (1697–1776) is one of the most remarkable Orthodox Jewish inclusivists speaking in highly irenic tones, commending both Christianity and Islam as offshoots of Judaism. His comments about Christians, Paul, Jesus, and the apostles are stunningly progressive, particularly when one remembers him to be an eighteenth-century rabbi.

---

30. Ibid., 54–55.

31. In addition to Sacks, Brill summarizes the views of many other advocates of universalistic pluralism.

32. HaLevi, Yehudah, *The Kuzari*, IV:23, quoted in Brill, *Other Religions*, 65.

[Jesus] strengthened the Torah of Moses majestically . . . and not one of our Sages spoke out more emphatically concerning the immutability of the Torah. And on the other hand, he did much good for the Gentiles . . . by doing away with idolatry and removing the images from their midst. He obligated them with the Seven Commandments (of Noah) so that they should not be as the beasts of the field. He also bestowed upon them ethical ways, and in this respect he was much more stringent with them than the Torah of Moses, as is well-known. . . .

If certain Christians who consider themselves scholars would understand this secret, who believe that they are commanded to abolish the Torah of Moses from the seed of Israel, they would not engage in such foolishness. The people listen to their self-conceived words, something which was never intended by the writers of the Gospels. Quite the opposite, they have written clearly that they intended the contrary.

Because of these errant scholars, hatred has increased toward the Jews who are blameless of any guilt and proceed innocently to observe their Torah with all their heart, imbued with the fear of God. They should instead bring their people to love the ancient Children of Israel who remain loyal to their God, as indeed commanded to Christians by their original teachers.

They even said to love one's enemies. How much more so to us! In the name of Heaven, we are your brothers! One God has created us all. Why should they abuse us because we are joined to the commandments of God, to which we are tied with the ropes of his love? We do this not to enjoy the pleasures of the (evil) inclination and emptiness of a passing world. . . .

You, members of the Christian faith, how good and pleasant it might be if you will observe that which was commanded to you by your first teachers; how wonderful is your share if you will assist the Jews in the observance of their Torah. You will truly receive reward as if you had fulfilled it yourselves—for the one who helps others to observe is greater than one who observes but does not help others to do so—even though you only observe the Seven Commandments. I have written similarly in my pleasant work *Torat Ha-Kena'ot*—that the Jew who observes the Torah, but doesn't support it, is considered among the cursed; and the Gentile who does not observe the 613 commandments, but supports it, is considered among the blessed.[33]

---

33. *Seder Olam Rabbah Vezuta*, translated by Falk, in *Jesus the Pharisee*, 17–23.

The end of the last quoted paragraph could well function as a commentary on Paul's statements in Romans 2:11–14. Emden not only attributes an irenic attitude to Jesus and the apostles, he himself exhibits an acceptance and validation of the Christian other which all today would do well to emulate.[34] Because he is so exceptional, we ought not to regard his views as typical of Jews of his day, or ours. Today, this viewpoint commonly transmutes into a patronizing stance that fails to maintain Emden's ethical heights.

LITURGICAL THEOLOGIZING ABOUT THE OTHER

The Jewish community has always conveyed and imprinted its theologizing through liturgy, with the Jewish daily prayer book, the *siddur*, remaining religious Israel's theological primer. Together with whatever life cycle and ritual observances or holy day participations the average Jew might encounter, the *siddur* shapes Jewish thought about God more than the Bible or the Talmud, closed books to many Jews. Two central prayers of Jewish life found in the *siddur* help capture the prevailing ethos of religious Judaism concerning mission.

Alenu ("It is for us," or, "It is our responsibility") is a prayer of commissioning that concludes every statutory Jewish service. Phillip Sigal suggests that internal evidence indicates it was written prior to the destruction of the Temple in 70 CE as a liturgical poem on creation, election, and redemption. He sees it to be a meditation on Isaiah 45, originally intended to express "the Jew's rage with paganism and his hope that it will cease to be."[35]

Sigal finds the prayer's universalistic thrust of special missiological interest, as indicated in the second paragraph:

> We hope therefore, Lord our God, soon to behold thy majestic glory, when the abominations shall be removed from the earth, and the false gods exterminated; when the world shall be perfected under the reign of the Almighty, and all mankind will call upon thy name, and all the wicked of the earth will be turned to thee. May all the inhabitants of the world realize and know that to thee every knee must bend, every tongue must vow allegiance. May they bend the knee and prostrate themselves before thee, Lord our God, and give honor to thy glorious name; may they all accept the yoke of thy kingdom, and do thou reign

---

34. Other rabbinic figures championing a universal particularist approach include Ovadia Sforno (fifteenth–sixteenth century) and Avraham Yitzchak Kook (twentieth century).

35. Sigal, "Early Christian and Rabbinic Liturgical Affinities," 77.

speedily over them forever and ever. For the kingdom is thine, and to all eternity Thou wilt reign in glory, as it is written in thy Torah: "The Lord shall be king forever and ever." And it is said "The Lord shall be King over all the earth; on that day the Lord shall be One, and His name One."[36]

One might argue there is nothing in this prayer to indicate that bringing all peoples to the knowledge of the Living God calls for any Jewish action. While this is true, it is also true that this text argues against certain pluralistic impulses, affirming that the highest culmination of history is for all humankind to come to know, acknowledge, and serve the God of Israel.[37] Brill holds that the Alenu is pluri-vocal and "can be read to support inclusive, exclusive, and universal visions."[38]

TOWARD A SYNERGISTIC, COMPLEMENTARIAN, CONVERGING DESTINIES PERSPECTIVE

This survey of Jewish exclusivism, pluralistic universalism, and inclusivism shows that there is no position one may fairly characterize as "the Jewish perspective on mission to the Christian other." The positions held are as diverse as the people holding them, their historical contexts, and the Scripture texts upon which they ground their views. Such diversity invites Christians and Jews to cooperate and interact more on missional matters, developing new and diverse avenues of self-definition and missional theory and praxis, not only as discrete communities, but more dynamically as coordinate peoples of God, or even as one people of God currently living in a state of schism destined to be healed. These communities would do well to assist each other in seeking to better discern God's way forward in the world, which neither community may find apart from the other. Indeed, I hold that these two communities are divinely destined for a synergistic relationship, with divinely ordained complementary callings.

---

36. Birnbaum, *Ha-Siddur Hashalem Daily Prayer Book*, 572.

37. Sigal suggests that the kenosis hymn in Philippians 2 was Paul's meditation on the Alenu, and that the already extant Alenu was added to the Jewish Rosh HaShanah (New Year's) liturgy at Yavneh (Jamnia—90 CE), "as part of the polemic with rising Christianity"; in other words, as a reiteration of the Jewish "party line" upon which Paul had been commenting and from which he was regarded to be departing when he wrote of every knee bowing and every tongue confessing Yeshua as Lord, in contradistinction to the Alenu's according that dignity solely to Israel's God. Sigal, "Early Christian and Rabbinic Liturgical Affinities," 75–78.

38. Brill, *Other Religions*, 60.

Contemporary Jewish Advocates of Complementary Mission by Jews and Christians

There have been and continue to be Jewish leaders who affirm that the One True and Living God of Israel has complementary purposes both for Israel and the church, leaders who view *keruv* within this broader context. Three such dynamic figures are Sholem Asch, David Novak, and Irving Greenberg.

Each of these authors helps lay the groundwork for the Converging Destinies perspective. Separately and together they challenge us to examine whether God is up to something other than the exclusivist, universalistic pluralist, and inclusivist models that we have been examining. They help point us to a complementarian mission of Jews and Christians living in humble service to the Living God and to a yet indistinct eschatological vision.

Sholem Asch

In his essay, *One Destiny: An Epistle to the Christians*,[39] Sholem Asch identified his service to the God of Israel as the call to highlight two great realities: the unique spiritual wonder of Israel's miraculous preservation despite all her historical depredations, and the miraculous spread of the Judaeo-Christian idea in the pagan world. He saw these developments as "a single, divine event . . . two poles of a world which are always drawn to each other, and no deliverance, no peace, and no salvation can come until the two halves are joined together and become one part in God."[40] He developed this paradigm in his 1945 monograph, *One Destiny*, where he views the Christian and Jewish historical experiences as two complementary aspects of the one mission of God.

Ten aspects of his treatment bear mention here as outlining his prophetic and iconoclastic approach to Christian-Jewish relations.

1. Jewish faith is universal in its intent from its earliest beginnings.

2. Jesus is unparalleled as an agent of the actualization of the Jewish ideal. Asch consistently admires him, finding fault only with those who he believes misrepresented him or betrayed his teachings.

---

39. Asch, *One Destiny*.
40. Ibid., 8–9.

3. The preservation of the Jews and the vitality of triumphant Christianity in the pagan world are a unique historical wonder. Christendom and Jewry are united, "two parts of a single whole."[41]

4. Christianity is a form of Judaism. This is reminiscent of the thought of Yehezkel Kauffman,[42] where he views both Christianity and Islam to be extensions of Judaism that alone could uproot idolatry from the pagan world. For Kauffman, "Islam and Christianity enabled the pagan world to turn from idolatry to the God of Israel, without having to become Jews."[43]

5. Christians and Jews benefit mutually from the riches of each other's heritage and history.

6. The sufferings of the Jews out of faithfulness to God, at the hands of anti-Semitic Christendom, demonstrate how these Jews were more aligned with the teachings and heart of Christ than were their persecutors.

7. Asch positions himself with Messiah within the Jewish community, and from there honors an indissoluble bond with Christians who await Messiah.

8. The key word to describe the interrelationship between Judaism and Christianity is *partnership*.

9. Asch speaks of "the Jewish-Christian Man,"[44] perhaps his version of Paul's "One New Man," as found in Ephesians, chapter 2.

10. He speaks of "the dominion of God . . . the commandments [God] has given us through his chosen prophets—both of the Old and the New testaments. . . . these teachings created our civilization, which we call the civilization of the Jewish-Christian idea. We live and die for this civilization, because it is the only one which contains the possibility of salvation for our life at present and hope for life after death in the expectation of the resurrection of the dead." In this, his concept of the kingdom of God is strongly continuous with history, positing the triumph of God's will and ways on the stage of humanity's strivings.

41. Ibid., 9.

42. Kauffman, *Christianity and Judaism*.

43. Ibid., 41.

44. Asch, *One Destiny*, 85.

David Novak

For Asch, neither religious group swallows the other in some inclusiv-ist fashion. Rather, he held that the two are destined to converge within a broader purpose of God beyond the horizon of history as we know it, while on this side of that ultimate horizon, the unique integrity of each group remains and must be honored. Writing more than half a century later, David Novak reflects similar insights:

> The world-yet-to-come *(olam ha-ba)*, this coming-future *(l'atid la-vo)*, is mysterious; it lies on the other side of our present ho-rizon. Therefore Jews and Christians cannot see their past tradi-tions or their present efforts and differences as the last word. The different claims of Judaism and Christianity are only tentative. Surely what God will do at the end of history will be radical enough to surprise everyone—Jews, Christians, and all others who wait for that time here and now.[45]

Asch's prophetic paradigm was far ahead of its time in 1945. But Novak's opinion, coming some fifty-five year later, is no less bold, as provocative in Novak's circles as was Asch's in his own. All concerned with the integrity and future of Jewish Christian dialogue should digest what Novak has to say.

He holds that human persons come into differentiated personhood in the image of God as they know themselves to be addressed, and respond to such address. On the matter of such address, Novak postulates three possibilities: theonomous morality where one responds to having been addressed by God, heteronomous morality where one responds to having been addressed by others, and autonomous morality, where one addresses oneself. While autonomous morality pits part of the self against the self (one responds to a part of oneself that does the addressing), heteronomous mo-rality subjects oneself to the will of others who are likewise creatures. Being governed by such an outside address as one's reference point is essentially idolatrous. It is only in responding to the voice of the Creator, rather than a creature, that the human person rises to his/her true self, neither frag-mented nor subjected to that which is finite and must inevitably pass away. Additionally, addressing oneself is idolatrous because such conduct often involves planning and vowing concerning future events, while in truth, the only one who knows what the future may hold is God. Therefore, autonomy is also fundamentally idolatrous.

And what is the content of that manner of address from God of which we speak? It is his commandments. For Novak, true dialogue between

---

45. Novak, "What to Seek and What to Avoid," 6.

Christians and Jews is only possible because both communities know themselves and each other to have been addressed and commanded by the God of the Hebrew Bible. This dialogue between Christians and Jews takes place along a resultant common border of ethical concern, and members of both communities authenticate themselves if and as they respond worthily to having been so addressed. Because true knowledge of the other's religious tradition remains inaccessible to outsiders, for Novak, there cannot be a Judaeo-Christian faith, but there can be a Judaeo-Christian ethic. This ethical discussion is what constitutes the common border where dialogue with integrity may be conducted.

This common ethic is based on four assumptions, upheld by the Hebrew Bible as authentic revelation:

1. The human person is created by God for the primary purpose of being related to God;

2. This relationship to God is primarily practical, its content being response to the commandments of God;

3. The human person is created as a social being. This sociality is the human precondition for covenant with God . . . (and) the covenant presupposes a general morality of socially pertinent standards as well as entailing specific intercovenantal norms;

4. The ultimate fulfillment of human personhood, both individually and collectively, lies in a future and universal redemptive act by God, one as yet on the unattainable historical horizon.[46]

In considering what the tradition says about how the Jew is to regard the faith of the (Christian) other, Novak contrasts two views borrowed from Maimonides. The first holds that revelation comes to one at the pinnacle of philosophical insight. Maimonides considers it a vulgar view that prophetic insight will come as a matter of course to the morally qualified. He holds instead that moral worthiness must be accompanied by intellectual excellence. The two together constitute the necessary precondition but not the adequate cause of receiving Divine revelation, yet one must avoid imagining that God must provide prophetic insight/revelation when these two conditions are met. No! Prophetic insight is always dependent on the free initiative of God.[47] But all of this discussion indicates that the Christian community, which has received divine revelation, has been intellectually and morally worthy, and has in fact been graced with Divine revelation out

---

46. Novak, *Jewish-Christian Dialogue*, 141–42.

47. Ibid., 138.

of the freedom of God. This gives Christians stature in Jewish-Christian dialogue.

Christians and Jews must engage in their dialogues from within their respective encounters with the Voice of God. To bracket such matters for the sake of a quasi-dialogue will only more firmly establish secularism as the prevailing mind-set, and this "relegates both Judaism's Torah and Christianity's gospel to a corner of historical obscurity."[48]

Instead, Novak counsels this: "The horizon of the Jewish-Christian relationship must be not only what it is between these two communities, but the future of all humankind. Without such a horizon, the relationship is myopic. Each community, in moving toward relationship with the other, must be able to constitute a role for humankind as a whole, and it must be able to do this more compellingly than secularism."[49] And if what he says is true, as I believe it is, then the dialogical struggle in which the church and Israel are called to engage is nothing less a struggle for the redemption of the world.

Irving Greenberg

Modern Orthodox rabbi Irving (Yitzchak) Greenberg[50] repeatedly seeks clarity on the contours of Jewish/Christian complementary mission. He writes in a sorrowful voice preoccupied with the sufferings of Israel, and especially the Shoah. Deeply sensitive and empathetic, Greenberg's views have evolved slowly out of decades of Jacob-like wrestling with this dark reality, which for Greenberg is a struggle for psychological and spiritual survival. Novak seems more the objective philosopher, whose views have been modified out of the inherent implications of his philosophical commitments, while in reading Greenberg, we observe a nocturnal wrestler, over the years seeking to prevail through changing his grip on that Being whom Greenberg will not let go unless he blesses him.[51]

Moored in a deep concern for *tikkun olam* (repairing a broken world), he believes that God's mission is to make right what is wrong, restoring balance to a disordered creation. He regards Israel and the church as divinely

---

48. Ibid., 140.

49. Ibid., 13.

50. Greenberg formerly served as rabbi of the Riverdale Jewish Center, as associate professor of history at Yeshiva University, and as professor in the department of Jewish Studies of the City College of the City University of New York. He also served as founder and president of the National Jewish Center for Learning and Leadership (CLAL).

51. Gen 32:26.

destined partners in this endeavor. Pursuing this partnership is priority one, and "re-visioning the Christian-Jewish relationship through bi-lateral self-revision is the mission of this generation . . . . [P]ersistence will bring the needed permanent breakthrough."[52]

Tikkun olam comes from the lexicon of kabbalistic thought from which Greenberg also borrows the concept *tzim-tzum* (divine self-contraction). He sees God as limiting his actions, even at the cost of his own sufferings, in order to create the challenge and opportunity for human engagement in *tikkun olam*.[53] He sees Israel and the church to be especially called to so engage, exploring this idea in his essay, "Toward a New Organic Model," where he portrays Christianity more positively than is comfortable for many Jews. He highlights complementarity, treading on similar ground to Asch and Novak:

> [I have come to see] Christianity not just as a successful religion with which Jews must reckon, but as an organic outgrowth of Hebrew faith. Biblical Judaism looks forward to a future revelation/redemption that is more universal than the exodus. Therefore, a vital Judaism must stimulate messianic expectations and give rise to movements that seek to realize universal redemption. The question is whether such a messianic movement was meant to happen only once in Jewish history. Or could such a development happen constructively more than once? Could it have been God's purpose to start another religion alongside Judaism to bring the message of redemption to the world in accelerated fashion without breaking up the ongoing election and mission of the original covenanted children of Israel? If this is the case, then Christianity's birth was neither a sign of Judaism's senescence and termination (the classic traditional Christian claim) nor of deviant applications of fundamental Jewish values and concepts (the classic traditional Jewish claim). Rather, the founders of Christianity were being faithful to their remarkable religious experience with Jesus's life and were using Jewish visions, interpretive methods, and thought processes every step of the way, even as their conclusions led them out of Judaism. . . . However . . . they were mistaken in concluding that in order for their experience to be valid, Judaism must be finished.[54]

Greenberg's position bears a superficial resemblance to my own, yet with significant differences. His vision finds its vanishing point in the person

---

52. Greenberg, *For the Sake of Heaven and Earth*, 38.

53. Ibid., 27–28.

54. Ibid., 31–32.

and purposes of God, mine, in the person and purposes of God in Yeshua the Messiah, in whom the divine struggle is so clearly epitomized. Also, he disallows both the objective reality of the resurrection of Christ and its implications for Jews, each of which I affirm. Greenberg suggests that Jesus is not so much a false Messiah (the standard Jewish verdict on the matter), as a failed Messiah, who did not accomplish what he sought. Surprisingly, Greenberg expresses irritation that neither Jews nor Christians have embraced his viewpoint, which he regards to be a workable and ecumenical way forward. Because he develops his view quite deeply, it warrants extensive summation here.

The Voluntary Covenant

In his volume *For the Sake of Heaven and Earth,* Greenberg traces the slow and gradual unfolding of his *rapprochement* with the Christian world, the nature of divine contraction, and the complementary mission of the Jewish and Christian communities. He sees God as having abandoned Israel to the sufferings of the Shoah due to their not living up to his high standards. Through such non-intervention, God has lost the right to insist that Israel be faithful to him and to his commands. Still, Greenberg sees the righteous remnant of Israel as having taken up the challenge to love and obey God despite his having violated the covenant. Religious Jews therefore practice an obedience freely given whereby Israel goes forth with greater vigor, determination, and purity to address her mission as a light to the nations and repairer of a broken world. All of this despite God's having hidden his face from them in their hour of greatest need.[55] He calls this "the voluntary covenant," to which God has brought Israel and others at great cost to himself and to Israel in sufferings endured. For Greenberg, this move leads naturally to a kind of pluralism which "constitutes a divine statement of respect for human freedom as well as a conferral of legitimacy on the broadest expressions of human variety and uniqueness."[56] In a sense, God cut Israel loose to see what she might do.

In his essay, "Respective Roles," Greenberg seems to channel the spirit of Sholem Asch also echoing the sentiments of David Novak, arguing that "Judaism and Christianity share one central message: the triumph of life. Both faiths share the belief that the process of redeeming the world operates through the covenant, that is, a Divine-human partnership. . . . The two faiths *need each other* to maximize the good and to offset the negative

55. Ibid., 27–29.
56. Ibid., 31.

tendencies inherent in both as they follow their own distinctive paths. The two faiths must learn to see themselves as two aspects of a general divine strategy of redemption."[57]

He further argues that "the mission of this generation is to renew revelation, to continue the covenantal way, and to discover each other. . . . Let these two religions model the truth that the love of God leads to the total discovery of the image of God in the other, not to its distortion or elimination."[58] Furthermore, he sees that "the moral and cultural credibility of both Judaism and Christianity . . . depend . . . on overcoming the legacy of their interacting hatefulness."[59] Such ideas, formerly unthinkable for him as a Modern Orthodox Jew, are still off limits for many of his co-religionists who have marginalized and vilified him for moving ancient boundary markers.

Greenberg develops the complementary roles assigned to Judaism and Christianity in the *missio dei* in his essay, "Covenantal Pluralism" suggesting a joint role in history for the two faiths while maintaining a distinction between them. He suggests that the people of Israel have been chosen by God to witness to their loving God and to the divine plan for humanity and the cosmos. He astonishes us by suggesting that "Israel" is not a descriptor of Israeli nationals or Jews only, but of Christians and Muslims as well. The members of other faiths may be recognized as Abraham's cherished children, as theological Israel, but only when and as they have purged themselves of their hatred of Jews and supersessionist positions.[60] Of course, Christianity also postulates a wider-than-ethnic category for the seed of Abraham. Nevertheless, to hear a twenty-first-century Orthodox rabbi widen the term "Israel" beyond the confines of the Jewish people is astounding.[61]

Greenberg's pluralistic perspective, while not denying the ultimacy of religious authority, accepts limits. "The believer may accept the Gospels as the absolute word of God, yet believe that their authority was not intended to obliterate the norms of the Hebrew faith that preceded it (or of

---

57. Ibid., 38.

58. Ibid.

59. Ibid., 39.

60. Ibid., 40.

61. In "Postmodern Hermeneutics and Jewish Christian Dialogue," Lutheran ecumenical theologian George Lindbeck reaches similar conclusions suggesting that if God's covenant with Israel is not revoked, and if the church does not replace Jewish Israel then both the Jews and the church can safely be Israel, albeit in different senses. "If the church is non-supersessionist Israel, then it can see its election as a subset of Jewish Israel's election, thus affirming both." 163.

other religions that precede or parallel it)."[62] In part I can agree (about not obliterating the norms or validity of the Hebrew faith), yet his aspirations seem naïve. We cannot redesign the Scriptures and re-texture our faith so as to eliminate the tensions inherent in the differences between ours and other religious systems. Judaism and Christianity cannot view polytheistic Hinduism to be likewise valid. It seems that Greenberg imposes a certain postmodern moralistic agenda upon Scripture which precludes hearing certain things the text is saying.

Reflections from a Converging Destinies Perspective

We conclude this chapter by reflecting on the foregoing from a Converging Destinies perspective. We can best get to that reflection by the bridge of listening to two Christian voices, Father Lev Gillet and Sister Mary Boys.

Father Lev Gillet: Ministry With and Ministry To

Father Lev Gillet (Eastern Orthodox), a contemporary of Sholem Asch, advocated ideas similar to his, although the two never interacted nor do they refer to each other's works. In his *Communion in Messiah*, Gillet explores two main themes: a true dialogue between Judaism and Christianity, with each having a message to bring to the other, and the "communion" of Jews and Christians either explicitly, with both recognizing and believing in Jesus as Messiah, or implicitly, with both adhering to messianic values, a status widely available and capable of being enlarged.[63] He examines Christian and Jewish mission both together, and to each other.

Gillet focuses on what Christians stand to learn from Judaism's forward-looking messianic restlessness, an activated longing for the coming consummation, even where and when Jews do not believe in any personal Messiah. In contrast, he sees Christians as being too content to believe in a Messiah who came, with no expectation concerning what he is now up to in the world.[64] As for "communion," Christians and Jews commune when they look forward to an expected messianic outcome that ever makes demands upon them.[65] The church not only needs to learn from the Jews, she must also learn to help Israel discern and fulfill its own calling, that all Jews might

---

62. Greenberg, *For the Sake of Heaven and Earth*, 66.

63. Gillet, *Communion in the Messiah*, x.

64. Ibid., 194.

65. Ibid., 196–97.

recognize Israel's enduring chosenness, and the imperative to fulfill its holy destiny, apart from which the church cannot fulfill its own. In harmony with Paul in Romans 11, Gillet affirms that Israel and the nations can only get to the consummation as the fullness of the Gentiles and the fullness of Israel are both realized.[66]

Gillet believes that Judaism and the Jewish community have a mission to the church. In Gillet's words, "The people of the Law and of the Prophets is perpetually sent (missus, missio) by God to the Christian Church in order to witness to certain truths and powers. . . . The present task of Judaism is to maintain certain affirmations of which Christians are in need no less than Jews and for the proclamation of which Israel has a particular authority."[67]

He lists seven such affirmations: (1) the living and personal God—in contrast to the arid metaphysics of much theology; (2) the Scripture and its history of interpretation by Israel; (3) the Law, and the related concepts of justice, duty, and conscience; (4) the Prophets: "The spirit of the prophecy—to be found . . . in the synagogue—is the oxygen necessary for the life of the Christian church, if she is not to degenerate into clericalism and institutionalism. . . . This is not the only inheritance, but the continuous possession of Israel"; (5) the primacy of the spiritual; (6) Messianism, by which he means a restlessness in the present, longing for a future consummation; (7) Zionism. It seems likely that most Jews would gladly entertain this agenda of mission to the church.[68]

Gillet uses the term "convergence" when speaking of how the destinies of Israel and the church meet in Yeshua the Messiah. Writing of Hebrew prophecy and its interpretation, he says, "Jesus is the very centre of convergence. The scattered rays which gleam across the words of the prophets and rabbis are absorbed in the person of Our Lord. All of these elements are brought together and realized in Him."[69] While he used the term differently than I do, I found it startling that he used the term *convergence* I also employ. The more one examines Scripture, the more one notes that God has ordained a consummation involving both Israel and the nations—converging destinies.

---

66. Ibid., 211–17.

67. Ibid., 191–92.

68. Ibid., 192–94.

69. Ibid., 185. Most Jews would respond to this by saying, "Oh, really?"

Sister Mary Boys: Ministry With, But Not To

Gillet's theologizing is creative and innovative. But such new wine inevitably brings tensions with old wineskins and with those who prefer the old wine to the new. Mary C. Boys passionately explores just such tensions in the Roman Catholic context in her article, "Does the Catholic Church Have a Mission 'with' Jews or 'to' Jews?"[70] She proves conclusively that making pronouncements and releasing declarations such as *Nostra Aetate* is one thing, while creating consensus and agreement among either clergy or laity is quite another. Boys favors mission *with* the Jews "in furthering the reign of God" but not mission *to* the Jews which she views to be "no longer theologically warranted and . . . pastorally insensitive." She is especially vexed with the Hebrew Catholic movement which, in her view, is moored in a pre-Vatican II devotionalism and a hard-line conversionist mind-set. However, her dismissal of mission "to" the Jews in favor of mission "with" the Jews fails to persuade when one considers the truth claims of both Judaism and Christianity. Doesn't the church have anything to teach the Jewish world, and doesn't the Jewish community have anything to teach the church? Much! Since both are religions with a worldwide salvific vision, proscribing mission from one to the other seems a form of special pleading.

Equally unconvincing is her advocacy of postponement of any sort of mission by Jews or Christians to the other until eschatological times. Although many would view that course of action to be more politically correct and socially manageable, it is unpersuasive for at least two reasons. First, for Christianity even if not for Judaism, these *are* the last days, as specified on the Day of Pentecost by St. Peter, the first pope, to Roman Catholics.[71] Second, Scripture foretells the future specifically so as to order present action. The Second Letter of Peter makes this explicit when speaking of the final destruction of the present cosmos, the eschatological event par excellence, saying, "Since all these things are thus to be dissolved, what sort of people ought you to be in lives of holiness and godliness, waiting for and hastening the coming of the day of God."[72] Yes, there is a waiting for what was promised, but this is not a passive waiting. Instead, when Scripture prophesies future realities, even eschatological ones, we must ask and answer with our lives the question in this text: in view of what is coming, what sort of people should we to be now in order to hasten this foreordained consummation?

---

70. Boys, "Does the Catholic Church Have a Mission 'with' Jews or 'to' Jews?"

71. Acts 2:14–21. For St. Paul's concurrence, see 1 Cor 10:11.

72. 2 Pet 3:11–12.

SOME CONCLUSIONS

The question of whether Christianity and Judaism have missions to each other has already been answered by the truth claims of each religion: the answer is "yes." Three questions remain to be answered: (1) What is the eschatological vision we anticipate and which we see as "through a glass, darkly"? (2) In view of that vision, what is the mission toward one another appropriate to each group? (3) What conduct is appropriate and inappropriate in the name of mission? Answering each question in turn:

(1) The Converging Destinies perspective anticipates an eschatological vision in which Yeshua of Nazareth is the vanishing point. In his very being he will be both reproof and reassurance to both the Jewish community and the church. To the Jews, he will reprove those who dismissed or fought against the possibility of his messianic claims. He will remind them that he is not only the glory of God's people Israel, he is also a light for revelation to the Gentiles, or as Isaiah said,

> "It is too light a thing that you should be my servant
> to raise up the tribes of Jacob
> and to bring back the preserved of Israel;
> I will make you as a light for the nations,
> that my salvation may reach to the end of the earth."[73]

He will also reassure the Jewish community that he has always been their advocate and faithful King, despite their being a rejected, vilified, and persecuted people. Likewise the church will be reproved for its chauvinism, its history of supersessionism and anti-Semitism, for having forgotten and discounted Israel's status as God's beloved nation, of whom Jesus, the Lion of the Tribe of Judah was, is, and evermore shall be King.

In addition, the age to come will be a time of all nations living in loving synergistic celebratory harmony. With this in mind, we do well to mirror that relational culture in the world as we know it now.

(2) In view of the foregoing, the mission of each group is to present to their respective audiences a vision of who Jesus is, to live lives that honor God in accordance with a mission definition such as the following which I have developed, while each community assists the other in their respective missions.[74]

---

73. Isa 49:6.

74. I explore the respective missions of Israel and the church, and their paramissions, that is the missions in which they assist each other, in two monographs, *Christians and Jews Together* and *Son of David*.

Mission is the Triune God's extending and expressing Godself within and through the created order in blessing, judgment and redemption so as to call forth a people for God's own Name from among Israel and the nations, reconciling them to each other, and enlisting them in individual, familial, and communal obedience of faith for the sake of His name in all aspects of relationship with the social, spiritual, and material aspects of the created order. This bi-lateral *ekklesia* is sent by the Triune God to increase God's glory through mirroring God's self-extension and self-expression in its own self-extension and self-expression, and in calling others from among Israel and the nations into the life here described and into participation in local communities of the faithful, looking forward to and hastening the consummation of all things in the new heavens and the new earth, free from the curse of sin and death, where righteousness dwells, and all things visible and invisible live together in loving synergistic celebratory harmony to the glory of God, world without end.

In responding to such a definition, it is crucial to liberate the term "mission" from its imprisonment in a narrow sense of having a religious message. "Mission" involves not only what we are sent to do, but also who we are sent to be, and involves not only task behaviors but also relational behaviors. In this both Christians and Jews have much to learn from the wisdom of the Talmud. We read this:

R. Hama son of R. Hanina further said: What means the text: Ye shall walk after the Lord your God? Is it, then, possible for a human being to walk after the Shechinah; for has it not been said: For the Lord thy God is a devouring fire? But [the meaning is] to walk after the attributes of the Holy One, blessed be He. As He clothes the naked, for it is written: And the Lord God made for Adam and for his wife coats of skin, and clothed them, so do thou also clothe the naked. The Holy One, blessed be He, visited the sick, for it is written: And the Lord appeared unto him by the oaks of Mamre, so do thou also visit the sick. The Holy One, blessed be He, comforted mourners, for it is written: And it came to pass after the death of Abraham, that God blessed Isaac his son, so do thou also comfort mourners. The Holy one, blessed be He, buried the dead, for it is written: And He buried him in the valley, so do thou also bury the dead.[75]

75. T.B. 14a, *The Soncino Talmud*.

This imitation of God, one of the roots of Jewish ethics, is intrinsic to a right concept of mission. For what are we sent into the world? Is it not to lead lives in imitation of God?

(3) Not all conduct is appropriate in the name of doing God's mission. The ends do not justify the means, and the Jewish community is right to be skittish on these matters since the church has a long history of oppression, coercion, and persecution in these areas. In accordance with the definition given above, our conduct toward those deemed "other" must always "increase God's glory through mirroring God's self-extension and self-expression in our own self-extension and self-expression, calling others from among Israel and the nations into the life here described and into participation in local communities of the faithful." In service to such a vision, coercion, manipulation, and oppression have absolutely no place.

The Converging Destinies paradigm sees Jewish and Christian mission being properly both/and, not either/or. The Christian and Jewish communities have a mission to their own constituencies (the peoples of the nations, and the Jewish people), to be understood within the context of both communities having a mission together in furthering the reign of God. Each also has a mission to the other, all in view of a rehabilitated vision of who Jesus is, and the accountability awaiting all of us at the end of days. Toward preparing for such a consummation, we would all do well to determine carefully what is our definition of mission, for "mission" is what we have been sent to do, and it is for that we are all to be held accountable. In view of all the foregoing, the question with which both communities must wrestle every day is this: "How then shall we live," or to frame it in accord with what I view to be the predominant Jewish question, "What does it mean for us to honor God in this situation?"

PART THREE

Where Are We Going?

4

The Mission of God and the Mission of Protestant Churches in Relation to that of Israel

IN WHAT FOLLOWS, AFTER introducing the concept of the *missio dei,* I broadly trace the seedbeds from which emerged the World Council of Churches (WCC) and the Lausanne Consultation on World Evangelization (LCWE), summarizing the history, character, and development of each with special attention to their relationships with the Jewish people and their concepts of where today's Jewish people fit in the *missio dei.* From these contexts, I show how supersessionist assumptions suppress theologizing about the continuing and consummational role of the people of Israel in the *missio dei* and negatively skew Christian response to the Jewish state. This is a long chapter presenting data that may seem tedious. However, its intent is to make a point by detailing evidence.

MISSIO DEI: A HELPFUL BUT DIVISIVE CONCEPT

More than fifty years ago, the church began grounding its own mission in the *missio dei,* "God the Father sending the Son, and God the Father and the Son sending the Spirit . . . (and) Father, Son, and Holy Spirit sending the Church into the world."[1] Karl Hartenstein is credited with inventing the term in his reflections upon proceedings at the 1952 International Missionary Council Meeting in Willingen, Germany. Previously Karl Barth had

---

1. Bosch, *Transforming Mission,* 390.

touched upon the concept although not the term in a paper he presented at the Brandenburg Missionary Conference (1932). Six years after the Willingen meeting Lutheran theologian and missionary Georg Vicedom was the first to write a book about the *missio dei*, the mission of God.[2]

This concept supplied a much-needed alternative to paternalistic mission models lingering from the marrying of mission endeavors to European/American colonialism. Earlier paradigms of mission included the soteriological, saving individuals from eternal damnation; the ecclesiastical, the expansion of a given church or denomination; and the salvation-historical, the process by which the world would somehow be transformed into the kingdom of God.[3] The *missio dei* paradigm improved on all of these, grounding mission in the being and activity of the Godhead, providing a broader and less culturally linked base for missional action. The new term made such an impact that the historic ecumenical mission journal *International Review of Missions* changed its name to *International Review of Mission*.

DIFFERENCES OF OPINION FROM THE VERY BEGINNING

Enthusiasm should not be confused with unity. As soon as the term was introduced, delegates at the Willingen meeting disagreed sharply as to the nature and implications of the mission of God. Two factions formed which have been evident in theological politics ever since. Adherents of the *church-centered position* understood God's mission to be God's evangelizing work in the world through the church, while those favoring the *world-centered position* saw the mission of God as his work in the world apart from the church. Proponents of this latter view regarded the church as either too restrictive or too outmoded to serve as a vehicle for God's mission in the world.

By the 1960s, ecumenical advocates of the world-centered position were identifying the *missio dei* with good works of all kinds from all sources, Christian and non-Christian, secular and multicultural, ecclesial

2. *The Mission of God.* Christopher Wright decries collapsing the term "mission" into the "sending," arguing that the mission of God is broader and larger: "It seems to me that if we define *mission* only in 'sending' terms we necessarily exclude from our inventory of relevant resources many other aspects of biblical teaching that directly or indirectly affect our understandings of God's mission and the practice of our own." Wright, *The Mission of God*, 23. While Wright has a point, one needs to bear in mind that sending (and going) is the core of mission, whatever other aspects of mission there might be besides.

3. Bosch, *Transforming Mission*.

and non-ecclesial. Critics protested that this compromised the uniqueness of Christ as both message and sender of Christian mission, holding that the world-centered approach rendered forensic justification a mere provincial concern.[4]

Consequently, some conservative leaders and agencies sought to jettison the term altogether. However, the concept survived these threats. Today, the term is universally accepted. In a recent book, evangelical missiologist Christopher Wright, theologian of the Lausanne movement, defines mission as "Our committed participation as God's people, at God's invitation and command, in God's own mission within the history of God's world for the redemption of God's creation."[5] The *missio dei* has become part of the standard vocabulary of the missiological world, across the theological spectrum. The mission of God is alive and well.

Still, the world-centered and church-centered perspectives could not coexist as a house divided. Each produced its own institutional expression: the world-centered perspective took root in the World Council of Churches (WCC), and the church-centered approach in the Lausanne Consultation for World Evangelization (LCWE), conservative to the core.[6]

We will examine each of these institutions, beginning with the genesis, character, and development of the WCC. We will want to take special note of how the WCC conceived of the mission of the church with respect to Israel, and the mission of Israel under the mission of God.[7] After this we will turn to the LCWE and, in the following chapter, the Roman Catholic Church.

4. By the 1980s their concerns were vindicated as the world-centered approach gave rise to a more radical pluralism affirming the revelatory and saving power of God evident in other, even all religious traditions.

5. Wright, *Mission of God*, 23.

6. Actually the WCC, true to its name, does coordinate the work of churches in serving the mission of God. Still, its theologizing focuses on discerning and serving the mission of God as active in the broader context of world affairs and cultures. And the LCWE, while serving the church-based paradigm insofar as this focuses on Christian service to the mission of God, is actually an association of individuals and agencies involved in mission, all of them church or parachurch related, but it is not an association of denominations and church bodies, as is the WCC.

7. In this book I use the term *Israel* to refer to the Jewish people. When referring to the Jewish state, I refer to the State of Israel, the Jewish state, or the nation of Israel.

THE WORLD COUNCIL OF CHURCHES, THE *MISSIO DEI*, AND THEOLOGIZING ABOUT THE JEWISH PEOPLE AND JEWISH STATE

The WCC traces its genesis to the World Missions Conference (WMC, Edinburgh, 1910). Convened by John R. Mott, the WMC sought to foster cooperation between Protestant mission councils. If judged by modern standards of ecumenicity, the endeavor was unimpressive. Out of the 1,400 participants, only seventeen came from the global south, and as it was solely a Protestant endeavor—there were no Catholic or Orthodox representatives.

The WMC reflected a colonialist approach to mission, equating the proclamation of the gospel to the "heathen" world with the spread of Western civilization. The conference birthed the *International Review of Missions* (later, the *International Review of Mission*), and a continuation committee that prepared for the founding of the International Missionary Council (IMC) in 1921.

The Jews presented a unique challenge to these missional activists. Unlike the heathen in the regions beyond, the Jews had never been without the opportunity to hear the gospel. Their anomalous status helps account for how out of focus and even contradictory were the church's statements and attitudes concerning the mission of the Jewish people, and the church's mission to them.

In a positive direction, the Protestant missions world stepped forward during this period as a bulwark against a burgeoning European anti-Semitism.[8] Beginning in the middle of the nineteenth century, political figures employed vilification of the Jews as an acceptable political platform useful for uniting and mobilizing the masses, identifying the Jews as scapegoats for societal ills. In these years and in the early decades of the twentieth century, the missionary movement coalesced to speak out against these canards. Especially during the period following World War I the Protestant church began to view the Jews with a respect and curiosity contrasting with the contempt and stigma of former centuries.

At the same time, in a negative direction, theologizing about the Jews as a people was out of focus. Although prophecy enthusiasts like William Blackstone, David Baron, Dwight Moody, and Samuel Henry Kellogg, and

---

8. John Pawlikowski's definition of anti-Semitism is helpful: "a post-Enlightenment phenomenon following upon earlier forms of anti-Judaism, (referring to) the denigration of Jews rooted in a new form of thinking about biology and genetics, as well as in certain political and cultural trends associated with the emergence of modernity in Europe" ("Antisemitism"). For an in-depth study of the varieties of anti-Semitism and its definitions, see Falk, *Anti-Semitism*, 5–10.

movements like the Plymouth Brethren and Dispensationalism had a well-developed zeal for the eschatological future of the Jewish people, these views were generally regarded as sectarian and uncharacteristic of the church as a whole. And apart from eschatology, little if any theologizing about the Jewish people was taking place.

Christian concern for the Jews was a subset of a more general humanitarian concern for all persecuted minorities, combined with evangelistic zeal. Subsequent developments demonstrate that the more the Jewish people moved out of the subjugated and suffering status in which the church had been accustomed to viewing them, the more confused the church became as to how to theologize about and act toward them.

THREE CONFERENCES HIGHLIGHTING MISSIONAL CONCERN FOR THE JEWS

By the mid-1920s, the IMC had established study centers around the world related to major religions, but nothing had been done with reference to the Jews and Judaism. British members of the Council protested this omission, and a resolution was adopted at the IMC Oxford Meeting in 1923 whereby the Council bound itself to deal with the question of Jewish missions "at some early date."

The Council invited John R. Mott to preside over two conferences on "The Christian Approach to the Jews," both in 1927, one in Budapest and the other in Warsaw. These were passionately evangelistic events. Delegates at the Budapest conference proclaimed: "Our message to the Jews is the love of God revealed in Jesus Christ, crucified, risen, glorified, the fulfillment of the Law and the true Messiah. He is the incarnate Word, the Redeemer of the world, the Savior from sin, who is bringing Israel to her destiny—viz., to become a blessing to all humanity."[9] Here zeal for Jewish evangelism was linked to an anticipated eschatological benefit.

As a testament to prevailing ambiguities, such evangelistic zeal mingled with a provincial lack of Christian self-critical awareness about attitudes towards the Jews. At the third conference, on "The Christian Approach to the Jews" (1931, Atlantic City), Dr. Frank Gavin of the General Theological Seminary in New York stated,

> I don't believe that there is such a thing as "religious anti-Semitism" . . . . Judaism when practiced by observant Jews certainly appears to the non-Jew a religion apart from the ordinary world,

9. See Brockway, "General Trends," 125.

within this quite limited meaning of "religious intolerance"
there is some basis for its existence, but the creating word, the
determining factor, is not to be cast up to the gentile but to the
Jewish side of the ledger.[10]

In other words, if Jews are categorically disdained, it is their own fault, and
should not be regarded as a manifestation of Gentile anti-Semitism.

Such patronizing statements were juxtaposed with others where the
delegates sought the well-being of the Jewish people. Delegates at this
same conference issued a statement expressing "sympathy with the widespread suffering among Jewish peoples in Central and Eastern Europe and
commend(ing) all well-directed efforts to provide relief to the support of
Christian philanthropy." Christian attitudes toward the Jews were fraught
with ambiguities, simultaneously humanitarian and condescending.

Allan Brockway highlights these ambiguities to prevent us from being
enamored of sanguine statements that peppered the proceedings of such
conferences:

Whereas from the beginning of the Christian movement until
the Enlightenment, the Jewish people had been a theological
reality for the church, in the missionary movement it was de-
theologized, becoming "the Jews" or "the Jewish peoples." As
individuals, Jews were suitable targets for Christian evangelism
while, at the same time, they were subjects of Christian compassion when they were oppressed, just as were other deprived
or persecuted children of God. But, as the Jewish people, Jews
were perceived to have no significance for Christian theology or
ecclesiology.

Though Christian opposition to antisemitism could only be
of benefit to the welfare of Jews, it provided a way for the church
to sweep the theological significance of the Jewish people under
the carpet. The otherwise laudable emphasis upon antisemitism
as a violation of human rights became, therefore, a substitute for
wrestling with the critical issue of the theological significance of
the Jewish people for Christian self-understanding. Misguided
as it was, medieval persecution of Jews because they had "killed
God" nevertheless took the Jewish people with theological seri-
ousness, as the missionary movement, by and large, did not.[11]

It is important to heed Brockway's observation that humanitarian concern
and evangelistic zeal may coexist with a refusal, neglect, or inability to

10. Ibid.
11. Ibid., 125–26.

theologize seriously about the Jews. But what is at the root of this? Surely, not indifference. Humanitarian and evangelistic concern are the antithesis of indifference. Rather, the root of the failure to theologize seriously about the Jewish people is supersessionism. Wherever the church thinks of itself as the new Israel, it displaces the Jewish people who then have no place and function in Christian thought. Even a dispensationalist like Leopold Cohn, founder of the American Board of Missions to the Jews, who had a well-developed eschatological expectation concerning the Jewish people, was affected by this. In his brief autobiography and in its addendum, he indicates that it is "for the purpose of calling out from among Israel 'a remnant according to the election of grace' (Romans 11:5), that the American Board of Missions to the Jews, Inc., is in existence."[12] The term "calling out" is significant, and is related to the very nature of the *ekklesia* as an assembly of called out ones. In Cohn's schema, the Jewish people had a significant theological past as God's "ancient people," and a significant future in prophetic writ, but they have no current distinct role in the *missio dei*. This may be termed "the flaw of the excluded present," a position affirming the glories of the biblical Jewish past, and anticipating a glorious Jewish future, while having no real theology of the Jews *now*.[13] For people manifesting the flaw of the excluded present the Jewish people are at best a people on hold. And for supersessionists, they are a people no different than any other, a people with a wonderful past but with a present and future without discrete theological significance.

AMSTERDAM: THE FOUNDING OF THE WORLD COUNCIL OF CHURCHES

From their founding Assembly in Amsterdam (August 1948), the churches of the WCC evidenced both guilt about the Shoah and zeal for Jewish conversion. But the ambiguities ran far deeper than this. The Protestant Commission on the Witness to Israel of the Protestant Federation of France prepared an appalling statement for this inaugural Assembly. They held that the Jews should see their sufferings (in the Shoah) as not due to the death of Jesus (the church thus disputing the ancient charge of deicide), but were rather "an appeal to conversion and to turn from their unfaithfulness . . . [that] consists in their refusal to recognize him as Messiah foretold in the prophets." Don't miss their point: God allowed (caused?) the Shoah to awaken the

---

12. Cohn, *The Story of a Modern Missionary to an Ancient People.*

13. The name of this principle is a respectful variation of the name a renowned article by Hiebert, "The Flaw of the Excluded Middle."

Jewish people to their guilt for the rejection of Christ. One would think it could not get any worse, but one would be wrong. The statement goes on to say "unless we are to be at cross-purposes, a clear distinction should be drawn between anti-semitism and the anti-Judaism which is involved in every summons to conversion. . . . The aim of general conversion cannot be anything less than the spiritual destruction of Judaism."[14] They were making explicit this goal for Christian witness: the spiritual destruction of Judaism. Although the Assembly did not ratify this statement, it should not be considered anomalous. Rather, it baldly stated assumptions held by too many people, noxious weeds growing from the soil of supersessionism, ironically, among those who decried anti-Semitism.

In harmony with Brockway's observation, the French statement helps us see that it is possible to reject anti-Semitism, the categorical hatred of the "Jewish race," while embracing anti-Judaism. Supersessionism fails to provide a positive theological or ecclesiological category into which to fit the Jewish people as a people, and fails to nurture theological sympathy for the Jewish state beyond the common right of all people to live somewhere.[15]

OTHER TAMPERING WITH MISSIONAL CLARITY REGARDING THE JEWS

In 1931, prior to the founding of the WCC, the IMC established the Committee on the Christian Approach to the Jews (CCAJ) as a quasi-independent sponsored entity. It had its own constituency, independently raised budget, its own constitution, and was composed of representatives of agencies involved in mission to the Jews, as well as others with relevant knowledge or expertise. Eventually, it was to include members of the WCC (1951).[16]

14. Brockway, "General Trends," 128. When the Church posits itself as the enemy of Judaism and God as the one who abandons or consigns Israel to genocidal terrors, can one blame the Jews for not only rejecting but also despising the "good news" being proffered by the Church?

15. On the matter of the right of all people to live somewhere, and this being all the Jews should expect, a history lesson is in order. Before WWII, there were signs up in Europe which said, "Jews! Go to Palestine!" For many in Europe, the Jews were unwelcome strangers. Now that the Jews are in Palestine/Israel, many feel them to be intruders even there. Helen Thomas, for many decades the dean of White House reporters, consigned herself to infamy when she stated that the Jews should "get the hell out of Palestine" and "go home." When asked where that would be, she suggested Germany and Poland. No further comment is necessary.

16. In 1954, the Committee published a collection of essays, *The Church and the Jewish People*, which included a wide variety of articles expressing seminal thoughts at a seminal time. Of special note: the name of the collection speaks of the Jewish people

When the IMC merged with the WCC (1961) delegates vigorously debated whether the CCAJ should merge as well. Some felt that the committee would lose its traction by joining the WCC, but they were overruled. This proved unfortunate. While the CCAJ had formerly been primarily oriented toward mission, when the committee joined the WCC, the committee name was changed to the "Committee on the Church and the Jewish People" (CCJP). This was already a modification of her former character. The new name blunted the missional edge of the CCAJ. And subsequent events would show that the CCJP would not always think and act in ways Jews would view positively.

FOUNDING OF THE STATE OF ISRAEL

The founding of the Jewish state brought WCC ambivalence regarding the Jewish people into sharpest focus. The Amsterdam Assembly met within a few months of Israel's founding. Brockway observes that "delegates simply did not know how to respond to the Jewish people's claim to statehood because it added a political dimension to the Christian approach to the Jews."[17] To their credit, at this earliest stage, the Assembly chose to remain noncommittal on the comparative claims and conflicting rights of the various peoples in the region. Canon Henry Wolfe Baines of the Church of England added this sentence to the Assembly statement on the situation: "We appeal to the nations to deal with the problem (of the new State of Israel) not as one of expediency, political, strategic or economic, but as a moral and spiritual question that touches a nerve-center of the world's religious life." At this point, at least some of churches had some memory of a scriptural testimony of Israel's uniqueness. However, in future years, this kind of voice would be drowned out by others categorically critical of the claims and policies of the Jewish state.

Evanston (1954) and New Delhi (1961)

The more the Jewish people moved out of the subjugated status to which the church had grown accustomed to assigning them, the more confused the church became as to how to theologize about the people Israel. From the time of the founding of the WCC, the sign of Israel's overcoming subjugation

---

as a collective entity, a sign of some ideological movement taking place in WCC circles concerning the Jewish people as a collective entity.

17. Brockway, "General Trends," 131.

was the founding of the Jewish state, something with which the Council has not fully been able to come to terms even now. By 1954 a separation became apparent between the churches concerned for the theological significance of the Jewish people and Jewish state and those that saw the Jews and their statehood purely in political terms, and as an inconvenience.

The uniqueness of the Jewish people was itself in dispute, and the issue arose sharply at the Evanston Assembly (1954). Originally the theme of Assembly was "Jesus Christ: The Hope of the Word—The Hope of Israel." Opposing voices contended that any mention of Israel would undermine the WCC cause in the Middle East. They rejected "any suggestion that political events at present befalling the Jews were associated with the fulfillment of the Christian hope." The motion to eliminate all references to Israel passed. To this day, this remains the prevailing position of the WCC. There were dissenting voices: "The next day, a minority report . . . was submitted by twenty-four theologians expressing the conviction that the Christian hope include hope for the conversion of Israel. This report was published as an appendix in the Assembly report, in essence shunted off to the back pages."[18]

Following the Evanston Assembly, the WCC Central Committee requested that a joint consultation be held together with the IMC's Committee on the Christian Approach to the Jews on Christian convictions and attitudes in relation to the Jewish people. The meeting was held, but its proceedings were not deemed representative of the WCC constituency. More marginalization.

To summarize briefly, in its early stages, while the WCC decried anti-Semitism, Judaism was generally negated or derided as a primitive religious stage transcended through the gospel, and the existence of the Jewish state was a topic to be avoided or dismissed as without theological significance. The generalized liberalized humanitarian ethos of the WCC worked against particularism while the church's tradition of supersessionism neutralized any impulse toward thinking theologically about the Jews. When the church identifies itself as the new Israel, it should come as no surprise that she has great difficulty knowing what to do with the old one. A supersessionism

18. Ibid., 133–34. Attempting to account for the heated division on even including the phrase "The hope of Israel" in the assembly theme, general secretary of the WCC Willem Visser t' Hooft suggested that the division was along the lines of which groups had had the most experience with Hitler's national socialism. Those who had had an intimate experience of this were driven to recognize the demonic nature of hatred for the Jews, and the significance of Romans 9–11. Those who had not had this experience felt that to single out the Jews and to give them a special place in history was a sort of discrimination. These, together with the small number of Near Eastern Christians, constituted the prevailing majority (Visser t' Hooft, *Memoirs*, 313–14).

founded on the premise of Israel being set aside has difficulty dealing with a Jewish state front and center.

Even at this early stage then, less than a decade after its founding, the die was cast in the WCC concerning its posture toward the Jewish people and the Jewish state. And at New Delhi (1961), when the Council took the Russian and Eastern Orthodox churches into membership, Brockway reminds us, "It was no occasion for acrimonious theological debate (about the Jewish people and Jewish state) and the Council leadership made sure it didn't happen." Willem Visser t' Hooft offers interesting reflections on what happened and why. In the process he confirms our analysis of the WCC's inability to deal with the Jewish people and Jewish state when he says, "We knew that we could speak out together against antisemitism [on humanitarian grounds] but that we had as yet no common mind about the theological question of the destiny of the Jewish people or about the deeper significance of the creation of the state of Israel." As has been the case from the beginning, the WCC defaulted to a generalized humanitarian ethos, passing a resolution that "concentrated on the issue of discrimination and which made the important point that the historic events which led to the crucifixion should not be so presented as to fasten upon the Jewish people of today responsibilities which belong to our corporate humanity and not to one race or community."[19]

As in the past, minority voices rose up to explore the theological significance of the Jewish people and the Jewish state, and once again these were marginalized and neutralized. Rev. Christophe Schnyder of the Swiss Protestant Church Federation proposed an amendment that would have inserted the sentence: "On the contrary, the Jews remain God's chosen people (cf. Rom. 9–11), for even their rejection for a time must contribute to the world's salvation." At Visser 't Hooft's urging, however, Schnyder withdrew the amendment and the debate was over. Writing in the 1980s Allan Brockway reminds us how "since 1961 there has been no attempt to revive the question of the Jewish people's place within the ecumenical theological spectrum at a World Council of Churches Assembly."[20] This remains true today. Political correctness makes such a fine garrote with which to strangle theological progress.

19. Visser t' Hooft, *Memoirs,* 313–14.
20. Brockway, "General Trends," 136.

Uppsala (1968) and Nairobi (1975)

Despite the policy of marginalization, contrary voices concerning the Jewish people and Jewish state continued to make themselves heard. Just prior to the Uppsala Assembly (1968), the Commission on Faith and Order produced "the Bristol Document" which represented fresh thinking on the relationship between Christians and Jews. Its vision of Christian-Jewish solidarity was far ahead of its time:

> It is possible to regard the church and the Jewish people together as forming the one people of God, separated from one another for the time being, yet with the promise that they will ultimately become one. Those who follow this line of thinking would say that the church should consider her attitude towards the Jews as theologically and in principle as being different from the attitude she has to all other men who do not believe in Christ. It should be thought of more in terms of ecumenical engagement in order to heal the breach than of missionary witness in which she hopes for conversion.[21]

We ought not to miss the visionary newness of this proposal. This sort of language is quite popular today and is commonly used by postliberal theologians who speak of a schism destined to be healed between Israel and the church. This paradigm is at diametric variance with supersessionist triumphalism, and has much to commend it biblically. However, it is largely neglected by many from both the right and the left. Many on the right cannot conceive of the Jewish people having any theological profile unless and until they explicitly believe in Jesus Christ, while those on the left cannot conceive of the people of Israel as an elect theological datum in God's endgame, as necessary partners with the church. Their instinct is to regard Israel's theological claims to be spurious, troglodytic, or even fascistic. However both sides neglect how Paul himself views the Jewish people to be home base to the people of God, such that Gentiles (read "pagans") were without hope and without God in the world precisely because they were "strangers to the commonwealth of Israel" (Eph 2:12). Furthermore, the apostle conceives of God's endgame strategy as encompassing both the fullness of the Gentiles and the fullness of Israel, two fullnesses, not one, neither subsumed by the other.[22]

21. "The Church and Her Witness," Section Four of *The Church and the Jewish People*.

22. While some Christian exegetes like John Gager hold that Israel enters her fullness apart from faith in Jesus/Yeshua, others insist Paul's assumption is otherwise—that all reaches its culmination in and through the Triune God, with Christ as the

Unlike some who conceive of this healed schism as precluding any evangelistic action, when all scriptural evidence is taken into account, it seems more appropriate to hold that the only evangelism which should be precluded is that which fails to preserve and celebrate Jewish communal cohesion and fidelity to the sacred patrimony that has been in her custodial care for millennia.[23]

The Bristol document speaks also of the State of Israel, pleading "in view of the changed situation in the Middle East as a result of the war of June 1967, that also the question of the present State of Israel, and of its theological significance, if any, has to be taken up." In a context where the subject is invariably avoided, this plea for theologizing about the State of Israel is revolutionary! However, even though carefully couched in diffident language, this plea went unheeded. Apparently any discussion of Israel's theological significance was to remain off limits for the WCC.

In defiance of the intent of the framers of the Bristol document, almost nothing was said about the theological significance of the Jewish people at the Uppsala Assembly (in 1968, less than a year after the Six-Day War). Instead, emphasis shifted to the general political situation in the Middle East and the troubles between Israel and her Arab neighbors, under the general rubric, "Towards Justice and Peace in International Affairs." Again, we see in process the generalizing tendency of philosophical liberalism, and a chronic avoidance of particularism, especially Jewish particularism.

The Assembly Statement on the Middle East expressed concern about the situation in the Middle East, and spoke of how "occupation continues." We should note that very term "occupation" is a partisan political statement. What for some are the disputed territories, and for others, the rightful possession of a people who gained these territories in a defensive war, for the WCC remains evidence of Israel's illegal and oppressive occupation. Krister Stendahl, a delegate from the Lutheran Church in America later to become moderator of the Consultation on the Church and the Jewish People, introduced a motion seeking to add an additional sentence to the statement:

---

cornerstone of the entire enterprise. However, in this case, we do well to remember that for Paul the fullness of Israel, which comes through the same Messiah as the fullness of the nations, is not subsumed into the latter fullness. Interestingly, elsewhere in Scripture this distinction is likewise maintained, as in Isaiah 49 where the Servant of the Lord not only gathers the tribes of Israel but is *also* a light to the nations. I hold that people on both the right and left tend to forget who Israel is to God, the differentiated consummatory union of which Paul speaks, and the full identity of Jesus Christ, who is not only the Savior of the world, but still, and indeed first, the Son of David, through whom God's destiny for the Jewish people must, will, and does move forward to an altogether glorious consummation.

23. Rom 9:4.

"It is the special responsibility of the World Council of Churches and of its member churches to discern ways in which theological and religious factors affect the conflict." A reasonable request, framed in the most polite of terms. But in response, a delegate from the Greek Orthodox Patriarchate of Antioch proposed that the word "theological" be removed, to which Stendahl demurred. When put to a vote, the deletion was accepted, though the remainder of the sentence was incorporated into the statement.[24] Here we clearly see theologizing about Israel nullified, Israel's status as a nation disputed, and the groundwork laid for seeing her as the habitual aggressor in the region. We see here a decline in the fortunes of Jewish people and Jewish state in the WCC. "The mood and center of attention at Uppsala relative to the Jewish people was radically different from what it had been at Amsterdam, Evanston, and even New Delhi." Matters had deteriorated since Amsterdam, Evanston, and New Delhi, none of which was a highwater mark for the status of the Jewish people and Jewish state. So marked was the deterioration that "Stendahl's cautiously-worded addition to the Uppsala statement and its reception indicate that the Amsterdam plea *probably* would have gotten short shrift at Uppsala."[25] In other words, what was a matter for consideration in 1948 was by 1968 a dead issue.

At the Nairobi Assembly (1975) attempts to place Israel in an overtly theological context were defeated during debate. This demonstrates hardening resistance against any prospect of seeing the people of Israel as currently elect, and their land claims as having any biblical basis. Today any voices advocating such ideas are stigmatized and disallowed as "Christian Zionism" as if this label was self-evidently a term of opprobrium. Even in a body as international and consensus-governed as the WCC, minority voices advocating theologizing about the Jewish people and the Jewish state are neutered by countervailing voices and voting blocks, through the passivity of some unprepared to step forward on Israel's behalf, and due to officials prevailing upon minority voices to be silent in the interests of preserving group tranquility. To be fair, it is also true that appeals from delegates from Middle Eastern churches for more explicit affirmation of the Palestinian cause went unheeded at Nairobi. The Nairobi statement on the Middle East avoided making theological or even religious statements, content to affirm three points that have since become the basis of World Council policy: "Withdrawal by Israel from territories occupied in 1967; the right of all states including Israel and the Arab states to live in peace within secure and recognized boundaries; the implementation of the rights of the Palestinian

24. Brockway, "General Trends," 136–37.
25. Ibid., 137.

people to self-determination."[26] Again, the language of occupation is anything but neutral, framing the debate in a manner that predetermines how
the state of Israel will be regarded.[27]

Vancouver (1983)

At Vancouver, the Sixth Assembly took positions about interfaith dialogue
and mission, but said nothing about the Jewish people as such. Instead, the
theological stance evident at Uppsala and Nairobi intensified, centering in a
concern for peace and justice through standing with the poor and oppressed.
Again we see in place a liberal tendency to prefer the general to the specific,
an antipodal antipathy to particularism, and surely, to Jewish particularism.
Israel is assumed to be the destabilizing factor in the Middle East. We also
note an antipathy toward, and stereotyping stigmatization of what is commonly termed Christian Zionism, that is, any theological enthusiasm for the
Jewish state and its eschatological significance. This is why the Introduction
of the Assembly's Statement on the Middle East laments how "historical factors and certain theological interpretations have often confused Christians
outside in evaluating the religious and political developments in the Middle
East."[28] This is code language for disparaging and stigmatizing Christian
Zionism as an unhelpful source of confusion and instability. It seems clear
that the WCC feels obligated to side with the (Arab) churches in the Middle
East, their representation of who is at fault, and what must be done about it.
It also seems clear that Israeli Jews would do well to look elsewhere than to
the WCC for fairness, support, and understanding. This would include the
many Israeli Jesus believers whose protest against such WCC construals of
the situation remain unaddressed.

It would be naïve to imagine that WCC friction concerning the Jewish
state is solely due to Israeli governmental policies and actions. At its root,
the problem lies with the dissonance between supersesssionism and Israel
redivivus. The State of Israel is for supersessionist Christianity an irritat-
ing and unacceptable symbol of Jewish strength. From long experience, the
church knows how to deal with Jewish weakness, neediness, and depreda-
tion: it does not know how to deal with Jewish strength. The church has
learned to deal with Jewish impotence, but not Jewish virility. Apart from

---

26. See Paton, ed., *Breaking Barriers*, 162ff.

27. For the role of framing as a political strategy, see Lakoff, *Don't Think of an
Elephant!*.

28. Gill, ed., *Gathered for Life*, 147ff.

keeping these things in mind, analyses of the root of Christian concern about the sins of the Jewish state will always be flawed.

Canberra (1991)

In August of 1992, The Central Committee of the World Council of Churches adopted a statement on "Christian-Jewish Dialogue Beyond Canberra '91" which in its opening paragraph bears witness to continuing tensions in the WCC concerning theologizing about the Jewish people and the modern State of Israel:

> The relationship between the World Council of Churches and the Jewish community is as old as the Council itself. It has grown and changed over the years. Much progress has been made after many centuries of controversies in the history of Christian-Jewish relations. On several painfully divisive issues we have come closer to reconciliation. New problems and concerns have, however, come up that need to be addressed.[29]

Reading between the lines, this is quite a way to begin an ecumenical document. This language signals that the underlying issues to be unearthed are going to be unpleasant, perhaps unwelcome, but, in the view of those drafting the document, critical. It is like one spouse telling the other the other, "You and I will need to have a talk." Storm clouds are gathering.

The document highlights the theme of the Canberra Assembly, "Come Holy Spirit Renew the Whole Creation" and the themes of unity, peace, and justice, which none can gainsay. The reference to peace and justice anticipates the bone of contention in the document: the Jewish state and "the occupied territories." On a related note, the section "Developing Commitments" in article B acknowledges that "issues of Jewish-Christian relations . . . can and do divide churches." Although these issues are not named, the statement seems to intimate the kinds of tensions we have been tracing since the WCC was founded.

After a preparatory and unambiguous disavowal of anti-Semitism the document names the disputed issue, the Council's critique of the Jewish state, couched in characteristically careful rhetoric:

> We assume that criticism of the policies of the Israeli government is not in itself anti-Jewish. . . . Expressions of concern regarding Israel's actions are not statements regarding the Jewish people or Judaism, but are a legitimate part of the public debate. The same

29. "Christian-Jewish Dialogue Beyond Canberra '91."

> holds true for a critique . . . of states and political movements
> that claim a Christian foundation for their basic values.

Fair enough, but it is wearisome that this critical stance concerning Israeli policy is the only voice heard within WCC circles. Where is the appropriate tension one would expect in an organization that advocates diversity, pluralism, and an openness to hearing everyone's voice? It seems clear that only anti-Zionist voices prevail in WCC circles when the Middle East is discussed.

SOME IRENIC AND MARGINALIZED VOICES

The "Christian-Jewish Dialogue Beyond Canberra '91" document references another: "The Churches and the Jewish People: Toward a New Understanding," a statement issued by the Consultation on the Church and the Jewish People at the conclusion of its meeting in Sigtuna, Sweden, October 31 to November 4, 1988. On a positive note, the Sigtuna document speaks within the context of a general commitment to irenic pluralism, and acknowledges "a special relationship between Jews and Christians because of our shared roots in biblical revelation."[30] It speaks as well of "our Jewish neighbors" and the "Jewish and Christian faiths" and "faith communities."[31] The second section of the paper, "Toward a Christian Understanding of Jews and Judaism," is remarkable in its careful language and nuanced insight into how Christian knowledge and attitudes on Jews and Judaism have matured. The Sigtuna document references another, the Consultation on the Church and the Jewish People, which was commended to the member churches by the WCC Executive Committee in 1982 as "Ecumenical Considerations on Jewish-Christian dialogue." Skillfully crafted and wide in scope, it bears close consideration.

In the second section of this document, "Toward a Christian Understanding of Jews and Judaism," eighteen points are listed assessing how dialogue with the Jews has helped the church revise its prior negative stereotypes about Judaism, its sources, and its leaders; how the legacy of supersessionism birthed a Christian tradition of negatively portraying Jews and Judaism; and the need to balance understandings of the commonalities and differences between Judaism and Christianity. The final five points, 2.14—2.18, concern Israel's relationship to the Land, how even though the

---

30. "The Churches and the Jewish People: Toward a New Understanding," Article A (Preamble).

31. Ibid.

Jewish people learned to live in Diaspora, in varied ways and with varied intensity they viewed the Land to be their true home from which they were dispersed and to which they longed to return. However, the document states that Jews, Muslims, and Christians all equally view this Land to be "the Holy Land," and that all have an equal claim. The final point states, "the need for dialogue is the more urgent, when under strain the dialogue is tested. Is it mere debate and negotiation or is it grounded in faith that God's will for the world is secure peace with justice and compassion?" Although these are irenic words, since this is a document on Jewish-Christian dialogue, what is being asked is for Jews to relinquish their sense of ownership of the Land and any sense of divine grant or of Jewish priority, and to view the matter of their rights as open to negotiation with Christian and Muslim dialogue partners to whom they should grant provisional trust. However, the very historical experience touched upon in the prior thirteen points justifies Israel's distrust of Christian intent, as does the WCC's proven bias toward Palestinian claims and contemporary experience with the Muslim world. This, combined with Israel's justifiable scriptural reading of the prior claim to the land of the descendants of Jacob, makes it a virtual certainty that Jewish decision makers will pass on the proposal, even if it is always possible to find Jewish academics and leaders prepared to dialogue on such utopian bases.

After a well-crafted section 3 on "Hatred and Persecution of Jews—A Continuing Concern," the document closes in section 4 with eight statements concerning "Authentic Christian Witness." These are of special interest as they touch upon how the church sees itself serving the *missio dei* with reference to the Jews in particular. They outline how mission is a non-negotiable imperative for the church (4.1), that coercive proselytism is illegitimate and that Jews should be protected from it (4.2–3), that the church remains committed to mission, whether world-based or church-based, and that there are those who insist mission remains explicitly evangelistic (4.4).

Section 4.5 names four perspectives on mission to the Jews represented in WCC churches, of which the first and second view generally coalesce: "There are Christians who view a mission to the Jews as having a very special salvific significance, and those who believe the conversion of the Jews to be the eschatological event that will climax the history of the world. There are those who would place no special emphasis on a mission to the Jews, but would include them in the one mission to all those who have not accepted Christ as their Saviour. There are those who believe that a mission to the Jews is not part of an authentic Christian witness, since the Jewish people finds its fulfilment in faithfulness to God's covenant of old." While this is very helpful in characterizing the variety of positions on mission to the Jews in WCC circles in the context of the *missio dei*, it also demonstrates that the

WCC has no agreed upon "party line" on this matter.[32] This is not surprising when one remembers the WCC's tradition of avoiding theological discussion about the people and Land of Israel, and the foundation of supersessionism which so influences presuppositions, nullifying any expectation of a continuing role for an Israel that has been replaced in God's economy of dealings with the world.

Harare (1988)

Two developments from this Assembly especially impact the concerns we have been pursuing. First is document 5.6, "Statement on the Status of Jerusalem." The document is quite comprehensive, and cannot be handled here in detail. It makes ten points, of which the first four have numerous subpoints. Point 1 reaffirms and summarizes earlier positions of the WCC, especially concerning the status and disposition of holy places, and the perpetuation of the local communities that venerate these shrines. These matters are presented as "seen as part of a general settlement of the wider Middle East conflict" (1.4), which then becomes the general concern of the rest of the document. I find it significant and vexing that the Israelis are presented as the sole troublemakers in their region, which flies in the face of the facts, as if neither Muslims nor Christians had any political agendas or militant factions.

So it is that Section 2 *"condemns once again* the violations of fundamental rights of Palestinians in Jerusalem which oblige many to leave." In general the document pleads for Jerusalem to be a *corpus separatum,* basing this on Resolution 194 of the United Nations General Assembly (December 1948), and resolutions claiming a right of return for Palestinian refugees (Resolutions 181 and 194). These and other international rulings are invoked, chiefly those of the United Nations, without any attention to their historical context, to the ways in which votes were assembled to pass these measures, or to disputes about their interpretation. An incautious or uninformed reader of this WCC document could reach only one conclusion: that Israel is at fault and to be condemned on every issue addressed. However, there are two sides to every story, and as we have seen the other side of the

32. This section of the paper closes by indicating that interfaith dialogue properly includes bearing forthright witness to one's faith (4.6), the varied ways Jewish believers in Jesus are viewed by the Jewish community or view themselves in relationship to the wider Jewish world, (4.7), and an offer by the WCC to remain open to growing in new understandings and language about Judaism as discovered by Christians of various traditions who engage in dialogue with Jews in local, national, and international contexts (4.8).

story pertaining to Israel's theological and political status has been silenced and marginalized from the very founding of the WCC.[33]

Porto Alegre (2006)

Although its interfaith pronouncements about the Jewish people are often couched in well-tooled, careful, and respectful language, the WCC has adopted a hard line in Jewish-Christian relations concerning theologizing about the Jewish people and the about the Jewish state. As has been chronicled here, since its founding three months after Israel declared statehood, the WCC has been at best noncommittal about the Jewish state, even while calling for the rights of all peoples in the region to live in peace with their neighbors with secure borders. It is in this last respect that the WCC has been most rejectionist about the Jewish state, holding that the borders of the state are illegitimate and calling for a retreat to the borders that prevailed before the Six-Day War. Israel's failure to do so has led to be being labeled an occupying force, and the Palestinians labeled as victims. This hard-line stance remains the WCC position today, as is evident in this comment recorded by Dr. David Hilborn, an observer representing the World Evangelical Alliance, confirming our assessment of the WCC's stigmatization of Israel as the source of trouble in the region:

> The Porto Alegre Assembly marked the mid-point of the ecumenical Decade to Overcome Violence, and many proposals and resolutions related to this concern. . . . While this issue proved uncontroversial from an Evangelical point of view, a later presentation on the Middle East regrettably confirmed widespread Evangelical suspicions of WCC's political and theological bias. All the images of violence presented here were of Israelis harassing Palestinians; but we saw nothing of the carnage caused by Islamist suicide bombings.[34]

33. For a brief and informative alternative to the WCC's portrayal of the history and interpretation of international rulings on these matters, and of Israel as the troublemakers as recalcitrant troublemakers in the region, see Bard, "Myths and Facts Online." Also of value, and in greater depth, see Peters, *From Time Immemorial*; Baker, ed., *Israel's Rights as a Nation-State in International Diplomacy*; and Dershowitz, *The Case for Israel.*

34. Rev. Dr. David Hilborn, Head of Theology, Evangelical Alliance UK, Member, World Evangelical Alliance Theological Commission, reporting on the Porto Allegre Assembly of the WCC (2006).

The situation in the area is portrayed monolithically, with the Jews cast as militarist aggressors, and the Palestinians as hapless and innocent victims of the implacable domination of Zionist oppressors.

Preliminary to the tenth Assembly of the WCC, held in Busan, Korea, October 30–November 8, 2013, an "International and Ecumenical Conference: Christian Presence and Witness in the Middle East," was convened May 21–25, 2013 in Beirut, Lebanon. This conference was cosponsored by the WCC and the Middle East Council of Churches (MECC).

The seventh fundamental principle undergirding the Beirut gathering stated, "Christians who promote 'Christian Zionism' distort the interpretation of the Word of God and the historic connection of Palestinians—Christians and Muslims—to the Holy Land, enable the manipulation of public opinion by Zionist lobbies, and damage intra-Christian relations."[35] For the WCC and MECC, whatever Israel is doing in the region, it has no biblical claim to be there. For these participants, it was axiomatic that Israel is not only responsible for unrest in the region, but also guilty of conspiratorial manipulation of public opinion through the actions of "Zionist lobbies." This is an old and pernicious anti-Semitic meme. Similar statements may be found nearly word for word in the Nazi propaganda paper *Der Sturmer,* or in *The Protocols of the Learned Elders of Zion,* a Tsarist forgery from the early twentieth century, which purported to be reports on secret Jewish meetings about taking over the world. The document is touted by various figures in the Arab world.[36]

Having received and ratified this advisory Beirut document, the tenth WCC Assembly itself attributes all turmoil in the Middle East to the Israel/Palestine issue. This is clear in their November 8, 2013 "Statement Affirming the Christian Presence and Witness in the Middle East."[37] Throughout the document, there is no doubt about who is being positioned as the culprit in the Middle East, responsible for instability in the region. "This tension and violence around the Middle East and in North Africa are taking place in the midst of the on-going and long-standing Palestine/Israel conflict in the region, and the Israeli occupation of Palestinian and Arab territories

35. http://www.oikumene.or/en/resources/documents/wcc-programmes/public-witness-addressing-power-affirming-peace/middle-east-peace/statement-on-christian-presence-and-witness-in-the-middle-east.

36. For corroboration and further details on the history and current distribution of this document, see "A Hoax of Hate: The Protocols of the Learned Elders of Zion," on the website of the Anti-Defamation League, http://www.adl.org/anti-semitism/internatioinal/c/a-hoax-of-hate-the-protocols.html.

37. https://www.oikoumene.org/en/resources/documents/wcc-programmes/public-witness-addressing-power-affirming-peace/middle-east-peace/statement-on-christian-presence-and-witness-in-the-middle-east.

since 1967."[38] As with any such document, take note not only of what is said, but more importantly, the language used to frame the discussion, which predetermines how one interprets the issues being addressed. The term *occupation* frames Israel's presence in the disputed territories as aggressive and illegitimate. "Disputed territories" would have been a more appropriate, value-neutral term. But you will read none of that here, because the verdict is already settled, and such documents are published as a means of swaying public opinion for political ends, even in the name of theology.

The WCC adds, "Resolving once and for all the conflict between Israelies and Palestinians in accordance with United Nations resolutions and internal law, addressing all final status issues, including the right of return, can only help in resolving the other conflicts in the region."[39] But United Nations resolutions have been monolithically against Israel and are widely known to be the result of power blocs voting in collusion. The Palestinian right of return as interpreted by the United Nations is so broad as to spell the death knell of the Jewish State if adopted. And the document is significant not only for what it says and how, but for what it does not say. Israel finds no friends here, no sympathetic words. As in the first Assembly meeting in 1948, here again we see the WCC not knowing what to do with the Jewish State, long ago written out of the theological script, and now so inconvenient.

In the next-to-last paragraph of the document, Israel is stigmatized once more as the WCC "reiterates its call to the United Nations to secure and protect the integrity of the holy sites of all religions in Jerusalem and make them accessible to all as well as to end the occupation of East Jerusalem by Israel." It is well known and easy to demonstrate that Israel is the only political force in the region that has kept holy sites open to all, but such a statement has its purposes: it serves to label Israel as obstructionist, even if falsely so.

THE LAUSANNE MOVEMENT, THE *MISSIO DEI*, AND THEOLOGIZING ABOUT THE JEWISH PEOPLE AND JEWISH STATE

With its first international gathering in 1974, the Lausanne Committee of World Evangelization (LCWE) emerged as the standard bearer for church-related evangelical perspectives on mission. As with the WCC, one

---

38. WCC, *Statement Affirming*, section 3.5.
39. Ibid.

cannot rightly understand the character and genesis of the movement apart from considering tensions and events in the late nineteenth and twentieth centuries.[40]

In the 1890s to 1940s, Evangelicalism/Fundamentalism, especially in the United States, lost momentum. This was due in part to the influx of immigrant Jews and European Catholics, both resistant to Protestant missions. Dispensationalism's social pessimism, which viewed the world as fated to grow worse and worse while focusing on an anticipated rapture and return of Christ, neutered engagement in social causes and slowed its growth. The movement appeared irrelevant and backward to outsiders. As theological liberalism gained vigor and influence, and Darwinian views began increasingly to prevail, Evangelicalism and Fundamentalism reacted and retrenched, engaging in disputes about "the Fundamentals" such as the inerrancy and authority of the Bible. And while Evangelicals/Fundamentalists rejoiced over the conviction of John Scopes for violating the Butler Act making it unlawful to teach anything but Creationism as a theory of origins in schools, much of America viewed Evangelical posturing, grandstanding, and jubilation to be proof that the movement was irrelevant, ignorant, anti-intellectual, and stifling to freedom of thought, a movement preferring superstition and fideism to the certainties of science. For many in the general culture, this remains the unappealing stereotype of conservative Christians.

Evangelicalism was strongly reactionary in its response to theological liberalism. A. C. Gaebelein, one of Evangelicalism's champions, insisted "God's greatest call is separation."[41] Commitment to the centrality of separation and to the overruling priority of waiting and working toward the coming of Christ rather than repairing a crumbling social order led to a policy of double separation and to the founding of the American Council of Christian Churches (1941).[42]

---

40. For the structure of material tracing the history of the Lausanne Movement, I am largely following, paraphrasing, and supplementing material found in chapter 5, "The Background and Emergence of the Lausanne Movement," in Lundström, *Gospel and Culture in the World Council of Churches and the Lausanne Movement With Particular Focus on the Period 1973–1996*, 181–204. For primary documents of the Lausanne Movement, I rely chiefly on John Stott, ed., *Making Christ Known*, as supplemented by materials on found on the LCWE internet site at http://www.lausanne.org/en/

41. Gaebelein, "The Present Day Apostasy," 154.

42. While separationists insisted that one not associate with those judged theologically liberal, the related doctrine of double separation insisted that the shunning extend also to anyone who associated with theological liberals, also called modernists. Thus, many shunned Billy Graham, who, while not liberal himself, associated with others who were.

Some Evangelicals viewed these battle lines to be ill-conceived. In the 1940s, 1950s, and 1960s, a new American Evangelicalism emerged, shaped by younger, moderate fundamentalists weary of an acrimonious and strident Fundamentalism. Preferring to center their efforts on evangelistic effectiveness instead of separationist purity, they cultivated a more intellectually grounded faith expressing itself in relevant political and social action.

In April, 1942, the new evangelicals founded the National Association of Evangelicals (NAE) to help spearhead this new movement. While indistinguishable doctrinally from the fundamentalist American Council of Christian Churches, they were non-separationist. Ringing in on these differences, Carl Henry wrote *The Uneasy Conscience of Modern Fundamentalism* (1947), critiquing Fundamentalism's social and political apathy, a world-resisting rather than a world-changing religion. Rather than the "Christ Against Culture" model named by H. R. Niebuhr, the new evangelicals, also termed neo-evangelicals, favored a "Christ Transforming Culture" model. In that same year, Fuller Seminary was founded as the flagship of this new breed of evangelicals.

However, purveyors of new paradigms can expect resistance, and beyond that, militant attack from gatekeepers of the old order.[43] This was war, and as in all wars, there were casualties.

One casualty was Edward James Carnell, appointed president of Fuller Theological Seminary in 1957, who brought down upon himself constant criticism and vilification by old-guard Fundamentalists. Troubled by depression and insomnia, he was dead of barbiturate poisoning ten years later. Another vilified pioneer was George Eldon Ladd, who served Fuller as associate professor of New Testament and Greek from 1946–50, head of

---

43. David Bosch, speaking of Thomas Kuhn's work on paradigm theory and applying it to mission theology, writes:

"[A shifting of paradigms] seldom happens without a struggle. . . . Since scientific [and theological] communities are by nature conservative and do not like their peace to be disturbed; the old paradigm's protagonists continue for a long time to fight a rearguard action. . . . Proponents of the old paradigm often just cannot understand the arguments of the proponents of the new. Metaphorically speaking, the one is playing chess and the other checkers on the same board.

. . . This explains why defenders of the old order and champions of the new frequently argue at cross-purposes. Protagonists of the old paradigm, in particular, tend to immunize themselves against the arguments of the new. They resist its challenges with deep emotional reactions, since those challenges threaten to destroy their very perception and experience of reality, indeed their entire world" (Bosch, *Transforming Mission*, 184–85). In part, Bosch's argument paraphrases Hiebert, "Epistemological Foundations for Science and Theology," and Hiebert, "The Missiological Implications of an Epistemological Shift," 12.

the department of New Testament from 1946–49, in 1950–52 as associate professor and then professor of biblical theology from 1952 until his death in 1980. He was another paradigm-shifter, like Carnell. On the right, he battled Dispensationalism's pretribulationist rapture theology, arguing for historic premillenialism and a posttribulatonist stance. This departure from the received wisdom of the conservative power structure brought swift and continual rebuke and vilification. He was also savaged from the left, from which he received something of a coup de grace. In the 1960s, he completed ten years of work on *Jesus and the Kingdom*, through which he hoped to gain a place at the table of liberal scholarship for a biblical theological paradigm. Norman Perrin reviewed the book, administering a blistering and dismissive attack on the validity and quality of Ladd's scholarship. As a result, Ladd became convinced that his entire life and career had been a futile sham. He spent his final years as an out of control alcoholic, his marriage and relationship with his children in disarray, estranged from the seminary that had formerly lionized him. He died a broken man, leaving behind not only a sad story, but also a body of work more respected after his death than during his life.[44]

These tragic accounts highlight the rancorous tensions attending the birth of what is widely termed neo-Evangelicalism. In 1962–1963, some left Fuller Seminary over definitions of inerrancy, and the title of Harold Lindsell's 1967 book, *The Battle for the Bible,* underscores how the field of theological discussion was redolent with the smoke of verbal musket fire along battle lines first mapped out by separationist Fundamentalists.

Neo-Evangelicalism survived to fight another day due to three factors. First, the founding of Fuller Seminary, as embattled as it was. Second, Billy Graham's break with Fundamentalist separationism in his 1957 New York Crusade. Third, Graham's founding of *Christianity Today* in 1956 as a magazine laying claim to middle-of-the-road Evangelicalism and social engagement. While Evangelicalism spawned a plethora of mission groups, parachurch organizations, and schools of various kinds, as a movement it was and is highly diverse, including peace churches like the Mennonites, the Southern Baptists, white and black Holiness strains, immigrant/ethnic churches like Missouri Synod Lutherans and the Christian Reformed, Pentecostals, and Bible churches, etc. Amidst this diversity, the Fuller/Graham/ *Christianity Today* strand is somewhat homogenous, well integrated, well organized, decidedly middle class, and centrist.

It was from such a milieu that the Lausanne Movement grew, a middle of the road, neo-evangelical missiological alternative to Fundamentalism

44. For details of Ladd's theological and personal battles, see D'Elia, *A Place at the Table.*

on the right and liberal theology on the left. In a Billy Graham Evangelistic Association sponsored event, in August of 1960, thirty-three international evangelical leaders met in Montreux, Switzerland, under the theme "God's Strategy in Missions and Evangelism." This meeting led to the Berlin Conference (1966) and what would prove to be the first Lausanne Conference (1974).

The main missiological influences in the founding of the Lausanne Movement included a brain trust from Fuller Theological Seminary's School of World Mission. Among these, Donald McGavran, Alan Tippett, Ralph Winter, Win Arn, Edward Dayton (MARC), C. Peter Wagner—first chairman of the Lausanne Strategy Working Group (1975–81)—Charles Kraft, and Paul Hiebert. British Anglican Evangelical icon John R. W. Stott served as the movement's chief theologian, and it is he who drafted the Lausanne Covenant, which defined the movement and formed a basis for vetting out prospective members.

Since its inception, Lausanne has sustained its ethos and served its mission through a variety of consultations, congresses, and meetings, both regional and international. The larger of these were the 1974 founding conference in Lausanne, Switzerland, the one held in Manila, 2007 (known as Lausanne II), and the largest, in 2010, the Lausanne World Congress at Capetown (Lausanne III). As the 1974 conference produced the *Lausanne Covenant*, so the Manila Conference produced the *Manila Manifesto*, a ratification and upgrading of the earlier covenant in light of the deepening of the movement and changes in the world in the intervening years.

In keeping with the movement's slogan, "the whole church, bringing the whole gospel to the whole world," one may detect in the wording of the Manifesto a continued intention for the Lausanne Movement to eschew sectarianism:

> Our reference to "the whole church" is not a presumptuous claim that the universal church and the evangelical community are synonymous. For we recognize that there are many churches which are not part of the evangelical movement.[45]

On the other hand, the document bears witness to tensions among the signatories of the Covenant concerning just this issue:

> Evangelical attitudes to the Roman Catholic and Orthodox Churches differ widely. Some evangelicals are praying, talking, studying Scripture and working with these churches. Others are

45. "*The Manila Manifesto*: An Elaboration of the Lausanne Covenant Fifteen Years Later (1989)" in Stott, ed., *Making Christ Known*, 242–43.

strongly opposed to any form of dialogue or cooperation with them. All are aware that serious theological differences between us remain.

. . . Some of us are members of churches which belong to the World Council of Churches and believe that a positive yet critical participation in its work is our Christian duty. Others among us have no link with the World Council. All of us urge the World Council of Churches to adopt a consistent biblical understanding of evangelism.[46]

Clearly, it is one thing to disavow sectarianism and entirely another to avoid it. Despite its rhetoric, aware observers and participants in Lausanne see it to be controlled by Reformed theology and white power brokers. When I attended Lausanne III in Capetown, South Africa, a black Pentecostal scholar commented to me how the bookstore at the conference had not one Pentecostal book. Indeed, with the exception of the Bibles for sale there, all were Reformed books. If Lausanne wants truly to avoid sectarianism, it will need to confront its own paternalism. This is not a nice word, I know, and the Lausanne people are good, earnest, dedicated people. But even such people as these would do well to note and critique the trends evident in the organizational culture that they serve, and the tensions acknowledged by some if not by all.

THE LAUSANNE COMMITTEE FOR JEWISH EVANGELIZATION (LCJE)

The LCJE developed out of a subgroup, "Reaching Jews," that was part of the LCWE-sponsored Consultation on World Evangelization held in Pattaya, Thailand, 1980. Mission leaders in attendance sought to prolong their fruitful association, giving rise to the creation of a task force, which is now called the Lausanne Consultation on Jewish Evangelism.

Speaking of the roots of the LCJE in the LCWE and the relationship between the two, missionary theologian and historian Kai Kjaer-Hansen, for many years International Coordinator of the LCJE, states, "Even before LCJE (Lausanne Consultation on Jewish Evangelism) existed, LCWE was. . . . LCJE is part of this worldwide evangelistic movement which has the *Lausanne Covenant* (1974) as its basis. There is no reason to hide that, from time to time, there have been some tensions between LCWE and LCJE."[47]

---

46. Ibid., 243.

47. Kjaer-Hansen, "What Do We Stand For?"

By examining events at the Lausanne III (Capetown), we may guess the nature of these tensions, which have much to do with how the LCWE compares to the WCC, and much to do with how the LCWE understands the church's role and that of the Jewish people under the *missio dei*.

LAUSANNE III (CAPETOWN): THEOLOGIZING ABOUT THE JEWS AND THE JEWISH STATE

Major documents were crafted in connection with each of the Lausanne World Congresses: the *Lausanne Covenant* (Lausanne I), the *Manila Manifesto* (Lausanne II), and the *Capetown Commitment* (Lausanne III).

The *Capetown Commitment* takes pains to make clear the LCWE perspective on God's mission and its relationship to the mission of Christians and churches in its section 10, "We Love the Mission of God." Here, in keeping with the writings of Christopher J. H. Wright, theologian of the LCWE and heir to the mantle formerly worn by John Stott, the Bible is represented as essentially a missional document: "The whole Bible reveals the mission of God to bring all things in heaven and earth into unity under Christ" and the related paragraph goes on to unpack what that consummational and redemptive unity will look like. In the first subsection of this portion of the *Capetown Commitment*, the mission of the church is explicitly related to the mission of God: "God calls his people to share his mission."

But it is the very next sentences that us that the Lausanne Movement restricts the God-ordained mission of the Jewish people to a formative stage in the saga of redemption. "The Church from all nations stands in continuity through the Messiah Jesus with God's people in the Old Testament. With them we have been called through Abraham and commissioned to be a blessing and a light to the nations. With them, we are to be shaped and taught through the law and the prophets to be a community of holiness, compassion and justice in a world of sin and suffering." The only partnership the church shares with Israel under the *missio dei* relates to Old Testament Israel. It is clear that this is a supersessionist document.

It would be a mistake to dismissively label this objection a form of ethnic chauvinism. A wide spectrum of theologians and textual scholars join in insisting on the continuing and eschatological role assigned to the seed of Jacob. Not only have the Jews not completed their divinely assigned task; the people of Israel are not nor can they be just like all the other nations.

Yet, a statement prepared by the Theology Working Group in connection with Lausanne III unambiguously positions itself in opposition to such conclusions, making unambiguous the supersessionist stance of the LCWE, demonstrating that when it comes to theologizing about the Jewish people and speaking of the Jewish state, any difference between the LCWE and the WCC is more a matter of style than substance:

> The one Church that God has called into being in Christ is drawn from every nation, tribe, people and language, with the result that no single ethnic identity can claim to be "God's chosen people." God's election of Old Testament Israel was for the sake of the eventual creation of this multi-national community of God's people . . . . We strongly affirm, therefore, that while there are multiple ethnicities within the one church by God's clear intention, no single ethnic group holds privileged place in God's economy of salvation or God's eschatological purpose. Thus, we strongly believe that the separate and privileged place given to the modern Israeli state, in certain forms of dispensationalism or Christian Zionism, should be challenged.

This statement met with vigorous protest from Jewish mission leaders present at Capetown. In a paper delivered at the meeting of the Lausanne Consultation on Jewish Evangelism on Meeting at High Leigh, Hoddesdon, England, on August 8, 2011, Mitch Glaser, executive director of Chosen People Ministries, points out that this statement cannot be embraced by a wide range of Lausanne delegates who come from churches and denominations that are premillennial, and/or that affirm some aspects of Christian Zionism. Glaser indicates that this is a rather divisive statement, especially for a conference emphasizing a commitment to unity through its study of Paul's Letter to the Ephesians.

He takes issue with the statement that "no single ethnic group holds a privileged place in God's economy of salvation or God's eschatological purpose," indicating that perhaps fifty percent or more of those at the Conference would disagree, holding on the basis of Romans 11:29 and other passages of Scripture that the election of the Jewish people stands, and has a God-preserved role in his eschatological purposes.

Glaser takes issue as well with the statement denying any "separate or privileged place given to the modern Israeli state, (as) in certain forms of dispensationalism or Christian Zionism." While acknowledging that some might take rightful exception to some Israeli policies, Glaser decries the partiality of this statement, since there was no statement at the Conference about terrorism, calling upon perpetrators to repent. There was no statement at or from the Conference protesting the terrorism of certain Palestinian groups or Al Qaeda.

He views the statement of the Theology Working Group to be a clear violation of what has been called "the spirit of Lausanne." He rightly characterizes the statements as sectarian.

In addition, Glaser protests activities on the second day of the conference, which focused on Palestine, and avoided calling the Jewish state by name. He points out how these moves "(revealed) a clear agenda that takes up the language and concerns of our Palestinian brothers and leaves Jewish Israelis in the cold." And that night a panel discussion was held on the Middle East with five participants—but no Jewish Israeli. As in the case of the WCC, Israel is an inconvenience to those whose supersessionist theologies long ago consigned the Jews to the dustbin of history.

An evening session featured a brief film clip and a conversation between a Palestinian Christian and Messianic Jewish believer on the subject of reconciliation. However, Glaser points out that the brief film included statements that can be seen as "in some ways anti-Jewish as they included a suggestion by the scriptwriter that one of the causes of tension in the Middle East has been the post-Holocaust immigration of millions of Jewish people to what Jewish people around the world view as their rightful homeland." In other words, the Jews were being portrayed as the problem in the area, unwanted outsiders, troublemakers. An old canard, echoing both in the WCC and the LCWE.

Glaser interprets the roots of these problems in a manner parallel to how I assess what has happened in the WCC: "Essentially, we believe they chose to 'lend their public support' to a stronger coalition of Arab believers, minimizing the role of Israel and the Jewish people in the Congress. This is unfortunate and yet consistent with the theological statements made by the TWG."[48] Indeed.

Clearly, there is little difference between the WCC and the LCJE in the stance each takes when theologizing about the Jewish people and when speaking of the Jewish state.

48. Comments drawn from Glaser, "Personal Reflections on the 3rd Lausanne Consultation."

5

The Mission of God and the Mission of the Roman Catholic Church in Relation to that of Israel

ALTHOUGH THE WCC AND LCWE have proven unable or disinclined to theologize about the Jewish people, this has not been so for the Roman Catholic Church, which has been at the forefront of rethinking and theologizing concerning the church and the Jews. In the main, this is due to three factors: the declaration *Nostra Aetate* from the Second Vatican Council; Pope John Paul II's labors to foster and implement changes inherent in that document; and the language of the Catechism of the Catholic Church (1995), which in its relevant sections, seeks to embody these changes.

Section four of *Nostra Aetate*, the declaration on "The Relation of the Church to Non-Christian Religions," proclaimed by His Holiness Pope Paul VI on October 28, 1965, reversed two millennia of what Jules Isaac named "the teaching of contempt." Eugene Fisher is not exaggerating when he says of this document, "it is easily the most significant document concerning Jewish-Christian relations in Church history since Paul in Romans 9–11."[1] Fisher highlights its rejection of anti-Judaic theological polemics, replacing these with foundations for a "renewed vision of the continuing role of the Jewish people in God's plan of salvation for all humanity."[2] Arguing on biblical grounds rather than from the writings of the church fathers, the statement explicitly exonerates the Jewish people of Jesus' day and ours from

---

1. Fisher, "Nostra Aetate," 320–21.
2. Ibid., 320.

wholesale responsibility for the death of Jesus, disemboweling in one-stroke millennia of assumptions that the destruction of the Jerusalem Temple and the diaspora of the Jews were divine punishments visited upon a nation of Christ-rejectors.[3] As later developed in the Holy See's 1985 *Notes on the Correct Way to Present Jews and Judaism in Catholic Preaching and Catechesis*, the diaspora is henceforth to be viewed positively, because it "allowed Israel to carry to the whole world a witness—often heroic—of its fidelity to the one God."[4] Unambiguously, *Nostra Aetate* affirmed "the Jewish origins of Christianity and that the Church draws (present tense) spiritual 'sustenance' from the people of God of the 'Ancient Covenant.' The Jews 'still remain most dear to God' and 'have (present tense) the glory and the covenant and the law and the worship an the promise . . . for the gifts and the call of God are irrevocable.'"[5]

Giving a full accounting of progress made in Roman Catholic theologizing about the Jews since Vatican II is beyond the scope of this or any other book. However, these are momentous changes and deserve comment, especially as they contrast so markedly with the inability and/or reluctance of the WCC and LCWE to theologize about the current status of the seed of Jacob and their homeland. I offer here a brief summation and adaptation of a nine-point summary penned by Eugene Fisher concerning the outworking of *Nostra Aetate* in the papacy of John Paul II,[6] who dedicated himself to making *Nostra Aetate* come alive in the life of the Church.[7]

1. *The Spiritual Bond Between the Church and the Jewish People: The Special Relationship.* John Paul II used the noun "brothers" and the adjective "fraternal" about the Jews. This is most significant because it reflects intra-Christian language, the same language he used in according to Orthodox and Protestant Christians a level of spiritual recognition formerly denied them.

He said the relationship between the Church and the Jewish people goes to the very essence of Christian faith itself, and that "to deny it is to

---

3. This dire portrait of Israel's alleged punitive history is laid out authoritatively in St. Augustine of Hippo's *Reply to Faustus the Manichean*, XII, 12 (fourth century).

4. Holy See, *Notes on the Correct Way to Present the Jews and Judaism in Preaching and Catechesis in the Roman Catholic Church.*

5. Fisher, "Nostra Aetate," 321.

6. Although as this writing there have been two further papacies, of Pope Benedict XVI and Pope Francis, since these do not advance in any substantial manner the considerable gains attributable to Pope John Paul II, in his implementation of *Nostra Aetate,* these papacies are not discussed in this chapter.

7. Quotations from Fisher in this summary are his "A Commentary on the Texts," hereafter Fisher, "Commentary."

deny something essential to the teaching of the Church."[8] For John Paul II, the spiritual bond with Jews, for John Paul, is to be properly understood as a "sacred one, stemming as it does from the mysterious will of God."[9]

Repeatedly John Paul II used bold metaphors to break new ground in Catholic-Jewish relations. His language contrasts sharply with the more measured and cautious rhetoric of the WCC and LCWE. At his allocution to the Jewish community at Mainz, West Germany (Nov 17, 1980), the Pope likened the relationship of Israel to the Church to the first and second parts of the Christian Bible. He undermined supersessionist assumptions, saying that this relationship "is a question . . . of reciprocal enlightenment and explanation, just as the relationship between the Scriptures themselves."[10] Over and again he will use the language of partnership for a relationship formerly characterize by the language of hierarchy and replacement.

One cannot help but be startled by his bold characterization of dialogue between Catholic and Jews "a dialogue within our Church."[11] Although many would differ, and some sharply, when the Pope suggests that the Jewish people are within the Church, that is not what he sought to emphasize. Rather, he was emphasizing the fraternal bond between the Church and Israel, and that for him as for many after him, the Church and Israel are one community currently living in a state of schism. He sees the Jewish and Christian world as living in a state of unfortunate tension, destined to be resolved.

John Paul II reinforces this foundational unity in his address at the synagogue in Rome. Commenting on the words of *Nostra Aetate,* "The Church of Christ discovers her 'bond' with Judaism by 'searching into her own mystery,'" he said, "the Jewish religion is not 'extrinsic' to us, but in a certain way is 'intrinisic' to our own religion. With Judaism, therefore, we have a relationship which we do not have with any other religion. You are dearly beloved brothers and, in a certain way, it could be said that you are our elder brothers."[12] Here his thoughts align with those of John Howard Yoder who terms Judaism "a non-non-Christian religion."[13]

---

8. Holy See, *Notes,* 1–2.

9. Pope John Paul II, "Address to International Catholic-Jewish Liaison Committee on the Twentieth Anniversary of *Nostra Aetate* (October 28, 1985)," 75.

10. John Paul II, "Address to the Jewish Community—West Germany (Nov 27. 1980)," 35. His Holiness is here referencing directives for the application of the conciliar Declaration *Nostra Aetate.*

11. Ibid.

12. Fisher, "Commentary," xxiii.

13. Yoder, *The Jewish-Christian Schism Revisited,* 147–59.

2. *The Jewish Patrimony as a Living Heritage.* In addressing the Jews at Mainz, the Pope referred to Judaism as "a living heritage, which must be understood and preserved in its depths and richness by us Catholic Christians" (November 17, 1980). He confirmed and deepened this thinking addressing delegates from Episcopal conferences gathered in Rome in March of 1982: "Christians have taken the right path, that of justice and brotherhood, in seeking to come together with their Semitic brethren, respectfully and perseveringly, in the common heritage, a heritage that all value so highly. . . . To assess it carefully in itself and with due awareness of the faith and religious life of the Jewish people *as they are professed and practiced today,* can greatly help us to understand better certain aspects of the life of the Church" (March 6, 1982, italics added).[14]

Here he is not simply validating the Older Testament, or speaking of God's ancient people, as is common in Protestant rhetoric. He is even going beyond representing Judaism as the Church's older sibling. Rather, he is validating the Judaism of today as a heritage from which all might learn. The Pope sees an analogy between the spiritual patrimony of the Church developed down through the ages by the doctors and saints of the Church, and that of Judaism, through rabbinic literature and Talmud, Jewish philosophers and sages, each community developing what was given it by God.[15]

3. *The Permanent Validity of God's Covenant with the Jewish People.* The Pope built on the insights of Vatican II, and in *Lumen Gentium*, commenting on Romans 11:28–29, said, "On account of their fathers, this people remains most dear to God, for God does not repent of the gifts He makes nor of the calls he issues."[16] He saw the Jews as fully chosen by God, in a manner that is "unequivocal and in no way diminishes the Church's own affirmation of its own standing as 'people of God.'"[17] In this regard, in his meeting with representatives of Episcopal conferences, he stressed the present tense of Rom 9:4–5, stating that the Jewish people "have the adoption as sons, and the glory and the covenants and the legislation, and the worship and the promises," while also affirming "the universal salvific significance of the death and resurrection of Jesus of Nazareth." He didn't seek to reconcile the two realities by subsuming one under the other, but affirmed both together, stating, "This means that the links between the Church and the

---

14. Both quotations in this paragraph from Fisher, "Commentary," xxiv.

15. This is explicitly stated in the 1985 *Notes On The Correct Way To Present The Jews And Judaism In Preaching And Catechesis In The Roman Catholic Church.*

16. *Dogmatic Constitution On The Church Lumen Gentium.*

17. Fisher, "Commentary," xxv.

Jewish people are founded on the design of the God of the Covenant."[18] He further amplified this when addressing the Anti-Defamation League of B'nai Brith: "The respect we speak of is based on the mysterious spiritual link which brings us close together, in Abraham and, through Abraham, in God who chose Israel and brought forth the Church from Israel" (March 22, 1984). Eugene Fisher adds, "Here there is not the slightest hint of supersessionism or of that subtler form of triumphalism that would envision Israel as having exhausted its salvific role in 'giving birth' to Christianity."[19]

Over and again the Pope startles us with his bold language and clear vision of a different theological relationship between the Church and the Jewish people. While the Protestant LCJE and the WCC decline to theologize about today's Jews, or relegate such theologizing to statements about continuities between the Old Testament people of God and the church of today, the Pope used the machete of metaphor to slash away centuries of theological undergrowth, forging new paths for thought and relationship, restoring to the Jewish people a living place in the mission of God and a dignity among Christians denied them for millennia.

4. Catechetics and Liturgy. One could argue that John Paul II dedicated his entire papacy to unpacking *Nostra Aetate* and making it live in the life of the Church. Accordingly, he wanted catechisms and liturgy to reflect the new day that had dawned. Referencing the 1974 *Guidelines* and the later *Notes on the Correct Presentation of the Jews and Judaism in Catholic Preaching and Teaching*, he spoke about catechesis in these terms: "I am sure that they will greatly help toward freeing our catechetical and religious teaching of a negative or inaccurate presentation of Jews and Judaism in the context of the Catholic faith. They will also help to promote respect, appreciation, and indeed love for one and the other, as they are both in the unfathomable design of God, who 'does not reject his people' [Ps. 94:14; Rom. 11:1]. By the same token, anti-Semitism in its ugly and sometimes violent manifestations should be completely eradicated. Better still, a positive view of each of our religions, with due respect for the identity of each, will surely emerge, as is already the case in so many places."[20] That words such as these came from the lips of a Polish Pope is preternatural to Jewish people when considered against the background of centuries of Polish anti-Semitism culminating in the Shoah, where more Jews died in Poland than anywhere else. This makes the next point all the more astounding.

18. "To Delegates to the Meeting of Representatives of Episcopal Conferences and Other Experts in Catholic-Jewish Relations," 38.

19. Fisher, "Commentary," xxvi.

20. "Address to the International Catholic-Jewish Liaison Committee on the Twentieth Anniversary of *Nostra Aetate*," 56.

5. *Condemnations of Anti-Semitism and Remembrances of the Shoah.* Fisher characterizes John Paul II's response to anti-Semitism as a "deep abhorrence," which he frequently communicated in his travels, especially in Europe. In his homily at Otranto, which Fisher terms "controversial," the Pope for the first time linked the Holocaust and State of Israel, saying: "The Jewish people, after tragic experiences connected with the extermination of so many sons and daughters, driven by the desire for security, set up the modern State of Israel" (October 5, 1980). Up to this point, the Vatican had traditionally avoided reference to the State of Israel, but here the Pope was sympathetically mentioning the founding of the State, a colossal leap of progress, and controversial because it was so at variance with the political climate of the day and with prior policies of the Church.

In Australia (November 26, 1986), John Paul said "no theological justification could ever be found for acts of discrimination or persecution against Jews. In fact, such acts must be held to be sinful."[21] In sharpest contrast to those prepared the glibly identify theological reasons for such, the Pope spoke of "the *mystery* of the suffering of Israel's children," summoning Christians to develop with Jews "common educational programs . . . which will teach future generations about the Holocaust so that never again will such a horror be possible. Never again!" (Miami, September 11, 1987). It is a measure of the Pope's passion for rapprochement with the Jewish community that be borrows the rhetoric of Jewish contemplation of the Shoah ("never again") in calling and pledging the Church to change and action.

He demonstrates this strong affinity when speaking at his childhood home in Wadowice, when he says, "In the school of Wadowice there were Jewish believers who are no longer with us. There is no longer a synagogue near the school. Let us remember that we are near Auschwitz" (*Catholic News Service,* August 15, 1991).[22] For the Pope to refer to Jews as "Jewish believers" is extraordinary, as it occurs in an ecclesial context which for centuries has disparaged the Jews and their religion.

His Holiness reiterated this theme in comments on August 16, 1991 in a meeting with representatives of the Jewish community in Wadowice, saying, "My thoughts go with deep respect to the great believers who even in those days of devastation—*yom shoah* in the words of Zephaniah (cf. 1:15].... We are here now to adore the God of Israel, who this time, too, has stretched out his protecting hand over a blessed remnant of his people. How often his mysterious ransom has been repeated in your history!"[23]

21. Fisher, "Commentary," xxvii-xxix.

22. Ibid., xxxii.

23. Washington, *Origins,* Catholic News Service Documentary Service. 13

6. The Land and State of Israel. We saw earlier how, at Otranto, the Pope provoked controversy by speaking positively of the modern State of Israel, sympathetically linking its founding with the Shoah. But he did more than just speak. On December 20, 1993, his representative signed the *Fundamental Agreement* which would lead to normalized relations. The first Ambassador of the Holy See was established in Israel as of August 16, 1994. In the midst of a wider church world so often uncommittal about the Jewish state, this committed action stands out like a beacon in the darkness.

7. Controversies and Dialogue. John Paul II's papacy was characterized by extensive controversy concerning both the Holocaust and Israel. Triggering incidents included his meetings with Yassir Arafat, with Kurt Waldheim, the beatification of Edith Stein, and the visit at the Carmelite convent in the Auschwitz-Birkenau compound. Fisher wisely stresses that the Pope of necessity acts within a Catholic context, and that his actions in each of these areas were understood differently by Catholics than they were by Jews. He pleads for members of both communities to learn to listen attentively and respectfully to members of the other reporting their interpretations of such events. He suggests that the time is or should be long past for simply telling people our own version of the truth without bothering to hear their version.

8. A Vision for the Future: A Call for Joint Action and Witness in History. I differ in my perspective from Christians on the left who take a dual covenant position and hold that Yeshua believers owe nothing to the Jewish people except gratitude, respect, and leaving them alone. Instead I believe that both Messianic Jews and Christians while owing respect and gratitude, ought also to embody and bear witness to who Yeshua is both for the church and for Israel. I differ with those on the right who *limit* their view of mission to evangelistic activity and who view the Jewish people as being nothing more than targets of this kind of mission, but in no sense partners in serving the *missio dei*. However, the mission to which God calls us is far broader than delivering a message. It is also an invitation to engage with him in "uniting all things in Christ," bringing nearer that day when the wolf will lie down with the lamb, embodying and hastening that unity between Israel and the church currently existing in a state of schism destined to be healed. Anything that hastens or foreshadows that healing is part of God's mission for all concerned.

Fisher reminds us that none of this is foreign to John Paul II. "Central to the Pope's vision of the Christian-Jewish relationship is the hope that it offers for joint social action and witness to the One God and the reality of the Kingdom of God as the defining point of human history."[24]

September 5, 1991, 203, quoted in Fisher, "Commentary," xxxii.

24. Fisher, "Commentary," xxxvii.

He adds that "such joint action, for the Pope, is more than simple 'good neighborliness.' It is a fulfillment of what is essential to the mission of both Judaism and Christianity." Mission together is part of our converging destinies. John Paul II in fact anticipates the core and language of the Converging Destinies paradigm. He even uses the key verb of the paradigm, saying "through different but finally convergent ways we will be able to reach, with the help of the Lord, who has never ceased to love his people (Rom. 11:1), true brotherhood in reconciliation and respect and to contribute to a full implementation of God's plan in history." This approximates the balance, vision, and burden of the Converging Destinies paradigm, expressing both the diversity and unity of the Church and Israel in service of "a full implementation of God's plan in history," the mission of God.[25]

9. *Papal Encyclicals.* Throughout his encyclicals, John Paul II sought "to integrate into his overall teachings the insights he . . . derived from his contacts with Jewish leaders and his continuing meditation upon the meaning of Jewish tradition for Catholic thought."[26] A few highlights from these documents help illustrate the fecundity of his theological imagination and its transformational substance.

In his very first encyclical, *Redemptor Hominis,* section 6, John Paul speaks first of the imperative to pursue unity among the various Christian churches, something to be sought "sincerely, perseveringly, humbly and also courageously."[27] He then speaks of seeking rapprochement with non-Christian religions, conscious that there is something of spiritual value to be learned from these traditions without sacrificing one's own religious truth claims and convictions.

In section 11, "The Mystery of Christ as the Basis of the Church's Mission and of Christianity," he delves more deeply into what may be learned from other religions, and especially from Judaism, speaking of *Nostra Aetate* against the background of earlier Church teachings:

> The Fathers of the Church rightly saw in the various religions as it were so many reflections of the one truth, "seeds of the Word" attesting that, though the routes taken may be different, there is but a single goal to which is directed the deepest aspiration of the human spirit as expressed in its quest for God and also in its quest, through its tending towards God, for the full dimension of its humanity, or in other words for the full meaning of human life. The Council gave particular attention to the Jewish religion,

25. Ibid., xxxviii.
26. Ibid., xxxix.
27. All quotations from Pope John Paul II, *Redemptor Hominis.*

> recalling the great spiritual heritage common to Christians and
> Jews.

These are generous words, highlighting and granting dignity to the spiritual longing and striving of all humankind, that all are reflections of the one truth, "seeds of the Word," with all, regardless of their various routes taken, seeking God and the full meaning of human life. What is especially interesting is how he accords special status to Judaism, noting "the great spiritual heritage common to Christians and Jews."

He goes on to highlight how it is in Christ that man finds both God and himself. This being the case, he calls Christians of all stripes to unite in the mission of both discovering and sharing the truth of God and of humanity as it is revealed in Christ who is also "the mystery hidden from the ages." Yet he acknowledges that this will take work. Here then he is speaking of one of those schisms that is destined to be healed, that between the churches, with the focal point of unity being "Jesus Christ [who] is the stable principle and fixed center of the mission that God himself has entrusted to man. We must all share in this mission and concentrate all our forces on it, since it is more necessary than ever for modern mankind." Within the context of a courageous theological imagination, his papacy sought to foster this unification, both unity among the churches and unity with other religions, most especially with Judaism, with which the Church shares a unique affinity.

It seems that wherever one dips in John Paul's writings, one finds newness, boldness, theological depth, and a new vision of possibilities of union, both with Christian churches, and with the people of Israel.

ONE STEP FORWARD, TWO STEPS BACK

We should not be so naïve as to imagine that since *Nostra Aetate* the Roman Catholic Church has only moved forward with regard to the Jewish people in its understanding, teachings, and ways of relating. An inevitable cultural lag will hinder any social system in implementing even authoritative changes. Those charged to implement change are often unaware of how older paradigms surface in their own rhetoric and writings, impeding the very progress they seek.[28]

---

28. As a measure of such a lag, a friend from an Orthodox Jewish background joined the Dominicans reasoning that she could teach among them and be allowed to maintain the rituals of Jewish life. She found that while this appeared quaint at first, in the end, her superiors could not tolerate her "strange ways." Indeed, theory is one thing, practice quite another.

In its concept of mission, *Lumen Gentium* operates very much in the conceptual field we have been exploring under the category *missio dei*. Here, the sending of the Church is linked to the sending of the Son and the sending of the Spirit, as in paragraph 5, which says in part, "When Jesus, who had suffered the death of the cross for mankind, had risen, He appeared as the one constituted as Lord, Christ and eternal Priest, and He poured out on His disciples the Spirit promised by the Father. From this source the Church, equipped with the gifts of its Founder and faithfully guarding His precepts of charity, humility and self-sacrifice, receives the mission to proclaim and to spread among all peoples the Kingdom of Christ and of God and to be, on earth, the initial budding forth of that kingdom." As the Father sent the Son, so we are sent by the Spirit and the Son to enter into their work: the *missio dei*.

> All men are called to belong to the new people of God. Wherefore this people, while remaining one and only one, is to be spread throughout the whole world and must exist in all ages, so that the decree of God's will may be fulfilled. In the beginning God made human nature one and decreed that all His children, scattered as they were, would finally be gathered together as one. (117) It was for this purpose that God sent His Son, whom He appointed heir of all things, (118) that be might be teacher, king and priest of all, the head of the new and universal people of the sons of God. For this too God sent the Spirit of His Son as Lord and Life-giver. He it is who brings together the whole Church and each and every one of those who believe, and who is the well-spring of their unity in the teaching of the apostles and in fellowship, in the breaking of bread and in prayers.[29]

Mark Kinzer finds *Lumen Gentium* especially problematic in how it exaggerates discontinuity and overuses the term "new" in its portrayal of the relationship between the Church and Judaism or the Jewish people. I have highlighted in italics this kind of problematic language found in section 9 of the encyclical:

> He therefore chose the race of Israel as a people unto Himself. With it He set up a covenant. Step by step He taught and prepared this people, making known in its history both Himself and the decree of His will and making it holy unto Himself. *All these things, however, were done by way of preparation and as a figure of that new and perfect covenant, which was to be ratified in Christ, and of that fuller revelation which was to be given through*

---

29. *Lumen Gentium*, paragraph 18.

> *the Word of God Himself made flesh.* "Behold the days shall come saith the Lord, and I will make a new covenant with the House of Israel, and with the house of Judah . . . I will give my law in their bowels, and I will write it in their heart, and I will be their God, and they shall be my people. . . . For all of them shall know Me, from the least of them even to the greatest, saith the Lord." Christ instituted this new covenant, the new testament, that is to say, in His Blood, *calling together a people made up of Jew and gentile, making them one, not according to the flesh but in the Spirit. This was to be the new People of God.* For those who believe in Christ, who are reborn not from a perishable but from an imperishable seed through the word of the living God, *not from the flesh but from water and the Holy Spirit, are finally established as "a chosen race, a royal priesthood, a holy nation, a purchased people . . . who in times past were not a people, but are now the people of God."*

While it is true that the paragraph uses biblical language, it does so in ways that presume a radical discontinuity between Israel and the Church. Israel is relegated to being "a preparation and a figure of that new and perfect covenant," while the church is "the new People of God not from the flesh but from water and the Holy Spirit, . . . finally established as 'a chosen race, a royal priesthood, a holy nation, a purchased people . . . who in times past were not a people, but are now the people of God.'" Israel has done its job, but now the church is here.

Later in the same paragraph, the contrast between Israel and the church, between then and now, between old and new, is made unambiguously specific through referring to the church as "the new Israel."

> Israel according to the flesh, which wandered as an exile in the desert, was already called the Church of God. So likewise the new Israel which while living in this present age goes in search of a future and abiding city is called the Church of Christ. For He has bought it for Himself with His blood.

From examples like these, we can see that the Roman Catholic Church, despite its ground-breaking pronouncements and intentions, remains a work in progress, needing to exercise diligence and vigilance if it would conform its behaviors to the kinds of aspirations outlined in *Nostra Aetate* and explored during the papacy of John Paul II. Indeed all branches of Christ's church and of Judaism would do well not only to learn from the Roman Catholic Church's capacity for change and imagination, but also to learn how to initiate safeguards to assure that good intentions get worked out as on the ground realities.

FOUR FINAL QUESTIONS

Answering four questions will point us on our way forward on the basis of this research, although other chapters in this book will take us further.

The First Question: What is the Hole in the Theological Bucket?

The first question is "What is the hole in the bucket that prevents many in the church from theologizing afresh about the role in the mission of God of the people and state of Israel?" The answer to this question is "supersessionism," also known as "replacement theology."[30] As has been demonstrated in these pages, by postulating that the Jews have been set aside, with their covenant status expired or revoked, now replaced by the Church as the New Israel, one removes the entire engine driving theologizing about the Jews and the Jewish state. Not only is there no need to theologize about the Jews in such a case: there is no sense to it. Why theologize about something which is no longer a living theological reality? Similarly, once one adheres to such a stance, the modern State of Israel becomes something of a secular anomaly, for if the State of Israel has theological signficance, then the people of Israel have theological significance. And if *that* is so, then the entire edifice of supersessionsist assumptions upon which the church bases its own identity begins to crumble. This being the case, there remains for supersessionist Christianity an enormous psychological bias against theologizing about the Jewish people and the Jewish state. We have seen that bias repeatedly evident, especially in the WCC and LCWE.

---

30. Kendall Soulen says the term is used of "the traditional Christian belief that since Christ's coming the Church has taken the place of the Jewish people as God's chosen community, and that God's covenant with the Jews is now over and done. By extension, the term can be used to refer to any interpretation of Christian faith generally or the status of the Church in particular that claims or implies the abrogation or obsolescence of God's covenant with the Jewish people. Supersessionism is thus substantially equivalent to replacement theology, and the two terms are often used interchangeably" (Soulen, "Supersessionism").

The Second Question: What of Conservative Biblicist Christians?

Our second question is "What of conservative Christians who *do* theologize about the Jewish people and Jewish state? Does their activity prove that supersessionism is not the pervasive problem we have named it to be? Is the problem not so much with how Christians think of the Jews, as with how Christians of a certain stripe think of the Jews?" No, this does not disprove my point at all. Almost all such Christians are imbued with cryptosupersessionism, an unconscious and entrenched cluster of presuppositions held by those who oppose supersessionism, and whose rhetoric is nonsupersessionist, who nevertheless affirm the expiration or setting aside of those identity markers that formerly applied to the Jewish people. This stance effectively nullifies Israel's unique chosen status in whole or in part, rendering her chosenness merely rhetorical, not actual. What differentiates cryptosupersessionism from supersessionism itself is that its proponents vigorously reject supersessionism while failing to see how their presuppositions and theology rob their Israel-affirming words of substance, leaving religious Israel a hollow shell.

What are these presuppositions? Among them is the setting aside of the Torah of Moses, allegedly replaced by the Law of Christ that serves as a standard of righteousness for all Yeshua believers, Jewish and Gentile. However, if the Law of Christ, seen as the commandments given by Yeshua and the apostles, replaces the Law of Moses, becoming the uniform standard of righteousness and rule of life for Jewish and Gentile Yeshua believers alike, how then are Jewish Yeshua believers actually, rather than simply rhetorically, a distinct chosen people? Such a stance empties Israel of her substance while greasing the skids for total assimilation into the church. Such Jews do not live in Jewish covenant faithfulness, do not eat kosher, do not keep the sabbath, and likely, will freely intermarry. Within a few generations at most their descendants will not claim Jewish identity at all, and certainly will not live as Jews. Their Jewish identity has been superseded by something else.

This raises the question for Christians as to whether Jewish covenantal living ought to be maintained for Jewish Yeshua believers. What a significant question. Those who treat Jewish covenantal living as a quaint option rather than a mandated way of life are declaring that the Jewish way of life has been superseded by something else even as they might speak vigorously in favor of maintaining a Jewish distinctive. This is crypstosperessionism— the rhetoric of continuity surrounding its effective denial. Sadly, those who adopt such a position, whether Jewish Yeshua believers or Christians, barter away the birthright of Jewish covenantal identity for a dish of foreign theological lentils. This is Esau, not Jacob.

The Third Question: What Will Progress Look Like?

Adapting categories from Eugene Fisher's analysis of John Paul's work among the Jews, the following list outlines areas where Christians can and should make progress in their theologizing about the Jewish people and Jewish state. Such a list helps us recognize that supersessionism is not one thing, easily defined. Rather it is a nexus of theological assumptions that marginalize the seed of Jacob, installing the church alone as central. These principles help bring Israel back into the center, which she is meant to share with the church.[31]

1. Explore and celebrate the spiritual bond between the church and the Jewish people as a special and unique relationship. Avoid language and thought which relegates the Jewish people to being no more than a people like all others.

2. Recognize and respect the traditions and teachings of the Jewish people. Avoid discounting these traditions and teachings as without value when these are at variance with Christian perspectives.

3. Explore and celebrate the permanent validity of God's covenant with the Jewish people. Avoid and critique theologizing and rhetoric that highlights discontinuity while eclipsing continuity.

4. Bring these insights to the laity through appropriate preaching, catechetics, liturgy, and teaching. Avoid limiting changes in rhetoric and theologizing to discourse occurring among a theological elite.

5. Make condemnation of anti-Semitism and remembrances of the Shoah unambiguous. Avoid and expose theological arguments or statements that insinuate or assert that anti-Semitism and the Shoah are due to Israel's sins and rejection of Christ.

6. Explore and consider perspectives that celebrate the land and State of Israel as providential, even prophetic realities, truly listening to how previously marginalized theological voices speak on these matters. Avoid unquestioned adherence to arguments to the contrary and consider the political motives behind the stigmatization of Christian Zionism.

7. Open up to transformational dialogue with Jewish others. Rather than being an occasion for each side to recite their party line, such

---

31. The Jewish people must also make changes in their theology to the extent that it denigrates or marginalizes the church. However, that is not discussed here as it is the theology of the church which is the burden of this chapter.

dialogue consists in believing that God may well have given Jewish people aspects of the truth needed by Christians to complement their assessment of their own role under the *missio dei*. Avoid imagining that Christian deliberations and hermeneutical procedures are by themselves sufficient to provide all the light from God that Christians need.

8. As nurtured by such respectful dialogue, explore a vision for the future which involves joint testimony and witness in history by Israel and the church. Avoid being insular, or imagining that joint effort is only possible if and when the Jewish people accept Christian leadership and perspectives as their own.

9. As interfaith groups meet and work together, from time to time issue major papers and joint statements meant to both inform and fertilize each community toward the kinds of progress being sought. Avoid perpetuating secrecy about such meetings beyond the kinds of privacy necessary in the early stages of dialogue. Open windows and doors.

The Fourth Question: What Kind of Procedural Safeguards Need to be in Place?

If progress is to be made by Christians in considering and theologizing about the role of the Jewish people in the *missio dei*, there are at least four procedural safeguards that should be implemented.

The first is for Christian leaders and scholars to cultivate openness to considering a variety of opinions and points of view from within their own circles, opinions on the Jewish people and the Jewish state that have traditionally been institutionally marginalized. While it may be far easier for authorities to marginalize or to silence dissenting voices, this has not proven to be life-giving. The Messianic group known as Hashivenu has a core principle which nicely captures a wise ethos on this matter: "Maturation requires a humble openness to discovery within the context of firmly held convictions." To the extent this openness is compromised or thwarted, a certain hardening supplants growth.

The second procedural safeguard is to seek out the feedback of responsible Jewish community leaders and scholars. As an example of this process, consider the role Abraham Joshua Heschel of Blessed Memory had in influencing the deliberations of the Second Vatican Council. In preparation for the Second Vatican Council, Pope John XXIII directed Augustin Cardinal Bea to prepare a draft on the relations between the Roman Catholic Church and the Jewish people. Bea sought advice from the American Jewish Committee (AJC), as well as other Jewish organizations. Abraham Joshua Heschel was the primary theological consultant for the AJC who then became the primary interpreter of Jewish views to the Vatican. He met with Cardinal Bea and other Church officials for four years, even meeting with Pope Paul VI, and had a considerable influence on the crafting of the extraordinary *Nostra Aetate*.

In view of the fruit they bore, one can only regard these meetings as having been providential. Such was the effect of listening to involved outsiders! May this example light the pathway for many Christians to find the courage and security to listen to Jewish voices. As the prophet said, "By people of strange tongues and by the lips of foreigners will I speak to this people" (1 Cor 14:31, referencing Isa 28:11). The prophet went on to say, "and even then they will not hear me." May such an indictment not fall upon a church that cannot be bothered to listen to Jews!

A third safeguard is to make room at the table for responsible Messianic Jewish voices. David Rudolph chronicles how, beginning in the second century, but coalescing in the late fourth and early fifth centuries, the voice and perspective of Messianic Jews living in solidarity with Israel has been marginalized and silenced in the church. The evidence is extensive, and need not be reproduced here. St. Jerome's opinions on the matter are typical, writing of Jewish Christians to St. Augustine in 404 CE, "since they want to be both Jews and Christians, they are neither Jews nor Christians," indicating that such Jewish Christians were numerous and widespread, "a heresy . . . to be found in all part of the East where Jews have their synagogues."[32] For Christian theologizing, just *being* a Jewish believer in Yeshua and living in solidarity with Israel was heretical.

Rudolph substantiates how even today, when Messianic Jews living in solidarity with Israel are more widespread than they have been for centuries, their voice and presence is almost entirely excluded from theological and interfaith discussion. In his conclusion, he outlines what is lost due to this exclusion, and therefore what may be gained for our purposes by restoring Messianic Jews to theological discussion in general, and Christian-Jewish discussion in particular. His discussion on this matter may be broken down to seven aspects, to which I have added brief comments:[33]

---

32. A. F. J. Klijn and G. J. Reinink, *Patristic Evidence for Jewish-Christian Sects* (Leiden: Brill, 1973), 201, quoted in Rudolph, "Messianic Jews and Christian Theology," 19, and footnote 80.

33. All quotations from Rudolph, "Messianic Jews and Christian Theology," 25–27.

1. "There should be a place for the Messianic Jewish perspective in Christian theology. For centuries, many theological questions went unasked because Messianic Jews were not there to ask them."

2. "Similarly, many supersessionist readings of the New Testament stood unchallenged because supersessionism conveniently eliminated the *ecclesia ex circumcisione*." Therefore, returning Messianic Jews to the discussion table will serve to alert and warn Christian participants of the supersessionist implications of positions they are proposing or discussing. Mark Kinzer's experience with Roman Catholic theologians has already corroborated that Messianic Jews detect supersessionist implications unforeseen by well-meaning Christians. Although dialogue partners from the wider Jewish community are also valuable in this respect, because of their *Sitz im Leben* Messianic Jews are especially sensitized to these issues.

3. "Contemporary Messianic Jews bring to the table practical theological insights that call into question traditional dogmas, such as the principle that Torah-obedience is antithetical to New Covenant spirituality and unity between Jew and Gentile. The Messianic synagogue is a veritable laboratory of discovery in this regard." Such questions go to the heart of supersessionism and cryptosupersessionism, exposing the paternalism, marginalization, and disparagement historically demonstrated against the Jewish voice in the *ekklesia* and the Jewish people in the mission of God.

4. "In addition to the active contribution of Messianic Jews to scholarship, the guild's simple awareness of the Messianic Jewish community leads to fresh reassessments. Engagement of this kind is healthy and long overdue." The presence of Messianic Jews at the table represents ecclesiological, theological and historical realities, just as their absence reveals ecclesiological, historical, and theological omissions.

5. "Perhaps the most pivotal question is the ecclesiological one: Are Messianic Jews a *tertium datur* or *tertium non datur*?" In other words, are Messianic Jews a logical necessity or a logical obstacle? "Mark Kinzer, . . . echoes Osten-Sacken in suggesting that Messianic Jews are the ecclesiological bridge between the church and Israel: 'Without Messianic Jews and Messianic Judaism, the *ekklesia* is not truly and fully itself.' . . . An all-Gentile church is an aberration, a deformity never envisioned by Jesus and his *shelichim* (apostles). Moreover, a *tertium genus* (third race) *ekklesia* is foreign to the New Testament. For Paul,

Jesus-believing Jews and Jesus-believing Gentiles together, in 'echad-like unity and diversity, form the body of the Messiah. Israel's irrevocable calling validates and necessitates this ecclesiological model." And if the Messianic Jews living in solidarity with Israel are a logical necessity for the very existence of the *ekklesia,* they must have a place at the table if healthy and balanced theological and ecclesiological discussion is to occur.[34]

Rudolph summarizes some reasons why he contends "that nothing fully substitutes for the inclusion of Messianic Jewish scholars in theological forums and colloquia."[35] His sentiments fully accord with sentiments I have interleaved with his prior statements:

> Their (Messianic Jews') epistemology is informed by living at the junction between church and synagogue, and by life in the Messianic synagogue. Their tangible presence in theological circles fosters a consciousness of Messianic Jews. Individually, theologians can develop broader epistemologies by contemplating how various readings and doctrines will impact twenty-first century Messianic Jews and Messianic synagogues. They can ask, "Does my treatment of Israel and Jewish Law ultimately displace, erase or patronize the Messianic Jewish community? Or does it affirm, sustain and show concern for the Jewish wing of the church?" By raising such critical questions about Messianic Jews, and including Messianic Jewish scholars in the conversation, Christian theology restores an historic voice to the contemporary discussion.[36]

The schism within the *ekklesia* which ecumenism seeks to address is but a widening of the tear in the *ekklesia* that occurred when the Jewish Christian/Messianic Jewish voice and presence living in solidarity with Israel was stilled and expelled. This expulsion and delegitimization is the site of the wound, and it is here the healing must begin.[37]

---

34. Ibid., 26.

35. Ibid., 27.

36. Ibid.

37. There have been a number of initiatives seeking just such a reconciliation. Among them is Toward Jerusalem Council II, which identifies itself as " an initiative of repentance and reconciliation between the Jewish and Gentile segments of the Church . . . that one day there will be a second Council of Jerusalem that will be, in an important respect, the inverse of the first Council described in Acts 15. Whereas the first Council was made up of Jewish believers in Yeshua (Jesus), who decided not to impose on the Gentiles the requirements of the Jewish Law, so the second Council would be made up of Gentile church leaders who would recognize and welcome Jewish believers in Yeshua

A final safeguard is an appropriate adoption of the practice of Scriptural Reasoning. According to a website devoted to the practice,

> Scriptural Reasoning (SR) is an open-ended practice of reading- and reasoning-in-dialogue among scholars of the three Abrahamic traditions. There are no set doctrines or rules of SR, since the rules are embedded in the texts of scripture and their relation to those who study and reason together. Individual practitioners of SR do find it useful, however, to reflect occasionally on their group practice and identify its leading tendencies. Such reflections differ from individual to individual and from time to time, but there are overlaps, and both the overlaps and the differences stimulate groups of SR reasoners to talk about, debate, and refine their practices.[38]

I am convinced that some version of this procedure can be a crucial channel for divine light to illumine Christian and Jewish contemplation of what one source nicely terms "moving together as partners in God's unfolding plans,"[39] which is what we mean by being jointly involved in the mission of God. I am reminded of the passage from the prophet Malachi (3:16) which reads, "Then those who feared the Lord spoke with one another. The Lord paid attention and heard them, and a book of remembrance was written before him of those who feared the Lord and esteemed his name." This passage speaks of human participants who fear the Lord and esteem his name, who speak with one another and who are treasured by God, before whom their names are written in a book of remembrance. Such listening to one another is precious to God, and something holy.

The Converging Destinies paradigm anticipates a day when the Jewish and Christian worlds will each give an account of themselves to God in the presence of each other. Each community will receive a mixture of

---

back into the Body of Messiah without requiring them to abandon their Jewish identity and practice" ("What is TJCII?"). Other initiatives in which Messianic Jews are likewise involved include the Helsinki Conferences on Jewish Continuity in the Church. The first was held June 14–15, 2010, and the second, June 24–25, 2012. These meetings included Jewish scholars from Franch, Germany, Israel, Russia, the United Kingdom, and the United States and Catholic, Orthodox, Protestant, and Messianic Jewish representatives. A press release for the 2010 conference may be found at http://istina.eu/uploads/MJTI-Press%20Release%20Stadium%20Catholicum.pdf, and for the 2011 conference at http://aronbengilad.blogspot.com/2011/08/second-helsinki-conference.html. There are other initiatives as well that have not been publicized.

38. The Student Journal of Scriptural Reasoning, "What is Scriptural Reasoning?" http://abraham.lib.virginia.edu/sjsr/sjsrwhat.html.

39. Cunningham et al., Introduction to *Christ Jesus and the Jewish People Today*, xxvi.

reassurance and rebuke. The kind of Scriptural Reasoning contemplated within this model is an anticipation of this final day. Participants will gather together, in the presence of God, to receive from Scripture a mixture of reassurance and rebuke. This is a level playing field on which community members from neither side claim to be there to teach, but all come to learn, and yes, in the process, to be God's instruments in teaching one another under the authority of that Word which is read and discussed. Foundational to this process is a settled awareness that none of us know all the answers, that all of us believe we are right even when we are wrong, that each of us needs to learn from another, and that all of us need to be humble in the presence of the Holy One who speaks in the midst. Most sobering, this enterprise is always a preparation for that day when each community will be assayed in the crucible of God's judgment.

6

Paths and Detours on the Journey toward Synerjoy

IN THIS CHAPTER I map six ways the Jewish and Christian communities have come to view themselves and each other with respect to the mission of God.[1] After considering these six ways, which I term Divergent, Intersecting, Parallel, Merging, Overlapping, and Complementary, I add a seventh closely related to the sixth, which I term the Converging Destinies model or paradigm.[2] The purpose of this chapter is to paint with the broadest of brushes a context for the perspective favored here. The final model I outline, the Converging Model, sketches this preferred option.

THE DIVERGENT MODEL

Under the Divergent Model, Christians see themselves to be moving toward a positive final destiny, and Jews moving toward a negative final destiny, with the exception of those Jews who are joined to the church through sacrament or some ritual of faith commitment. These final destinies are termed "heaven" and "hell." Only "true Christians" go to heaven, and Jews go to hell, unless and until they become Christians. The work of the church with respect to the Jews is to evangelize them and save at least some from certain perdition, while imagining the Jewish community's only proper role to be

1. Irving Greenberg says it well, issuing "a call to re-imagine the mission of the people of Israel to be a 'a holy nation' and to reconfigure two faith communities' respective roles as the people of God" *For the Sake of Heaven and Earth,* 4.

2. I will use the terms "model" and "paradigm" interchangeably in this work.

considering and accepting the claims of Christ or facing the consequences—everlasting perdition. Understandably, the Jewish community resents and rejects this construct, avoiding discussion and even interaction with its partisans.

One can find in Jewish writings a similarly polarized view, still held by some, but for the most part a relic of an earlier stage of intergroup theological polemics. As a rule, the Jewish community of today prides itself on being far more tolerant of religious diversity than are Christians holding to the Divergent Model.

Under such a winners/losers model, the winners tend to see their community as God's obedient servants, accomplishing his will in the world, with the losers neither serving God nor accomplishing his will, except perhaps in serving as a sign of the bad things that happen to people who resist God's will. This is precisely the position adopted by Augustine of Hippo in his doctrine of "the wandering Jew." The winners also tend to see the spiritual tradition of the losers as neither revelatory nor salvific, at most a once necessary but now vestigial organ in God's dealings with the world. Tragically, many, in my view, most in the Jewish missions world, hold to the Divergent Model, even if not so blatantly expressed.

THE INTERSECTING MODEL

The second model, the Intersecting Model, sees the Christian and Jewish faith communities as intersecting situationally in matters of common concern. Jews and Christians might unite to promote better educational standards in their neighborhood or nation, or to define and resist a perceived common threat such as militant Islam, or to lobby for governmental action in some area of civic concern. David Novak commends this approach, urging Jews and Christians to become dialogue partners engaged in matters of common concern to combat the secularist threat to both communities.[3] In this model, the issue of positive or negative final destinies is not discussed or explored, although the model favors seeing all good people, however defined, ending up in a positive state in the end, and bad people not so, depending upon how bad they are!

In the Intersecting Model, the final destinies of each community are not in focus, and adherents of this model tend to hope for the best for all concerned. Similarly, proponents of the Intersecting Model tend to assume

---

3. Similarly, in 1973, Irving Greenberg was influenced by Professor Yosef Yerushalmi to realize that Nazism was not the spawn of Christianity, but rather of the secularizing excesses of modernity (*For the Sake of Heaven and Earth*, 8).

the viability of the other community's claims to revelation and salvation, while avoiding detailed discussion on these matters.

THE PARALLEL MODEL

The third model, the Parallel Model, sees Christians and Jews moving on parallel tracks, each moving toward a positive final destiny. The only Christians and Jews who might be excluded from this positive destiny are those who betray the moral, communal, and faith commitments considered normative in their respective communities and foundational to human decency. This is commonly termed the two-covenant model, in which Jews have a relationship with God and positive final status through the Mosaic Covenant, while Christians have the same through the New Covenant.

This is not a winners/losers model, but more a winners/winners model. Each side assumes the other to have viable claims to revelation and salvation.

THE MERGING MODEL

Fourth, the Merging Model is the Judaeo-Christian tradition conceived of as a common ethical and cultural legacy, where discussion avoids differences, preferring to focus on perceived commonalities. This model often blends into a kind of generic feel-good/do-good spirituality. While it is possible to conceive of a Judaeo-Christian cultural tradition as a category of thought, it is impossible to live as a Judaeo-Christian, except in the most superficial lowest common denominator sense. One must either live as a Christian or as a Jew, aligned either with the Christian or Jewish historical stream. Living true to either religion demands ritual choices and a life ordered by the demands of the particular religion. One cannot successfully ride two horses at the same time, at least not for long.[4] I would argue that in this model, rather than riding two horses, one rides none at all. Matters of final destiny are not generally discussed by advocates of the Merging Model, but are assumed to be positive, while issues of revelation and salvation are generally avoided but assumed to be positive.

---

4. The Jewish tradition puts it more colorfully: "With one tuchas (*derriere*) you can't dance at two weddings."

THE OVERLAPPING MODEL

Fifth, the Overlapping Model describes Christians and Jews discovering and discussing areas of commonality, toward fostering mutual understanding, benefit, and respect. This differs from the previous model in that the integrity of both religious communities is preserved, and merging or blending is avoided. This model resembles the Intersecting Model, but features more of an ongoing affiliation between the two communities rather than simply a temporary situational coalition. In such a model, matters of final destiny are generally not discussed intergroup, but the general assumption is that the ultimate horizon of truth about God and humanity, while incorporating aspects of both traditions, will in the end prove to be broader, and in some sense, other that what was anticipated, while remaining for now beyond our view. The model assumes final positive outcomes for each community, while regarding each other's revelatory and salvific status to be positive, with neither side considering itself qualified to stand in judgment over the relative value of the other's commitments.

David Novak articulates this view. He holds that Judaism and Christianity each stand as a singularity against the general culture because they are each revelatory religions, suggesting that this commonality binds them together in a way that makes dialogue possible. Additionally, he explores how each community may affirm the revelatory experience of the other without standing in judgment over it since there is no genus to which they respectively and together belong.[5]

He speaks of the consummation of all things as follows:

> The final redemption will be such that "No eye but Yours O Lord will see what will be done for those who wait for you." Until that time, we are all travelers passing through a vale of tears until we appear before God in Zion. Jews and Christians begin at the same starting point, and both are convinced that we will meet at the all mysterious end. Yet we cannot deny that our appointed tasks in this world are very different and must remain so because the covenant is not the same for both of us. It is God alone who will bring us to our unknown destination, in a time pleasing to him.

5. Irving Greenberg instinctively sought out the same ground, saying, "If religions turned out to be as valid and dignified as their practitioners were, one must come up with a new conceptualization of the nature of absolute truth that would allow for the existence of two or more valid yet contradicting faiths. My response was the image of a shift from a Newtonian universe—to an Einsteinian universe, in which many absolute center points exist, each absolute center defined relative to the system in which it was embedded" (*For the Sake of Heaven and Earth*, 10).

That time has not yet come. In the meantime, the constitution of the Jewish-Christian dialogue might have a message for the large body of humankind for whose peace we must all be concerned. Our dialogue might be able to show the world that the hope it needs for its very survival can only be the hope for its final redemption. Neither nature nor history nor the self can supply hope in these days. Beginning with creation and nurtured by or respective revelations, Jews and Christians can and do hope for the future. From creation and revelation comes our faith that God has not and will not abandon us or the world, that the promised redemption is surely yet to come.[6]

THE COMPLEMENTARIAN MODEL

This is a model propounded by R. Kendall Soulen. In his studies at Yale under Hans Frei, he reached the conclusion that Paul the Apostle never thinks of humanity as a non-differentiated whole, but always as the sum total of Jews plus the sum total of Gentiles, Israel, and the nations. His model is a theologically grounded and self-critical reappraisal of Christian theological assumptions about the Jewish people vis-a-vis the purposes of God and the proper interpretation of Scripture. He exposes supersessionism as untenable and destructive not only to the well-being of Israel but also that of the church. This is because the only God the church rightly can claim is the God of Israel. Therefore, whenever the church takes positions positing a divine abandonment of Israel, it undermines its security with and faith in the only God the church can rightly name as its own.

In building his case, Soulen divides his treatment into two parts. In the first, "The Logic and Limitations of the Standard Canonical Narrative," he traces the development of Christendom's theological disenfranchisement of the Jewish people in a narrative of creation, fall, incarnation, consummation, which makes God's dealings with Israel to be mere scene setting and background for God's real story, his foreground engagement with the church. He presents a contrasting narrative in the second part of his treatment, "The Unity of the Canon After Christendom," where he proposes that God is the God of creation and of consummation, and that his will has always been and continues to be to bestow blessing through "the other." In striking language, he names the church of Christendom as incompletely converted:

> The crucial marks of that incomplete conversion are a triumphalist posture toward the Jewish people and a latently gnostic assessment of God's engagement in the realm of history. . . .

6. Novak, *Jewish-Christian Dialogue*, 155.

"Christendom" names the church's theological and social posture when it is triumphalist toward Jews and gnostic toward God's engagement in history. The God of Israel, in contrast, names the God who is identified by fidelity to the Jewish people through time and therefore by engagement with human history in its public and corporate dimensions. If it is true that the gospel about Jesus is credible only as predicated of the God of Israel, then the integrity of Christian theology after Christendom depends upon bringing traditional forms of Christian thought into a further degree of congruence with the God of Israel.[7]

I would add and emphasize that Soulen's position is deeply congruent with Paul's construct of the fullness of Israel and the fullness of the nations. God is pursuing a unified and coordinated destiny for the cosmos in which his workings among Israel and the nations are discrete, yet coordinate. Soulen puts it this way:

As attested by the Scriptures, God's work as Consummator engages the human family in a historically decisive way in God's election of Israel as a blessing to the nations. The resulting distinction and mutual dependence of Israel and the nations is the fundamental form of the economy of consummation through which God initiates, sustains, and ultimately fulfills the one human family's destiny for life with God. So conceived, God's economy of consummation is essentially constituted as *an economy of mutual blessing* between those who are and who remain different.[8]

He asks two questions from the vantage point of constructing a post-Holocaust theology. "First, how deeply is supersessionism implicated in the traditional fabric of Christian theology? And how can Christians read the Bible and articulate their most basic convictions in ways that are not supersessionist?" In short, can Christians be really Christian without being triumphalist toward Jews?[9]

Such questions also drive the model that follows.

THE CONVERGING MODEL

The Converging Model, our seventh and last, posits a divinely ordained distinction between the Christian and Jewish historical streams within an

7. Soulen, *The God of Israel and Christian Theology*, x-xi.

8. Ibid., 111.

9. Asking and answering these questions is foundational to my thought as well as I seek to outline and summon forth a postsupersessionist missiology.

underlying unity. In this model, regarding the past, the church from among the nations and Israel are seen as one great people currently living in a state of schism destined to be healed. The model names the final consummation as a time of ultimate convergence for Israel and the church, calling both to align thinking and doing now with this converging destiny.

Unlike some others we have considered, this is not a coalescing model where Israel and the church merge with a resultant loss of distinctives. The model goes beyond other models, being inexplicit in how the church and Israel ought to link their thought and action to each other and to the mission of God. While indebted to Soulen's model, the Converging Model is more explicit about the consummation, and about the implications of a revelation of Yeshua's identity to both the church and the Jewish people.

Here are some other aspects of this model:

1. This model holds that both the Jewish and Christian communities will maintain cohesion beyond history's final horizon, a time beyond time when both communities, in the presence of the other, will each be validated and corrected in the salvific and revelatory eschatological revelation of the Living God and the judgment that awaits us.

2. The model preserves and values the creational, covenantal, and existential distinctions that mark the particularities of Israel and the church, distinctions that remain in the eschaton and final state.

3. This model remembers and values how true encounter with God combines reassurance and reproof, as is evident from examining prophetic oracles, as well as the Letters to the Seven Churches in Revelation. In Revelation, the best example is the Letter to Ephesus, which states, "'I know your works, your toil and your patient endurance, and how you cannot bear with those who are evil, but have tested those who call themselves apostles and are not, and found them to be false. I know you are enduring patiently and bearing up for my name's sake, and you have not grown weary [thus, commendation, reassurance]. But I have this against you, that you have abandoned the love you had at first [thus correction and rebuke]."[10] In the Older Testament, Isaiah's Temple vision is one paradigmatic example of this phenomenon. On the one hand he knows himself to be "undone," "a man of unclean lips who dwells among a people of unclean lips." On the other hand, he is the one for whom the angel takes a coal from off the altar with which he touches his mouth, cleansing him of his uncleanness, while the Divine voice summons him to service of the Divine, thus, rebuke

---

10. Rev 2:2–4.

and reassurance. So shall it be for Israel and the church, when we see him as he is.

4. This model posits that Yeshua of Nazareth is the vanishing point at which the historical trajectories of synagogue and church converge. This revelation will come as both validation and corrective for both the Christian and Jewish communities. The Jewish world in general has long assumed that Jesus of Nazareth has little relevance to them, and the Christian world has long ago forgotten or denied his continuing bond with Israel, his validation of her pathways of holiness, and commitment to her positive final destiny. Yeshua will ultimately be fully known as both Lord of the church and Son of David. In the process, both communities will be reproved and corrected, in the presence of the other, that no flesh might glory in his presence.

5. The model mirrors the experience of the sons of Israel with Joseph their brother. Although given up for dead, he was yet alive, and, although unseen and unrecognized as their committed kinsman, he supported the descendants of Jacob throughout their years of travail as their champion and friend at the right hand of rulership. Joseph's self-revelation and Yeshua's apocalyptic unveiling are parallel.

6. The Convergence Model rejects seeing the fullness of Israel and the fullness of the nations as in any manner isolated from one another, or *separate*. Rather they are meant to be *distinct* and yet to have a synergistic relationship—each community learning from the other and from the mistakes each has made, coming to appreciate the other in the process, growing in mutual reconciliation and cooperation, with each community coming to *understand itself* better through the entire process in anticipation of the consummational convergence described here.

Four terms are helpful in understanding this model's richness. The first, borrowed from Soulen, is *complementarity*. The second is *convergence*, which both contemplates a converging consummation and advocates conforming present action and transforming our thinking around a partial and distorted vision of that consummation which becomes clearer as it draws nearer. The third term is *interfaithulness*, which is also the name of the organization I direct that develops this paradigm and its implications on multiple levels and in multiple contexts. The term *interfaithfulness* captures the both-and nature of the paradigm: yes, two faith communities (Christian and Jewish) living together without compromising their own distinctives, that is, both communities living in faithfulness to their own religious commitments, rather than making peace through unacceptable compromise. This is a paradigm that demands greater faithfulness from all parties rather than self-negating capitulation.[11]

Our final term captures the imagination as to the outcome of all of this: *synerjoy,* a neologism based on the term *synergy.* Ray French and his co-authors define synergy as "the creation of a whole that is greater than the sum of its parts,"[12] while Barb Rentenbach reminds us how "a designed beauty of synergy is that it serves only to add, never subtract."[13] Etymologically, "synergy" means working together, with the connotations of the term being unrelievedly positive. In the context of the missions of God, of Israel and the nations, this is a consummational synergy leading toward maximal fullness of joy for the entire cosmos, hence, *synerjoy.*

This book describes this synerjoy destination toward which we strive, and the synerjoy process, the roles to be played and the paths to be taken by Israel and the church along the way, each community carrying out its own mission within the mission of God. I am reminded of Robert Frost's poem about two paths diverging in a wood. However, in this model the two paths converge, having diverged millennia ago. Still, this model agrees with the poet's insight, when he states, "I took the one [the path] less traveled, and that has made all the difference."[14] So will it make all the difference if church and Israel will learn to walk different paths than those to which they have grown accustomed, converging paths now, in interactive and instructive partnership with each other on route to their final destination.

In the past, other paths have been taken and commended, while some guides have long ago pointed us in this converging direction. Along the way there have been all sorts of detours and obstacles. These too must be examined, with lessons learned, if the church and Israel are to find the best way forward.

Finally, as a Messianic Jew, part of the message and meta-message of this book is to suggest that advocates of a mature Messianic Jewish perspective have a crucial role to play in assisting Christians and Jews to discern their paths and journey onward to God's foreordained synerjoy.

Wherever you are in your journey, would it not be best if Jews and Christians could learn to arise and go *together*?

11. www.interfaithfulness.org.

12. French et al., *Organizational Behaviour,* 266.

13. Rentenbach, *Synergy,* 6.

14. Frost, *Mountain Interval.*

7

What Is the Gospel We Should Be Commending to All Israel?[1]

I WAS ABOUT TEN years old the first time somebody called me a Christ-killer.

I had just come out of Morris Schaeffer's candy store, on the corner of Winthrop Street and Nostrand Avenue, in Flatbush, Brooklyn. A bunch of kids whom I had never met jumped me, pummeling me to the ground, while making a profound theological query: "Why'd you kill God?" I had no answer for them. At that moment I didn't know what they were talking about. Only later, while tending to bruises and scrapes (some) and checking for broken bones (none), did I realize that they were talking about Jesus. Thus ends my first experience with interfaith dialogue.

My bruises and scrapes healed a long time ago. Still, about sixty years later, I am still hurting. But the pain of being picked on as a child is nothing compared to how I feel now when friends and colleagues in the missions and Messianic Jewish world, most of them Jews, beat up on the Jewish people. It isn't any prettier to lump the Jews or any group of Jews into a distrusted, despised class than it was for those kids to beat me up one cool, clear, autumn day in New York.

I confess that, in part, I am missiologically directed and driven by my sensitivity to theological Jew-bashing.[2] I know we all agree that this should

1. This chapter slightly edited from a paper delivered October, 2007 at the Boro Park Symposium, "What Is The Gospel We Should Be Commending To All Israel In These Times Of Transition?"

2. I use the term "missiologically" here to name my concern for appropriately understanding, serving, and communicating what God is up to in the world, especially as that is advanced and defined in the good news about Yeshua. Although the word

have absolutely no place in our outreach to our people. But, beyond contradiction, most of us are well-practiced in bashing Jews and Judaism. These old and deep prejudices are mostly hidden from us. In this chapter I want to demonstrate this to be the case, and to outline a better way for us to think about our people, and a better way to understand the message we are to bring to them.[3]

I treat my topic, "What Kind Of Gospel Should We Commend to Israel?"[4] in four ways: matters of context, matters of content, matters of controversy, and cumulative conclusions. My argument is inductive, making its case moving from particulars to a general conclusion; cumulative, because each component contributes to the credibility of the whole; and synergistic, because the contribution of each component can only be rightly perceived through appreciating how the components work together, with the whole being greater than the sum of its parts. Only by keeping the parts and the whole in dynamic tension will readers rightly understand, evaluate, and above all, respond to what I say here.

I want to pull the covers off a sleepy movement, rousing all of us to a unified, demanding, and sacrificial outreach mandate, appropriate to our times, to the full witness of Scripture, and to our identity as part of the Remnant of Israel. Mine is a call to inconvenience and radical change. Mine is a call to sacrifice, humility, and discomfort. And above all, mine is a call to envision, speak, and live a gospel that is good news for all Israel.

MATTERS OF CONTEXT

We communicate an eternal gospel[5] in the midst of time. Therefore, we can only do so at specific times, in specific places, to specific people. "Context" should not be dismissed as a trendy buzzword: it is instead an unavoidable

---

mission has been contaminated by association with a tradition of cultural negation and coercion, the intended connotation here is "what it is God has sent us to be, to do, and to say in the world," and in my case and that of my original hearers, what we have been sent to be, to do and to say among and to our Jewish people.

3. To prevent abuses of my own, I have chosen to leave unnamed the authors or published sources I criticize in this chapter. Anyone requiring further identification of these sources may contact me.

4. "All Israel" is a term borrowed especially from Romans 11:26, connected in this chapter to "all the people [of Israel]" in Luke 2:10–11. It is a phrase found 149 times in Scripture. In the present discussion, I believe the sense of the term is equivalent to "Israel as a whole," rather than "every single Jew." This is compatible with the Talmudic view: "All Israel has a share in the world to come: the following (out of Israel) do not have a share in the world to come" (M. Sanhedrin 10:1).

5. Rev 14:6.

reality. Since only those who properly assess the soil of context have a right to expect a good harvest, we would be foolish to omit this step in our rush to sow or harvest the seed. Accordingly, I begin by examining five contextual issues demanding our attention: Living in Times of Eschatological Transition; New Paradigms, New Tensions; The Bad News Gospel; Individualism, Community and Consummation; and Implications of Adopting a New Creation Eschatology.

Living in Times of Eschatological Transition

The first of our five contextual factors identifies five signs indicating these to be eschatological times, with the consummation of all things drawing near. I suggest, as prophesied in Scripture, that God's agenda has begun to shift from a focus on the ingathering of the fullness of the Gentiles to the ingathering of the fullness of Israel.[6]

The Founding of the Modern State of Israel

The prophet Zechariah tells us that at the time of the end the Jewish people will be living in the Land, with all the nations of the world gathered against them.[7] This could not have happened for 1,900 years, and only became a possibility again in 1948, with the establishment of the Jewish State. This is a sign of the times. We should be anticipating and preparing for the consummation of all things.

The Liberation of Jerusalem

The prophets remind us as well that Jerusalem will be a Jewish city at the time of the end. This was a nonissue for two millennia, until the Liberation of Jerusalem in 1967. This too is a sign of the times.

---

6. Often, Luke 21:24 is applied here: "Jerusalem will be trampled underfoot by the Gentiles, until the times of the Gentiles are fulfilled." The text appears to specify a sign of transition between the times of the Gentiles and the time of the Jews, the sign being a change in the fortunes of Jerusalem, which many view to have been fulfilled in June 1967.

7. Zech 12:1–3, 9; 14:2, 3; Mic 4:11–13.

The Regathering of the Jews to Israel From the Land of the North

Part of the nexus of events in the latter days is the regathering of Jewish exiles not only from the nations in general, but also explicitly "from the land of the north," commonly associated with the heartland of the Former Soviet Union. Many of us are old enough to remember when it was front-page news for one Jew from the former Soviet Union to emigrate to Israel. But all of this changed forever with the advent of *glasnost* and *perestroika* under Mikhail Gorbachev and Boris Yeltsin in the 1980s and 1990s, and the astounding break-up of the former Soviet Union in 1991. It was Ronald Reagan who said, "Mr. Gorbachev: tear down this wall," but it was God who swung the hammer.

Since the 1980s, well over a million Jews from the former Soviet Union have emigrated to Israel. When we combine this statistic with others such as the massive airlifts and repatriation to Israel of over 85 percent of Ethiopia's Jews, can we be blamed for seeing these events in the context of this prophecy from the prophet Jeremiah?

> So then, the days are coming when they will say, "As surely as the Lord lives, who brought the descendants of Israel up out of the land of the north and out of all the countries where he had banished them." Then they will live in their own land (Jer 23:7–8).

The Repentance-Renewal of the Jewish People

Deuteronomy 30 and Ezekiel 36–37 are among the texts connecting this return to the Lord with a renewal among Jews of covenantal faithfulness, when God will spiritually renew his people and cause us to "again obey the voice of the Lord, and keep all his commandments . . . and his statutes which are written in this book of the law."[8] Today we are seeing this spiritual renewal become a manifest reality, at least in nascent stages. Many Jews are becoming *ba'alei teshuvah,* returnees to observance. And ever since the Liberation of Jerusalem in 1967, Jews have been coming to Yeshua-faith in increasing numbers. Many who have come to Israel from "the land of the north" are already Yeshua-believing Jews. Today it is impossible to find an Israeli congregation of Jewish Yeshua-believers that does not include a substantial number of Russian speakers. In Israel today more Jews are coming to believe in Yeshua than at any time since the first century. Mitch Glaser

---

8. Deut 30:8–10; also Ezek 37:24, "They shall follow my ordinances and be careful to obey my statutes."

estimates that the numbers of Israeli Yeshua-believers have grown by 300 or 400 percent in the past ten years, with 60 or 70 percent of this growth among Russian speakers. Something is happening that Scripture foretold, and the times they are a-changing!

A New Concern for Messianic Jewish Covenant Faithfulness

In recent years, the issue of Torah-based covenant faithfulness has moved to the forefront of Messianic Jewish discussion. Consider this quotation from a definitional document ratified by the Union of Messianic Jewish Congregations on July 31, 2002: "Messianic Judaism is a movement of Jewish congregations and congregation-like groupings committed to Yeshua the Messiah that embrace the covenantal responsibility of Jewish life and identity rooted in Torah, expressed in tradition, renewed and applied in the context of the New Covenant."[9] The reference to "covenantal responsibility of Jewish life and identity rooted in Torah, [and] expressed in tradition" is nothing short of revolutionary when one considers how prior theological paradigms excluded or even negated the priority of Torah faithfulness for Jewish believers in Yeshua. The statement contravenes the older consensus that Torah observance was at most to be regarded as strictly a matter of personal preference, something to be pursued privately, in circumspect moderation.

Can it be that such indicators are heralding the promised shift of God turning his attention from accomplishing the fullness of the Gentiles, to pursuing the fullness of Israel? Opinions differ. But for those of us inclined to agree, or those of us who are uncertain of our doubts on this matter, now is an appropriate time for the church, the Jewish missions culture, and the Messianic Jewish Movement to reexamine their priorities and embrace paradigms and priorities suited to changing times.

New Paradigms, New Tensions

Times of transition not only bring new missional dynamism; they are also times of destabilization, threat, and jockeying for power.

Any of us who have been change agents in times of transition can attest to the controversies, denunciations, and resistance attending such efforts. I'm sure that all of us who are leaders of groundbreaking Yeshua-groups have been called on the carpet by concerned or outraged critics not only

9. From the statement affirmed by the delegates to the 23rd Annual UMJC Conference on July 31, 2002.

differing with us, but denouncing us for doing new things in new ways. This is true not only of our ideological opposites, but even of those who we might look to as allies, and people with whom we have no axe to grind. Today you can even discover "proof" on the internet that many of us are involved in a one-world, one-religion conspiracy! Yes, it's news to me, too.

Because we are serving a movement birthed in times of transition, we have all had to learn to live with opposition and vilification. Now new and different transitions are upon us—and with the growth of new paradigms come new tensions.

David Bosch traces the past and future of mission theology under the overall concept of paradigm shifts, helping us to better understand the stresses confronting us. Referencing the writings of Thomas Kuhn, the father of modern paradigm theory, he explains why advocates of new paradigms always meet with resistance. This insight forms a lens through which we may better understand relationships among ourselves and with our critics:

> [A shifting of paradigms] seldom happens without a struggle, however, since scientific communities are by nature conservative and do not like their peace to be disturbed, the old paradigm's protagonists continue for a long time to fight a rearguard action. . . . Proponents of the old paradigm often just cannot understand the arguments of the proponents of the new. Metaphorically speaking, the one is playing chess and the other checkers on the same board.
>
> . . . This explains why defenders of the old order and champions of the new frequently argue at cross-purposes. Protagonists of the old paradigm, in particular, tend to immunize themselves against the arguments of the new. They resist its challenges with deep emotional reactions, since those challenges threaten to destroy their very perception and experience of reality, indeed their entire world.[10]

Bosch and Kuhn are reading our mail. This is us, and this is now.

The Bad News Gospel[11]

Because our sojourn in Christian space, particularly the Evangelical camp, affects all our missional thinking and doing, we must recognize how, since

---

10. Bosch, *Transforming Mission*, 184–85. In part, Bosch's argument paraphrases Hiebert, "Epistemological Foundations for Science and Theology," and Hiebert, "The Missiological Implications of an Epistemological Shift."

11. Another aspect of the bad-news gospel is Christendom's habit of denigrating

the early second century, Christendom has not presented the gospel as good news for all Israel. This is not just a bit of historical reflection on second-century Christian rhetoric. It is a current reality. Messianic Jews have themselves been misshapen by such rhetoric. Comparing Scripture with this perspective reveals its misalignment.

In the famous Christmas story, we read words so familiar we routinely miss their import.

> And in that region there were shepherds out in the field, keeping watch over their flock by night. And an angel of the Lord appeared to them, and the glory of the Lord shone around them, and they were filled with fear. And the angel said to them, "Be not afraid; for behold, I bring you good news of a great joy which will come to all the people; for to you is born this day in the city of David a Savior, who is Christ, the Lord."[12]

Notice the phrase, "good news of a great joy which will come to all the people." Although most are apt to assume otherwise, this is not "good news of great joy which will come to all the peoples of earth." The context speaks of one people in particular, the Jewish people. Many will recoil from this aspect of our text due to reflexively regarding the Jewish people as fundamentally spiritually lost, eternal losers, and the coming of Christ as not being good news for *the* Jewish people, but at best, good news only for a small minority of enlightened, lucky, or spiritually elite Jews.

One ought not to accept this assumption of majority Jewish loss without slowing down to look its implications in the eye. Let one implication suffice for now. The year before Yeshua died and rose again, faithful Jews needed only seek to live faithful to God, trusting in his faithfulness to his covenants and promises to Israel and in the provisions he had made through the Temple sacrifices, in which they had a vested interest through the Temple taxes. Under such an arrangement, certainly there must have been tens of thousands, hundreds of thousands, even millions of Jews who knew their status to be covenantally secured, in this life and the next. But with the coming of Christ, all that changed. Now, according to the prevailing paradigm, all of these Jews were fundamentally lost, unless and until they accepted as their savior a crucified Jew whose ministry flourished for three and half short years. Stop for a moment and consider. Is *this* gospel good news of great joy for all the people of Israel or is it only such for a spiritually enlightened elite minority? It will not do to respond that Yeshua is good

---

Jewish faith and sancta, postulating that these are worthless when compared with the church's patrimony. This too is bad news, not treated here for the sake of space.

12. Luke 2:8–11.

news for all Israel as a medicine might be for cancer patients, who must however take the medicine if they would recover. To speak thus is to read back into the context something that is not there: the angelic messenger assumes the gospel to be good tidings for Zion for whom the triumphant and vindicating reign of their God is becoming evident in the birth of the Son of David.[13]

Terrance Tiessen reminds us that holding to the prevailing paradigm of salvation being a matter of one-by-one destiny, with no salvation except for those who accept Christ as their personal savior, means the coming of Jesus was bad news for the Jews of his generation, as myriads of Jews, formerly covenantally secure, and perhaps also many God-fearers, slipped into perdition or least into eternal jeopardy and insecurity because the basis of covenantal security had changed and narrowed with Yeshua's incarnation, crucifixion, resurrection, or ascension, take your pick.[14] This is like your car warranty becoming invalid because the warranty holder went out of business, with you needing to buy a new warranty involving new stipulations and costs if you want to regain coverage. Is this good news for you? And is the one-by-one gospel good news for all the people of Israel? Hardly. In addition, we need to step back and consider whether we misread such passages through our default lenses of one-by-one salvation. Usually, when speaking of "salvation," the biblical context is national rescue and deliverance for Israel, of the fulfillment of covenanted national blessings just at the time when all seemed lost. For example, consider the foundational text in Isaiah, "How beautiful upon the mountains are the feet of him who brings good news."[15] Reading the context underscores that this gospel is not one of individualistic salvation but of the fulfillment of covenanted national blessings in an act of divine rescue. The text speaks of the one who "who says to *Zion* 'Your God reigns,'" and thereby "all the ends of the earth shall see the salvation of God." Ten times chapter 52 reminds us of the communal— rather than individualistic—context as the good news is vouchsafed to Zion (5x), to Jerusalem (5x). And from here, onward to Isaiah 53!

Donald McGavran, founder of the Fuller Seminary School of Intercultural Studies, took as his watchword πάντα τὰ ἔθνη (*panta ta ethne*), "all the nations." Today I urge those thinking of outreach to the Jews to take up a neglected biblical mandate, παντὶ τῷ λαῷ, "all the people of Israel."

---

13. See Isa 52:7.

14. Tiessen, *Who Can Be Saved?*, 199. Tiessen will argue for "accessibilism," which asserts "God does save some of the unevangelized, but he has not raised up the world's religions as instruments for achieving this" (47).

15. Isa 52:7.

We have allowed mostly subconscious cultural and historical forces to crop, narrow, and misshape the gospel message and outreach to our people. This is due in large measure to our focus on individual soul salvation. The eternal lostness of those who fail to accept our "medicine" is always the backdrop of our presentation, even if unstated. Since the vast majority of Jews have not accepted the claims of Christ, and due to the assumption that the New Testament has replaced the Old, and that "the Jews rejected/killed Christ," the church has long held and conditioned us to feel and believe the Jewish people to be *especially* lost. This means we always present our Jewish "contact" the opportunity to be individually "saved" against the backstory that the vast majority of the descendants of Jacob, fifty generations (two thousand years) of his or her family, including the brightest and the best who died in Nazi camps and ovens, are of theological necessity irretrievably lost, in fact, burning forever in the lake of fire. Is *this* "good news of a great joy which will come to all the people (of Israel)"? Is this not the worst possible news for the Jewish people: once the most favored nation, once cradled in the promises and covenants of God, but now, due to events surrounding the coming of the Man from Galilee, eternal losers? Only a bigot or a fool would blame Jewish people for telling us to take our "good news" and peddle it somewhere else.

Years ago, I heard Mark Kinzer make an off-hand comment that informs what I am saying here: "I just think that somehow the coming of Yeshua the Messiah must have advanced the condition of the Jewish people." Do you disagree? Or do you instead believe that with the coming of Messiah, the condition of the Jewish people as a whole took a great leap backward? If so then, how is it good news?

I am suggesting that our paradigms and presentations of the gospel are unbalanced and distorted. Besides individualism, other forces warp our assumptions and approach. For example, consider the common category mistake many make concerning the Jewish people and their religion.

A Category Mistake

One reason for confusion about Jews, Judaism, and the gospel is the category mistakes the church, mission, and Messianic Jewish communities make about Jews and Judaism. The term "category mistake," devised by English philosopher Gilbert Ryle, names "cases where we talk of something in terms appropriate only to something of a radically different kind."[16]

---

16. Definition accessed online at http://www.philosophyprofessor.com/philosophies/category-mistake.php. For a related study on the history of Christian negative

Most missiologists, missionaries, and theologically motivated Christians act and think as if the seed of Jacob is a nation like any other, and Judaism a religion like any religion, except for Christianity. This is partly supersessionism's legacy whereby Jews no longer enjoy the status they once knew now that Christ has come "and his own received him not."[17] Of course, most engaged in any kind of gospel presentation to the Jewish people would insist that they hold the Jews to be a unique and chosen people, referencing numerous texts highlighting this uniqueness.[18]

Yet despite such protestations, the vast majority of missionaries, Christians, and Messianic Jews assume Judaism to be a religion no different from other religions, and by extension, Jews not believing in Yeshua to be no different from any other people when it comes to knowledge of God, spiritual experience and status, and eternal destiny. In feeling, thinking, speaking, and writing, practically all of these view the Jews as simply non-Christians, categorically bound for hell, without hope and without God in the world, effectively pagans, even if religious ones. But what's wrong with this picture? Much!

Those who think in this manner slot the Jewish people into a category Paul applied not to Israel, but to Gentile pagans. He thought of the Jews in a *different* category, as home base for the people of God. Paul writes that it is Gentile pagans who were without hope and God in the world because they were "alienated from the commonwealth of Israel and (therefore) strangers to the covenants of promise" (Eph 2:12). He viewed the Jewish religion and Jewish identity in positive terms sharply divergent from the disparaging rhetoric we usually hear. And when, in the second chapter of Philippians he discounts his former life in Judaism as "dung" in comparison to the life he has found in Messiah, he is hyperbolically highlighting the glories of Messiah's coming by comparing it to something which he finds intrinsically valuable. He is saying that knowing Yeshua the Messiah and making him know is so extraordinary, it is even better even than the high status he once enjoyed as an exemplary Pharisee. What he rejects about his former life in Judaism is not Jewish practice, which he maintained for the rest of his life, or Jewish religion, for which he commends the Jewish people in Acts 26:7. Instead he condemns himself for having harbored an arrogant pride of status due to his prior religious privileges and performance. Paul never

---

categorization of the Jewish people and Judaism, see Cameron, "Jews and Heretics—A Category Error?"

17. John 1:12.

18. For example, see Deut 7:6; 14:2; 32:8; Pss 33:12; 147:19–20; Isa 43:20; 65:22; Amos 3:2; Rom 3:1–2.

leaves Judaism behind. Rather he takes on a new attitude toward his Judaism, viewing it now through the lens of his Yeshua-faith.

In contrast, nearly all missionaries, Messianic Jews, and Christians view Judaism to be a fruitless religion, no different from Hinduism, animism, or Buddhism. It is a dead, false religion, devoid of the Spirit, and its practitioners squander their souls on a religion that can neither save them, commend them to God, nor mediate to them any measure of true spiritual knowledge or spiritual experience. Religious Jews are spiritually dead in their trespasses and sins, and unable even to understand the things of God apart from receiving Christ and the Holy Spirit. And within such ranks, woe to the person who questions such a position or takes an opposing stance. He or she is sure to be regarded as deviant, dangerous, and at best, confused.[19]

But something is very wrong here. Judaism is *not* a religion just like all the others, any more than the Jewish people are simply a people like all the others. Just as the Jews remain the chosen people, Judaism remains the context of this people's trans-generational communal devotion to the God and Father of Yeshua the Messiah, who has elected throughout time to be known as the God of Abraham, Isaac, and Jacob, and therefore, especially the God of the Jews.[20] Can this be said of any other people and their religion? Of course not! No, the Jewish people are in a different category from all others, and their religion is not simply just another non-Christian religion. Failure to acknowledge this difference is a colossal categorical error.

John Howard Yoder helps us here by referring to Judaism as "a non-non-Christian religion."[21] We are not speaking here of a two-covenant theory, or of the alleged impropriety or superfluity of gospel proclamation to this people. Saying, after Yoder, that the Jewish people are a non-non-Christian people brilliantly corrects the category mistake of slotting Jews as non-Christians and Judaism as a fruitless and fundamentally false religion.

---

19. One does not have to look hard or long to find explicit, bald, and strident statements from within the Jewish missions and/or Messianic Jewish world denouncing Judaism as categorically no different from other non-Christian religions. Thus, one missionary says this on his website, "Rabbinic Judaism is a false religion. The synagogues of today are deceptions, which lead Jewish people away from the way of salvation into a system that rejects Torah, substitutes Torah with human tradition, and leads them into destruction. Rabbinic Judaism is as much a false religion as any other false religion." (Since this was written, this quotation has been removed from the web. However, it was up for years and represents a viewpoint seldom discussed but widely held in some circles).

20. Along with Mark Kinzer, I believe Judaism to be a house still inhabited by Yeshua even though he is yet to be recognized and explicitly honored by the majority of those living there.

21. Yoder, *The Jewish-Christian Schism Revisited*, 147–59.

Paul was closer to the truth. When speaking to Herod Agrippa he claimed Jews and Judaism as his religion:

> My manner of life from my youth, spent from the beginning among my own nation and at Jerusalem, is known by all the Jews. They have known for a long time, if they are willing to testify, that according to the strictest party of *our religion* [not *their* religion] I have lived as a Pharisee. And now I stand here on trial for hope in the promise made by God to our fathers, to which *our twelve tribes* [not *their* twelve tribes] hope to attain, as *they earnestly worship night and day.*[22]

How many Jewish mission newsletters would publish articles categorizing religious Jews as "earnestly worshipping [God] night and day?" None that I know of. I have even heard of prominent mission agencies that hold that Jews worship a different God from the God to be found through faith in Jesus! One friend reported hearing a worker with a prominent Jewish mission agency telling a church crowd that Judaism is "a satanic religion!" I am sure his bizarre and biased reasoning was as follows: Satan tries to keep Jews from finding salvation in Jesus the Messiah; Judaism seeks to keep Jews from finding faith in Jesus the Messiah; therefore, Judaism is a satanic religion. Of course his position falls to the ground on biblical grounds alone once one notes that Paul referred to the Judaism practiced by other Jews as "our religion."

The Jewish missions community, very many Messianic Jews and many Christians must grapple with the extensive biblical evidence that contradicts their categories. And there are few things so hard for such people as admitting fundamental error. In fifty years I have hardly ever seen this happen. Yet the truth demands that those who would rightly commend the gospel to the Jewish people must vigorously repudiate the error of ham-fistedly thinking of the Jews as just like any other non-Christian people, and Judaism as no different from any other non-Christian religion. Although most Jews are not categorically Yeshua-believers, Judaism is a non-non-Christian religion, and we might even term Jews "non-non-Christians." To paraphrase the prophet Balaam, "This is a people . . . and a religion . . . that dwells apart, that shall not be numbered with the nations (nor with pagan religions)."[23]

---

22. Acts 26:4–7.
23. Num 23:9.

Cryptosupersessionism

In some ways, the river of Jewish missions and much missional, Christian, and Messianic Jewish thinking about the Jewish people flows between the banks of unawareness on the one side and denial on the other. For many this unawareness and denial flows from their Bible-based Zionist conviction that the Jewish people remain God's chosen people with a patrimony in the promised land. Such biblical Zionists vigorously oppose supersessionism and therefore imagine themselves to be axiomatically positive about the Jewish people in contrast to most of the church. However, a closer examination reveals this to a faulty assumption. This is because biblical Zionism is almost always joined to assumptions that vitiate the dignity of Jewish religion and identity.

Bye-Bye Torah, Hello Law of Christ

Consider the popular teaching that the Law of Moses has been rendered categorically inoperative, and that the only that applies to Yeshua-believers this side of the cross is "the Law of Christ." Since the church too is subject only to the Law of Christ, a moment's reflection will reveal that this teaching postulates the expiration of a major status marker formerly attached to the Jewish people. Yes, I know there are those who would say that the Abrahamic Covenant with the promise of blessing and the Land remains in effect, but in practical terms, the jettisoning of the Law of Moses and the substitution of what is termed "the Law of Christ" means abolishing Judaism for Jewish Yeshua-believers and greasing the skids for their assimilation into a code of conduct and way of life indistinguishable from Gentile Christians—the same law, the Law of Christ. I must protest, and suggest you join me. It will not do to imagine that maintaining pride in Jewish lineage, or attending periodic Jewish Yeshua-believer meetings and holiday events will sustain Jewish identity from generation to generation.[24] It will take more than nostalgia or eschatological expectation of a millennium to come to inform and sustain Jewish continuity, covenantal living, family cohesion,

---

24. Although they say much on other matters for which I am grateful and with which I heartily concur, Craig Blaising and Darrell Bock are among those who unwittingly grease the skids for the assimilation of Jewish believers in Jesus when they say "progressive dispensationalism . . . teaches that Mosaic covenant law has ended dispensationally, it also teaches that it has been replaced by new covenant law" (*Progressive Dispensationalism*, 199.) If this is so, then the on-the-ground distinction of Messianic Jewish life and community rests on an exceedingly narrow bed. In their paradigm, in practical terms of lifestyle and legacy, how are Messianic Jews fundamentally different from other Yeshua-believers?

and trans-generational identity. If we accept that Messianic Jews are subject to no religious law other than the same Law of Christ to which the average white-bread Gentile in Tulsa subscribes, then we are fitting Jewish identity and intergenerational continuity into a plain pine box. It's time to say *kaddish*.

Defining Cryptosupersessionism

This doctrine of the expiration of the Law of Moses for Messianic Jews is but one example of cryptosupersessionism, an often unconscious cluster of presuppositions assuming the expiration, setting aside, or suspension of that status and those status markers formerly attached to the Jewish people. Unlike supersessionism itself, cryptosupersessionism is a virus epidemic even among those who repudiate supersessionism. Examples of its effects surround us like Spanish moss in the bayou. For example, a contemporary Jewish mission newsletter said this:

> Scripture teaches that God has called a social community into being, a community comprised of both Jews and Gentiles, what one early church writer even called a "third race." . . . We are not advocating that Jewish believers distance themselves from their Jewish heritage. May it never be! But our primary spiritual and social home must be among those whom we allow to influence us the most and that should be the body of believers.[25]

While I applaud the author's caveat concerning not distancing ourselves from our Jewish heritage, his wider context and choice of language enfeebles its force. The Jewish covenantal calling is a communal calling, requiring of us an ever-renewed engagement with the wider Jewish community, rather than the stand-offish caution proposed here, or worse, our opting to bond with another community, the church, as our "primary spiritual and social home" instead of the Jewish people. And when he says "We are not advocating that Jewish believers distance themselves from their Jewish heritage," while at the same time advising us to distance ourselves from Jewish community, he reveals an all too common flaw: the individualization of Jewish identity. To be Jewish is not a statement of individual identity but of communal identification, and distancing oneself from the Jewish community weakens one's claim to Jewish identity. It is a matter of covenantal calling, which the author, Rich Robinson, vitiates by terming it our "heritage." And whenever the holy obligations of the Jewish people are treated like cultural

25. Robinson, "The Challenge of Our Messianic Movement, Part 2."

souvenirs, the stuff of nostalgia, instead of mandates from on high, we encounter cryptosupersessionism.

More alarming still is the Robinson's telltale reference to Christians as "a third race." This expression echoes the second century *Epistle to Diognetus*, and means that in Messiah, Jews are no longer Jews, and Gentiles no longer Gentiles, that the two constitute a third race. I imagine we all find this rather repugnant when so stated. The concept feels Neoplatonic, treating Jew and Gentiles in the body of Messiah as discarnate and deracinated souls, negating the persistence of Jewish communal identity. Only the virus of cryptosupersessionism could cause a Jewish Yeshua-believer to issue a caveat about one's bond with the Jewish community, advocating a superseding bonding with the church, in view of the third race nature of the people of God.

Dan Juster's views, while not identical to mine, resemble my views about cryptosupersessionism. He uses a different term, "hidden replacement theology." He is concerned with how these views persist in the church, while my concern is with Jewish missions and Messianic Jews. Juster refers with approval to the views of Michael Wyschogrod on the matter:

> Wychogrod's assertion is that "The church will not have fully repented of its replacement theology until it teaches its baptized Jews that they are responsible to live a Jewish life based on Torah." [Wyschogrod] realizes the logic that anything less is still replacement theology, since it does not really value the ongoing continuity of the Jewish people.

Our light for evaluation (of Wyschogrod's position) is based on Romans 11:29, where Paul argues that the gifts and call of God to Israel are irrevocable and Romans 11:5 where he calls Jewish disciples of Yeshua the saved remnant of Israel. Therefore, if we want to see the growth of identifiable Jewish disciples of Yeshua, and do not desire to see Israel diminished, it would seem that Wyschogrod's argument is airtight.[26]

Individualism, Community, and the Consummation

Because its erosive influence is so pervasive, more needs to be said concerning individualism, which corrupts the relationship Jewish Yeshua believers have with other Jews and our understanding of their status, while desensitizing us to the communal context of our gospel proclamation. Bosch unmasks the problem:

26. Juster, "Do We Want the Jews to Disappear?"

> The gospel is not individualistic. Modern individualism is, to a
> large extent, a perversion of the Christian faith's understanding
> of the centrality and responsibility of the individual. In the wake
> of the Enlightenment, and because of its teachings, individuals
> have become isolated from the community which gave them
> birth.[27]

How many Jewish Yeshua believers are isolated from the community which
gave them birth? And how many preach a gospel that isolates Jews from
Jewish community?

While most missionaries, Messianic Jews, and well-meaning church
people would defensively recoil from the indictment, a moment's reflection
validates Bosch's assessment. It will not do to say, as so many Jewish believers in Jesus have said, "I feel more Jewish than ever." After all, being Jewish
is not a feeling, and regardless of how we might feel, we contradict the claim
to strengthened Jewish identity when we raise our children and marry them
off within the world of the church, reducing our relationship to the Jewish
community to photograph album memories, a visit to the folks in Florida,
and a commitment to the Jewish people as a target group for our efforts to
bring "them" to believe what "we" believe. Such constructs underscore how
many Jewish believers in Yeshua treat the rest of the Jewish community as
"other." Although some naively imagine it to be sufficient, our Jewish identity is blinking out if nurtured simply by paying tribute to it every Passover,
Rosh Hashana, and Yom Kippur.

We need to recover or discover for the first time a deep sense of communal identity and responsibility, and become convinced of the communal
nature of God's eschatological purposes for Israel and the nations. Although
some argue well for a certain secularized, Woody Allen, pastrami sandwich,
Shoah-obsessive Jewish identity, surely Jewish identity rightly understood
retains a core of covenantal and ritual continuity. And the covenants with
God that Yeshua-believing Jewish religious professionals name are covenants with people groups, not with individuals. Even the New Covenant
is with the House of Israel and the House of Judah. It is not an individualist
covenant, but communal, a covenant that binds us not only to Israel's God
but also to the people of Israel themselves and to their covenantal way of
life. The challenge then is for Jewish believers in Yeshua to deeply ask and
answer this question: how deeply and truly are we honoring our covenantal
bond with other Jews?

Ezekiel 37:21–28 provides a glimpse of how this covenantal bond
is to be lived out in eschatological times, listing seven aspects of God's

---

27. Bosch, *Transforming Mission*, 410–11.

eschatological purpose for the Jewish people. In these times of transition, we can only faithfully serve God's purpose among the Jewish people as we treat each of these facets as a non-negotiable priority. Notice they are all communal—good news for all Israel as a whole, *communal* and covenantal good news.

Ezekiel lists the facets of this good news in this order:

- ✓ The regathering of the Jewish to our homeland, Israel (thus, Aliyah)
- ✓ The restoration of the unity of the people of Israel
- ✓ Repentance-renewal[28] for the people as a whole
- ✓ Messiah reigning in the center of this gathered people
- ✓ Torah living as the communal life of this people
- ✓ National experience of the divine presence
- ✓ And because of the foregoing, and in the sight of the nations, the vindication of the Jewish people as the people of God, and the God of Israel as faithful to his promises

In varying degrees, many of these priorities are being addressed by some in the Messianic Jewish movement, even if in an unfocused or inconsistent manner. This is to be expected in a movement as young as ours. Yet for many Jewish believers in Yeshua this list bears little if any resemblance to their current mentality, practice, and message. These factors do not shape the agendas and lives of cryptosupersessionist and individualist Jewish believers, estranged as they are from the communal covenantal world of the Bible and "isolated from the community that gave them birth."[29]

I call this list of seven items "the Ezekiel Agenda" or "the New Messianic Agenda," but it might best be termed "God's Agenda for the Jewish People." This is the kind of communal Jewish covenantal gospel we should be proclaiming to the Jewish people. Ezekiel places Messiah in the center of these items, reigning as king over a covenantally obedient people, bringing communal blessings to the whole people of Israel and thus to the cosmos. God calls us, infused with his Spirit, to vigorously, joyously, and communally incarnate and serve these synergistic priorities. Anything less and anything other is at best someone else's truncated gospel. If we neglect this agenda, our Jewish people will rightly continue to find an individualistic message of

28. I hyphenate the two terms, because repentance itself is the fruit of the Spirit at work, and the renewal we value and long for is evident in repentance and not possible without it. The two realities, repentance and renewal, are inseparably hand in hand. As perceived by the human observer, they can occur in either order.

29. Bosch, *Transforming Mission*.

soul salvation and communal extraction, one which fails to highlight God's continued commitment and consummating purposes for the community of Israel, and will find it to be stale, suspect, irrelevant, and foreign—far less and far other than God's invitation to participate in the anticipated vindication and blessing of the seed of Jacob outlined here. We must repent and return to gospel that is good news for the Jews.

Adopting a New Creation Eschatology

Craig Blaising identifies yet another of our hindering habits of thought: our explicit or tacit acceptance of a spiritual vision eschatology, a view of the final state "which sees eternal life as a timeless, changeless, spiritual existence consisting primarily in the human soul's full knowledge of God . . . a direct view, a beatific vision."[30] Such a vision imagines the redeemed with spiritual bodies composed of some sort of spiritual substance, with earthly life as a mere prelude to these "more spiritual" eternal realities. Blaising insists that "a future for Israel literally has no place in a spiritual-vision eschatology,"[31] which disconnects us from the prophetic expectation that drove the apostles. While we may continue to pay lip service to a glorious eschatological future for the people of Israel, spiritual vision eschatology makes something else, something disembodied and other worldly to be ultimate, and therefore, as Blaising says, there is no place . . . no terra firma . . . where actual Israel is planted.

Some want to have it both ways, seeing the physical promises for Israel fulfilled in a Millennium, with the eternal state and some sort of spiritual-vision eschatology to follow. Blaising dismisses this kind of tokenism when he says "a limited duration [millennial] kingdom alone does not do full justice to the biblical vision for Israel and the Gentiles."[32] I concur.

Blaising commends an alternative we should fervently embrace. It is new creation eschatology that restores the communal dimension individualism destroys, providing a holistic vision of time and eternity fully compatible with the thrust of Scripture and the call to identify and serve a gospel that is good news for all Israel. He defines new creation eschatology and contrasts it with the spiritual vision variety:

> New creation eschatology emphasizes the liberation of the cosmos from sin, the bodily resurrection and glorification of

30. Blaising, "The Future of Israel as a Theological Question," 448.

31. Ibid., 449.

32. Ibid.

the righteous, and the liberation of the cosmos to share in the
liberty of the children of God. It does not see the eschaton as
simply a continuation of the past, but does emphasize its continuity with the past as seen in the resurrection of the body.
New creation does not see the eschaton as a timeless, changeless or essentially visionary-like epistemic state. It is not eternal
in the classic timeless sense but everlasting. New creation has
a place for the earth, the cosmos, for the fullness of created
life, but especially for resurrected human life living under the
lordship of the resurrected Jesus Christ in fellowship with the
Triune God. It would see human life in created wholeness—not
as undifferentiated individuals but as differentiated individuals.
But neither would it see them as just differentiated individuals,
but rather differentiated in ethnic and communal dimensions
as well, since these form an essential aspect of our identities.
And what will we find here except Israel and the Gentiles who
are together blessed by God, living under the lordship of Jesus
Christ to the glory of God.[33]

Blaising's description is wholly consonant with the outreach revolution
commended here. Such an eschatology not only uproots post-Enlightenment individualism, it also unseats a tunnel vision focus on heaven and
hell issues, while disempowering the seduction of cryptosupersessionist assumptions such as third-race ecclesiology. Through this lens we instead see
a panorama of the covenantal and communal future of the Jewish people,
and the promise of resurrection to communal life in a new heaven and a
new earth where righteousness dwells. In keeping with such a vision, God is
glorified not simply by the salvation of nationals, individuals extracted from
the nations and incorporated into a homogenous new people of God, but
by his saving work among nations and people groups, all destined to retain
their creational distinctiveness and communal identity into the eschaton:
resurrected, glorified humans living in community, not a non-diffentiated
crowd of disembodied souls gazing forever in adoring wonder at the one
seated on the throne.

John Stackhouse reminds us that "salvation is about heading for the
New Jerusalem, not heaven: a garden city on earth, not the very abode of
God and certainly not a bunch of pink clouds in the sky. . . . And salvation
is not only about what is to come but also about what is ours to enjoy and
foster here and now."[34] His last phrase lies at the heart of the outreach revo-

---

33. Ibid. For a fuller treatment on the roots and contrast between spiritual vision
eschatology and new creation eschatology, see Blaising, "Premillennialsm."

34. Stackhouse, ed., *What Does It Mean to be Saved?*, 10.

lution I believe God is calling us to in our remnant role. We are being called to prepare the way of the Lord by being a sign, demonstration, and catalyst of God's consummating purpose for Israel, and calling the church as well to live as a foretaste of the age to come.

Second Peter captures the dynamic tension between waiting and preparing:

> Since all these things are to be dissolved in this way, what sort of persons ought you to be in leading lives of holiness and godliness, waiting for and hastening the coming of the day of God, because of which the heavens will be set ablaze and dissolved, and the elements will melt with fire? But, in accordance with his promise, we wait for new heavens and a new earth, where righteousness is at home.[35]

It will not do to wait passively, holding fast to some millennial doctrine while failing to do all we can to prepare the way for the future we anticipate. And since, as Blaising points out, even that millennial expectation is too feeble a fulfillment for the promises of God, we are doubly bounden to do all we can to be signs, demonstrations, and catalysts of God's future for Israel as sketched for us by Ezekiel. We must be both "waiting for and hastening" this longed-for consummation. Anything other and anything less is neglectful disobedience and a dereliction of our calling.

MATTERS OF CONTENT

For some people, defining the gospel seems a simple straightforward assignment. Charles Dickens explains why.

In the second chapter of *Hard Times,* Dickens draws an indelible portrait of Victorian education at its worst, describing how the strict school master Thomas Gradgrind torments sweet little Sissy Jukes over her inability to define a horse with the bloodless exactitude he demands. Sissy's father works with horses, and she certainly knows and loves them. But the abrasive and pro forma Gradgrind gets her flustered and tongue-tied.

Predictably annoyed, Gradgrind turns instead to a pupil more to his liking, a lad named Bitzer, who does not disappoint him.

> "Bitzer," said Thomas Gradgrind. "Your definition of a horse."

> "Quadruped. Graminivorous. Forty teeth, namely twenty-four grinders, four eye-teeth, and twelve incisive. Sheds coat in

---

35. 2 Pet 3:11–13.

the spring; in marshy countries, sheds hoofs, too. Hoofs hard, but requiring to be shod with iron. Age known by marks in mouth." Thus (and much more) Bitzer.

"Now girl number twenty," said Mr. Gradgrind. "You know what a horse is."[36]

Didn't Sissy Jukes understand better than either Gradgrind or Bitzer what a horse is? Did Bitzer's definition really capture the wonder that is a horse? Is it not clear that Bitzer's definition, however accurate, remains wholly inadequate to describe what we encounter when we encounter a horse? Obviously, we all want to avoid duplicating Bitzer's blunder in "defining" the gospel. Yet too few do.

Conditioned by Evangelicalism and post-Enlightenment conceits, we may at first think that defining the gospel is a straightforward matter, and simple, really: begin by quoting 1 Corinthians 15:3–4, and throw in some discussions of the etymology and uses of the term *euangelion*. I advise against this approach! The gospel should not and cannot really be defined in the same manner as other terms. We must not convert the wonder that is the gospel into some slot in our systematics. We can define philosophical terms, because they are constructs of the mind devised to facilitate thought, but the gospel is something else entirely—it is fundamentally a report we have received and which we pass on, an authoritative, empowered, but always fragmentary report concerning God's rescuing intervention in Jesus Christ.

Which brings us to 9/11.

We all saw news reports about the 9/11 tragedy. Some of us were eyewitnesses, or nearly so, while others of us were a continent or even an ocean away, glued to some television set. But, whatever the case, whenever we speak of 9/11 we are exchanging fragmentary impressions and perceptions of something always far greater than what we know, think, and say.

The gospel is not a concept, nor even a term to be defined. Rather, the gospel is fundamentally a report (Isaiah 53), good tidings of great joy for all the people of Israel (Luke 2), and yes, a message to be delivered (1 Cor 15), that is always a reduction of the reality being reported. Although the gospel is not whatever one says it is, nor everything in general, it remains more than we can grasp and define. After all, when we speak of the gospel, angels bow. Paul says that there were aspects of the gospel, mysteries, that were long hidden but revealed in his time, as God revealed to Paul his mandate to "bring to light for everyone what is the plan of the mystery hidden for ages in God who created all things, so that through the church the manifold wisdom of God might now be made known to the rulers and authorities in

36. Dickens, *Hard Times*, chapter 2, "Murdering the Innocents."

the heavenly places."[37] The gospel is not a static term, but a living expanding reality, and our understanding of its nature and implications should have a growing edge.

In *Be My Witnesses,* Darrell Guder repeatedly visits this issue:

> Only through its pilgrimage through time can the church discover the vast dimensions of the meaning and application of the gospel. The early Christian community, although evangelized and instructed by the apostles themselves, did not fully grasp what the gospel meant. In fact, the church has not yet grasped the full meaning of the gospel.[38]

Reflecting further, he calls for a theological modesty often lacking in conservative Christian and Messianic Jewish circles:

> It would be wise for us to approach with modesty the task of gospel definition. . . . When we assume that our confidence is to be placed in the accuracy of our dogmatic formulations, the reliability of our particular confessional definitions of the gospel, or a particular version of the inspiredness of scripture, we have transformed the gospel into a subtle kind of Gnosticism.[39]

Theological immodesty and certitude addiction leads to truncated, mangled, domesticated truth. Worse still, convinced partisans will often denounce others, who may, like Sissy Jukes, actually sense or know aspects of the gospel invisible to their attackers who have a tightly reasoned and tersely expressed approved definition in hand.

MATTERS OF CONTROVERSY

Before turning to a concluding and summational report, or description, of the gospel, we should clear from our path matters of controversy blocking our way.

"Find Heaven, Avoid Hell"

In 2002, I attended the annual meeting of the Evangelical Theological Society at the Opryland Hotel in Nashville, Tennessee. Riding from the airport to the hotel, a missionary to the Jews whom I hardly knew, without any

37. Eph 3:8–10.

38. Guder, *Be My Witnesses,* 39.

39. Ibid., 76.

foreplay whatsoever, badgered me with one question: "Do you believe that a Jew who does not believe in Jesus goes to hell?" Aside from being put off by his abrasive approach, I was mystified as to why, of all questions he might have selected, he chose *this* one to test my orthodoxy? Why this preoccupation with the population of perdition?[40]

Of the eighteen evangelistic sermons in the book of Acts, none uses the find-heaven-avoid-hell approach as a motivation either for missional engagement by the apostolic messengers, or for repentance by their hearers. Neil Rees, international coordinator for World Horizons International, forcefully reminds us that "the basic apostolic kerygma fails to mention hell as a motive for accepting the gospel message," adding that "the apostles were perfectly capable of evangelizing without threatening their hearers with hell . . . [and] this is never developed in evangelistic preaching."[41] He states further that using the prospect of others going to hell as a goad for missionary action or financial support "succeeds only in producing feelings of self-condemnation rather than considered and solid commitment."[42] Many find such statements so threatening to the status quo that they feel obliged to fight them off and denounce them. But if evidence matters at all, Rees is right.

"You Are Going to Destroy the Engine Driving Outreach to the Jews"

I would not and do not deny the reality of hell, nor do I minimize its significance in Holy Writ. But I do question why heaven/hell was such a focus of attention for my tram-mate and for many others, whether explicitly or implicitly, considering its total absence from the apostolic kerygma. Hear this again: the apostles don't talk this talk and walk this walk! It wasn't their issue or motivational goad. Yet I am sure that some imagine that my call to ease off on this approach is nothing less than an attack on mission to the Jewish people, through disassembling its engine.

The reverse is true. This hoary "find heaven, avoid hell" motivation undermines the success of all we seek to achieve, in addition to not being in

40. I have since renewed contact with this person, and learned to my delight that what I perceived to be aggression and attack was simply his ardor for the subject. We are now good friends.

41. Rees, "Snatch Others from the Fire and Save Them."

42. Ibid. After providing a succinct and helpful historical survey of Protestant motivations for mission, Van Rheenen traces the contemporary shift in such motivations in his aptly titled essay, "Changing Motivations for Missions: From 'Fear of Hell' to 'the Glory of God.'"

evidence among the apostles themselves. I want to replace this non-apostolic engine with an older one—better rooted in the Bible and better behaving on the road God is calling us to. This engine has four "pistons" helpfully summarized in the opening verses of "The Lord's Prayer."

The First Piston of Our Missional Engine: Sharing Our Relationship with God

The Lord's Prayer begins "Our Father." Our first motivation for missional action is to call others to the depth of relationship with God we ourselves enjoy. A moment's thought will prove that this is what energized the apostles. Through their encounter with Messiah and their infusion with his Spirit, God had become so luminously real to them that they could not help but tell others what they had seen and heard which had brought them to this joy, this power, this intoxication. Our first missional motivation should then be to share with others the vital relationship with God driving us. But what is *our* experience with God? The early church was awash in wonder. Are we? Or are we practiced professionals, with a Bible verse and answer for anyone who asks us for a reason for the hope that is in us, while, to tell the truth, we're out of touch with the God of hope? I know that when I was in my forties, I had to repent of how my relationship with God had become peripheral to me, even while I was preoccupied with "ministry." Can anyone relate?

The Second Piston of Our Missional Engine: The Doxological Motive

The second phrase of the Lord's Prayer, "Hallowed be Thy Name," names what missional literature terms "the doxological motive," a passion to see God glorified and worshiped. Contemporary scholars are nearly unanimous in emphasizing this to be the most powerful piston of all, able to drive the entire engine, and do it well.

After tracing throughout the Bible the centrality of the glorification of God, Steve Hawthorne applies his findings to the contemporary missional task, contrasting the doxological motive with other motives, including "find-heaven-avoid-hell." "Guilt-based appeals to care for billions of people continues to soften our hearts a little. In practice, however, they weary and harden believers to a minimal token obedience. . . . Now more than ever believers need to be nurtured into a jealousy for God's glory."[43]

Today, John Piper is the leading advocate of the preeminence of God's glory. His perspective on this matter is a much-needed counterbalance to task-oriented, statistically driven approaches:

> Worship is ultimate, not missions, because God is ultimate, not man. . . . Worship, therefore, is the fuel and goal of missions. It's the goal of missions because in missions we simply aim to bring the nations into the white-hot enjoyment of God's glory. The goal of missions is the gladness of the peoples in the greatness of God.[44]

Some might imagine that Piper wins adherents to his view from Reformed circles alone. However, this is not the case. In a fascinating article, Fundamentalist pastor and educator Sam Horn tells how he encountered, resisted, and was eventually converted to Piper's views. Using the same missional engine metaphor as I do, he makes the issue unmistakable:

> I was also forced to consider that God's desire to be worshipped by men of all nations is actually the engine that drives biblical missions rather than the need of lost men to be saved from an eternal hell. In short, my perspective on missions was too man-centered.[45]

He goes on to highlight a related concept that Mark Kinzer and I highlighted in our flyer, "The Emerging Messianic Jewish Paradigm," and not without controversy. We said this:

> Such outreach proclaims the Name of Jesus, not the neediness of Jews. Sometimes mission approaches to the Jewish people include the assumption or even declaration of the emptiness and inadequacy of Jewish religious practice and faith. In contrast, the apostolic motivation for outreach to Jewish people was driven by the realization that in Yeshua, the long awaited Messiah had come. The oft-quoted passage, "There is no other name given among mortals by which we must be saved," comes in a context where Peter and John were seeking to lift up the name of Jesus rather than put down the Jewish people: "for we cannot keep from speaking about what we have seen and heard" (Acts 4:12, 20). We would do well to imitate their example and lift up

43. Hawthorne, "The Story of His Glory."
44. Piper, *Let the Nations Be Glad!*, 17.
45. Horn, "The Heart of Biblical Missions."

the name of Yeshua without denigrating the holy things already given to the Jewish people (see Romans 3:1–4; 9:1–5).[46]

Sam Horn helps to silence outcries that many raise against such a call to leave off a preoccupation with Jewish "neediness" and instead lift up the name of Yeshua.

> At the heart of biblical revelation is God's self-revelation to man. Part of what God chose to reveal in the scriptures concerns His primary motive for the activities ascribed to him in the words of the Book. That motivation can be summed up in the phrase, "God does what He does for the sake of His name." God's primary motive in the salvation of lost men is doxological, "for the sake of His name" (Isaiah 63:7–14; Acts 15:14; Romans 1:5). The scriptures reveal God's primary motive in delivering His children from their troubles is "the sake of His name" (1 Samuel 12:22; Psalm 106:8). God's primary motive in showing mercy to sinning people is "the sake of His name" (Isaiah 48:9; Ezekiel 20:44). God's primary motive in dealing with the wicked is "the sake of His name" (Exodus 9:14–16; Romans 9:17). Finally, God's primary motive in His dealings with saved men is "the sake of His name" (I John 2:12; Acts 9:16).[47]

Sam Horn, John Piper, and Steve Hawthorne are right in redirecting our attention to the centrality of lifting up the name of God and the name of Yeshua. Can we deny that the supremacy of lifting up Yeshua's name rather than the alleged spiritual bankruptcy or neediness of the Jewish people or of a hell-bound Sanhedrin was uppermost in the minds of Peter and John when they said there is no other name than his by which we must be saved? I challenge all of us to examine deeply why it is that some of us fight so energetically to maintain our habitual preoccupation with the neediness of Jews, a habit that necessarily leads to repeatedly proving to ourselves and to others the alleged futility, vacuity, and impotence of the Jewish way of life. This is not the engine that drove the apostles who lived to glorify Yeshua and the one who raised him from the dead. Isn't their focus and motivation good enough for us? And isn't majoring in the inadequacy and futility of Jewish life an engine driving us away from our people and driving them away from Yeshua, the King of the Jews?

---

46. Dauermann and Kinzer, *The Emerging Messianic Jewish Paradigm.*
47. Horn, "The Heart of Biblical Missions."

The Third Piston of Our Missional Engine: Hastening the Consummation of All Things

The Lord's Prayer reminds us, "Thy Kingdom come," expressing a longing for the consummation. When we speak of ourselves as "the remnant of Israel," what do we mean? And what relationship does this have to the consummation of all things?[48]

Dan Johnson[49] demonstrates how Scripture presents two contrasting modalities of remnant identity, one being survivors of a time of judgment, the other being the seed from which God's continuing purposes will move forward. Both of these perspectives are to be found in Romans chapters nine to eleven. Johnson finds the earliest reference to the remnant as the seed and earnest of future blessing in the verb form used in Genesis 7:23 (CJB), "only Noakh was *left (vayisha'er akh noakh)*, along with those who were with him in the ark," the term, *vayish'er* being related to the term *sh'erit* (remnant). As Noakh/Noah, his family, and the animals in the left with them in the ark (as a remnant) were a sign of God's continuing purpose for the earth, and instruments for its realization, so the eschatological remnant of Israel of Romans chapters nine to eleven is meant to be a sign, demonstration, and catalyst of God's continuing purposes for the Jewish people—a seed of good things to come. This is our calling.

In Romans, chapters 9 to 11, Paul speaks of two "fullnesses": "the fullness of the nations" (11:25) and "the fullness of Israel" (11:12). In Romans 11:12, Paul calls Israel's fullness greater than the fullness of the Gentiles (πόσῳ μᾶλλον τὸ πλήρωμα αὐτῶν, "How much greater will their fullness be?"). Therefore if the fullness of the Gentiles is associated with the Great Commission, the fullness of Israel, then that "greater riches" (Rom 11:12, NIV) God will bring to pass, may be termed "the Greater Commission," a commission that directly relates to our remnant responsibilities.

Because we are so used to operating out of an older paradigm, these concepts, and terms like "the Greater Commission" may come as a shock. However the distinction between the fullness of the nations and the fullness of Israel are biblical realities reflected in these terms. The Great Commission might also be termed "the Penultimate Commission," as it is the magnificent prelude to something greater. Surely this language is strange to our ears. But it would not have been strange to Paul! And this Greater Commission, to expedite Israel entering into her fullness, is our remnant calling.

48. Dauermann, "Seeds, Weeds, and Walking the High Wire."
49. Johnson, "The Structure and Meaning of Romans 11."

If we are nearing the pivotal juncture when the gigantic wheel of God's purpose is turning toward the fullness of Israel, we cannot simply go on with business as usual, living by older more conventional paradigms. Our responsibility is as great as our privileges.[50] Our role in the consummation of things is crucial and it is pivotal.

The Fourth Piston of Our Missional Engine: Obedience

Obedience to God, "thy will be done, on earth as it is in heaven," is our fourth powerful piston. And even if this were the only one, it would be more than enough to drive our engine. We must speak to our people about Yeshua because we have been commanded to do so. Paul's words apply to us: "For if I preach the gospel that gives me no ground for boasting. For necessity is laid upon me. Woe to me if I do not preach the gospel!"[51] Cannot such a piston drive our engine as well? Of course it can! And beyond that, should we not be passionate to "bring about the obedience of faith for the sake of His name" among all the people of Israel, as was Paul's passion for the nations?[52]

Such a mighty missional engine roars at the curbside like a Bugatti Roadster, its door open, waiting only for us to get in the driver's seat to go zero to sixty in less than three seconds. By comparison, the find-heaven-avoid-hell motivation seems like a donkey, energized by a carrot and a stick! I may be taking away our donkey, but our Father in heaven has given us the keys to the Bugatti. Let's take her out for a spin![53]

"The Law of Moses Has Been Rendered Inoperative"

On the basis of a lexical meaning of *katargeo* ("render inoperative"), some argue that the Law of Moses has lost all force and authority, having now been replaced by the Law of Messiah, by extension making inoperative any argument for God's preordained return to Torah-based covenant-faithfulness

---

50. "Every one to whom much is given, of him will much be required; and of him to whom men commit much they will demand the more" (Luke 12:48),

51. 2 Cor 9:16.

52. Rom 1:5; 16:26.

53. Johannes Verkuyl, writing in the late 1970s, reached similar conclusions, naming six motivations for mission, including all four I identified. His list, in order: obedience; love, mercy and pity; doxology; the eschatological motive (where he makes mention of the Lord's Prayer!); haste; and the personal motive—the arousing of ourselves through arousing others. Verkuyl was the pre-eminent missiologist of the mid-twentieth century. *Contemporary Missiology*, 164–68.

by the seed of Jacob. Is there any answer to this objection? Actually, many answers.

First, defining "the Law of Christ/Messiah" as is commonly done, as "all the individual commandments from Christ and the Apostles applicable to a New Testament believer,"[54] should not be regarded as either the unanimous or majority view of the exegetical community. Todd Wilson introduces his survey of recent opinion on the matter in a manner that should preclude our confidently asserting the Law of Messiah is a code of law replacing the Law of Moses. "While the phrase [the Law of Christ] has traditionally been harmonized with Paul's negative portrayal of the law by treating the phrase either as a circumlocution for Christian living or as a reference to some other "law," a growing number of interpreters want to treat the "law of Christ" as a reference to the *law of Moses*." Wilson also surveys the widening group of exegetical opinion viewing Paul's "law of faith" and the "law of the Spirit of life" as referring likewise to the Law of Moses.[55]

My point here is not to summarize or advocate for any of these arguments in the literature but instead to caution against accepting as self-evident a position which is by no means a settled issue. The Messianic Jewish community and the missions world still has homework to do.[56] It is clear that the Law of Christ as having replaced the Law of Moses has traction with some because it is compatible with their cryptosupersessionist theologies and sentiments, among these, Dispensationalism.

But I have a stronger argument against those who would confidently discount the persistence of the Law of Moses on the basis of the alleged meaning of *katargeo*. D. A. Carson names sixteen word fallacies, of which the eighth is "false assumptions about technical meaning," in which cases, "an interpreter falsely assumes that a word always or nearly always has a certain technical meaning—a meaning usually derived either from a subset of the evidence or from the interpreter's personal systematic theology." He notes that one of this fallacy's corollaries occurs whenever such interpreters "go one step further and reduce an entire doctrine to one word which they

---

54. Fruchtenbaum, "Messianic Congregations May Exist Within the Body of Messiah as Long as They Don't Function Contrary to the New Testament," 121.

55. Wilson, "The Law of Christ and the Law of Moses," 125–44.

56. Some of our finest minds have done much of the groundwork for us, although space does not permit a review of their argumentation here. Among them, see Fischer, "Messianic Congregations Should Exist and Be Very Jewish; Stern, "Torah"; Juster, *Jewish Roots*; and Kinzer, *Postmissionary Messianic Judaism*. For succinct, illuminating treatments of all the relevant texts, see Stern, *Jewish New Testament Commentary*. For a detailed presentation of the Law of Messiah as an alternative code to an inoperative Law of Moses, see as well Fruchtenbaum, *Israelology*.

have understood to be a technical term."[57] Later, he names and discusses a related error, "unwarranted restriction of the semantic field," by which he means "misunderstanding the meaning of a word in a particular context by illegitimately restricting the word's semantic range."[58] Carson's analysis takes the Torah-dismissive *katargeo* argument and spears it through the heart.

Words are best defined not from lexicons but always from contexts—and often, slightly differently from context to context. Besides, lexicographers have theological commitments, interpretative traditions, and communal interests affecting their interpretations of word meanings. This being the case, those who base their doctrines and stances on lexical data may wrongly attribute objectivity and dependability to lexicons neither objective nor dependable. Furthermore, those who consult lexicons have theological commitments of their own, interpretive traditions, and communal interests, all of which cause them to eagerly welcome lexical "evidence" when it appears to confirm prior preferences. Lexical evidence is helpful, to be sure, but must always be regarded as provisional, its validity contingent upon rigorous historical, cultural, and semantic analysis of each textual context.

Context is king, not lexicography. Those who "prove" the nullification of the Law's authority by alleging that *katargeo* means "to render inoperative," commit methodological error. They illegitimately and prematurely foreclose discussion on a matter that can only be rightly resolved by means of exacting examination of each context where the word is used. Such contexts may illumine or may, on the contrary, contrast with one another when examining how the term in question is being used elsewhere. And Carson notes that despite our best interpretive efforts, disputed interpretive matters may not be resolved at all, and surely not by a lexicon: "The fallacy lies in thinking the correct interpretation of a passage can be discovered anyway; and in many instances, that is not possible"[59] This calls for us to exercise far greater exegetical humility than is our habit, and certainly not to base doctrines on the authority of a lexical entry.

I am urging us to recall the jury on many arguments that have, in the past, seemed settled on lexical grounds. These cases deserve to be reopened, and discussion resumed to rightly understand both how each specific context influences, shades, and determines meaning, and how these contexts may properly be compared with one another. But such a project demands courage, because it requires us to be prepared to acknowledge how fealty to

---

57. Carson, *Exegetical Fallacies*, 45, 47.

58. Ibid., 57.

59. Ibid., 60.

our theological systems has too often predetermined our exegetical conclusions. This is a hard and bitter pill to swallow.

Nor does this exhaust the problems created by those who confidently assert that *katargeo* spells the death-knell of the Law of Moses. Here we can apply the lesson of a strong argument against those who dismiss any distinction between Jew or Gentile on the basis of Galatians 3:28, "There is neither Jew nor Greek, there is neither slave nor free, there is neither male nor female; for you are all one in Christ Jesus." We must always ask in what *sense* there is neither Jew nor Greek, neither slave nor free, and neither male nor female. Applying this criterion to the case at hand, we must be careful to ask, "In what sense, under what conditions, and for whom is the Law of Moses rendered inoperative now that Messiah has come?" Asking these questions cuts down those who, on lexical grounds, dismiss the law as a dead issue. Not so.

Two more arguments, briefly noted. First, it is not possible to separate the Law from the narrative of the Older Testament, where the narrative justifies and explains the setting and rationale of the laws there imbedded. The law can no more be successfully extracted from the narrative (or vice versa) than the skeleton can be extracted from a human without killing the patient. Second, and closely related, if the Law of Moses is rendered inoperative, does this not have implications for messianic prophecy? Is this too rendered inoperative now that Messiah has come? And if not, on what basis do we make an exception for the persistence of messianic prophecy from within a body of law and inextricable narrative now declared dead?

"Aren't You Arguing for 'the Wider Hope'?"

Having argued for the gospel being good news for all Israel, and not just for a certain theological elite, I have on occasion been regarded as theologically naïve, untaught, or dangerous. As one person put it, I am being seen as "deviating," as inviting censure by arguing for the wider hope. But I argue not *for* the wider hope as much as *against* the wider ego.

It has been decades since I have heard anyone in conservative Jewish mission or Messianic Jewish circles, speaking on a theological or missiological issue, say, "I don't know." Not many manage to mumble these monosyllables. As it stands, those who say, "I don't know," especially when asked questions about the census of perdition, are regarded as confused, deviant, or dangerous. I am suggesting that this kind of marginalization and stigmatization of the diffident is uncalled for, likely rooted not only in theological commitments but also in an appalling lack of theological humility. The wider ego.

It is encouraging to discover that even missiological giants like David Bosch and Paul Hiebert had smaller egos than these. We would do well to heed them, who, being dead, yet speak:

> Our theologies are partial, and they are culturally and socially biased. They may never claim to be absolutes. Yet this does not make them relativistic, as though one suggests that in theology—since we cannot really ever know "absolutely"—anything goes. It is true that we see only in part, but we do see. We are committed to our understanding of revelation, yet we also maintain a critical distance to that understanding. In other words, we are in principle open to other views, an attitude which does not, however, militate against complete commitment to our own understanding of truth. We preface our remarks with "I believe . . ," or "As I see it" . . . . It is misleading to believe that commitment and a self-critical attitude are mutually exclusive.[60]

Applying such theological humility to our missional task, Bosch says further, "The commitment we give to any theological paradigm is therefore wholehearted and provisional, wholehearted because we hold back nothing from our Lord, provisional because our Lord makes us his witnesses, not his know-it-alls."[61]

I wonder if we got the memo.

Some no doubt remain dissatisfied with what they would view to be "theological squishiness," demanding a verdict on the status of others, even hypothetical others. Again, I must demur, especially in the case of God's chosen people, whom he hardened for his purpose, but who remain beloved for the sake of the fathers. The full outworking of the drama of the Jews and the Holy One remains to be played out. And by divine design a cloud of incense obscures our view of the mercy seat. I prefer to echo the roar of another giant, Lesslie Newbigin, one of the most seminal missiologists of the past hundred years. We would do well to hear him:

> I confess that I am astounded at the arrogance of theologians who seem to think that we are authorized, in our capacity as Christians, to inform the rest of the world about who is to be vindicated and who is to be condemned at the last judgment. . . .
> I find this way of thinking among Christians astonishing in

---

60. Bosch, *Transforming Mission*, 186–87, referencing Hiebert, "Epistemological Foundations," 9.

61. Bosch, *Transforming Mission*, 47.

view of the emphatic warnings of Jesus against these kinds of judgments which claim to preempt the final judgment of God. Nothing could be more remote from the whole thrust of Jesus' teaching than the idea that we are in a position to know in advance the final judgment of God. It would be tedious to repeat again the innumerable warnings of Jesus in this matter, his repeated statements that the last day will be a day of surprises, of reversals, of astonishment. In his most developed parable of the last judgment, the parable of the sheep and the goats, both the saved and the lost are astonished. Surely theologians at least should know that the judge on the last day is God and no one else. . . . If a theologian is really serious he must learn to understand the impossible possibility of salvation.

In St. Paul we find this same tension of confidence and awareness of the abyss that lies underneath. Paul, who is certain that nothing can separate him from the love of God in Christ Jesus, also tells his friends that he has to exercise severe self-discipline "let having preached to others I myself should be disqualified" (1 Cor. 9:27). The Christian life, lived in the magnetic field between the two poles of the amazing grace of God and the appalling sin in which I share, has a corresponding synthesis of a godly confidence and a godly fear.[62]

Perhaps we should exchange our wider egos for wider souls—like that of Newbigin. I would trade. Would you?

CUMULATIVE CONCLUSIONS

Some important disclaimers, lest all I have said be misconstrued:

1. When I speak of the gospel as good news for all Israel, I am neither saying nor implying that all Jews who have ever lived, nor which Jews in particular, will be in the world to come. I am no more entitled to claim expertise on the census of the redeemed than are others to claim foreknowledge of the roll call of perdition. God alone is judge, and many surprises await us all. I am instead calling us back to a fundamental theme of both Testaments ignored or marginalized by the church and by Jewish missions for centuries, if not for millennia. The Law and the Prophets point to a glorious hope for all Israel. This concern motivated the apostles and informed their preaching, and is entirely absent from

---

62. Newbigin, *The Gospel in a Pluralist Society*, 177–78.

the evangelistic practice, expectation, and communal life or too many Jewish believers in Yeshua.[63]

2. When I speak of the gospel as good news for all Israel I am not saying or implying that helping Jews come to Yeshua-faith is a superfluous non-issue. It is a matter of sharing with others our intimacy of relationship with God, of glorifying him, of our remnant responsibility in helping to bring in the consummation, of obedience, and allegiance to the Son of David. Neglect of this responsibility is a matter for which we will all give an account of ourselves to God.

3. Although there is scarcely any mention in this chapter of God's will for the nations, this must not be taken to mean that I am unconcerned about the nations or hold that the Great Commission has no place in my missiology. Nor should my silence on these matters be taken to mean that I am negative about the church and/or its role. Rather, since this chapter was originally a paper delivered to a group of professionals concerned with the progress of the good news of Yeshua among the Jewish people, I have focused solely on the people of Israel and the role my audience might play as part of the remnant of Israel.

INTEGRATIONAL THOUGHTS

First, I affirm that repentance and faith play a central role in the message we are called to proclaim. But I also believe that mission culture has had an

---

63. Some confirmation of the instinct to see the gospel as good news for all Israel comes from *Dispensationalism, Israel and the Church,* where Darrell Bock speaks of "The Reign of the Lord Christ." His stated goal is "to argue that any reconstruction of New Testament eschatology [indeed of Messianic eschatology] must take into account the perspective of both Acts 2 and Acts 3" (37). In discussing the kingdom concept in Luke's gospel, he stresses the immanence of the kingdom, and the fact that kingdom period begins with Jesus' ministry and message. "While the kingdom has not arrived in its fullness, it *has* come in its initial stages. In that inauguration the deliverance of God has come, and the future full rule of God has been guaranteed" (40). Bock sees in Luke-Acts a tension between kingdom present and kingdom to come (Acts 1:6). When seen in context, the time of the consummation of the kingdom *vis-a-vis* Israel is tied in with Yeshua's return (v. 11). Bock sees Acts 2 and 3 as being answers to the disciples question in 1:6, demonstrating the already of Jesus' kingdom reign (Acts 2), and the not yet when the political promises to Israel will be consummated (Acts 3). What we should not miss is the seamless connection between the gospel and the consummation: the one who tabernacled among us will return to consummate God's good news for all Israel. This deserves to be central to our gospel during these times of transition. See Bock, "The Reign of the Lord Christ."

inconsistent and sub-biblical concept of what repentance means and what it entails for Jews. R. Kendall Soulen helps us with this clarifying statement:

> According to the biblical witness, God's work as Consummator takes enduring shape in the history that unfolds between the Lord, Israel, and the nations. Accordingly, *human sin is never merely the sin of the creature against the Creator-Consummator. Human sin is also always the sin of Jew and Gentile, of Israel and the nations.*[64]

The sins of Messianic Jews and of all Israel are more dire and extensive than simply the record of individual human failings. The sins of all Israel, including Messianic Jews, foundationally consist of our failure to live in covenant faithfulness with our God.

Do Jews need the atonement Yeshua provides? Yes, by all means, yes, but for reasons deeper than we have yet realized and proclaimed. Jewish missionaries and Messianic Jews have always called for other Jews to repent and believe. But we fail to ask, "Repent for what?" By default, we would say, "Repent for being a sinner, for your sins," or perhaps, "Repent for not recognizing the Messiah whom God sent for us."

But this will not do because we can only know what sin is when we compare our conduct with what God demands of us. We, the seed of Abraham and Sarah, whose ancestors, standing at the foot of Sinai, said "*na'aseh v'nishmah*—we will do and we will hear/obey—all that the Lord has spoken we will do"—must repent not of being sinners in general, but of being *Jewish* sinners in particular. The sins of all Israel, including Messianic Jews, include continual and pervasive neglect of the covenant to which we are all obligated.[65] Although we may confidently say, "There is therefore now no condemnation for those who are in Messiah Yeshua," we may *not* say "there is therefore now no responsibility for those who in Messiah Yeshua." "Yeshua paid it all," but not that we might go back to each of us turning to his own way.[66] Surely, if our sin was fundamentally covenant violation, our repentance must involve not simply faith in the sin-bearer, but also a return to that covenant-faithfulness from which we departed. And is it of no significance that it is precisely to the restoration of this kind of obedience (communally) that God's consummating actions are directed?[67]

Second, under the influence of Enlightenment rationalism, evangelicals have for too long been too focused on the gospel being true news. We

---

64. Soulen, *The God of Israel and Christian Theology*, 153, emphasis added.

65. Deut 29:10–15.

66. Isa 53:6.

67. Deut 30:6; Jer 31:33; 32:39; Ezek 11:19–20; 36:27; 37:24b, 26.

zero in on apologetics and Messianic prophecy, good in their own right. However, when the subtext of our message is the certain perdition of the vast majority of the Jews who ever lived, including the intimate family members of those whom we evangelize, anyone who is reasonably astute, particularly those influenced by those opposing our message, is likely to turn to us a deaf ear and rightly so. The "truth" of the gospel is not likely to make inroads when the news is unwelcome, oppressive, and when it implies, or even theologically *requires*, that the evangelized be eternally separated from their people, who are axiomatically viewed to be lost forever. Nor will it do to try and hide these implications from those we evangelize: Jewish people are not stupid, and, sooner or later they know when they have been duped. With our prevailing propositions, we have news for the Jew standing before us: God is going to take her away from her family for ever and ever to be in heaven with him, with most if not all of her loved ones tormented eternally in the lake of fire. Not so good. Can we get back to a gospel that is good news for all Israel without betraying the text of Scripture, leaving matters of judgment where they belong, in the hands of God? I believe we can and I believe we must. I have tried to help point the way.

Third, we have been too focused on the salvation of individuals, and on individual response. In the process, we have forgotten that the Bible portrays the gospel as good news for *Zion*. It is news of the vindicating and merciful reign of God displayed and accomplished in the one whose goings forth have been from of old, from everlasting days, whose incarnation, death, resurrection, ascension, high priestly ministry, and Davidic reign need to be restored in our thinking to their central place as the means toward prophesied national blessings.

Fourth, we have been too focused on the gospel as atonement, as if this were all there is or the main point, failing to see atonement as part of a "package deal" of sorts, which includes the regathering, renewal, reunification, return to covenant faithfulness, and messianic fulfillment of all Israel. We have also seen atonement as monolithically individual, which is a strange concept considering the biblical evidence. (See as but one example the prophecy in Daniel 9 which couches the atonement in this broader context of national vindication and salvation.)

Who Has Believed Our Report? Toward a Gospel for All Israel

With all of this in view, consider the following description of the gospel we are being called to commend to our people.

1. The gospel of God for the Jewish people is above all else good news for *all* Israel rather than for a fragmentary spiritually enlightened elite.

2. It is not entirely new news, for the arm of the Lord has rescued Israel time and time again. But it is the good news of God, in covenant faithfulness, doing again what he has done before—coming to rescue his people—but outdoing himself this time, in the foretold ultimate deliverance, through the faithfulness of Yeshua the Messiah in his incarnation, atoning death, resurrection, and ascension as Great High Priest and ruling Son of David.

3. It is the good news of God vindicating his name and his people Israel in the sight of all nations in victorious strength and faithfulness, to be consummated in the regathering, reunification, repentance-renewal, and return to Torah-based covenant faithfulness of the community of Jacob, gathered around Yeshua the Son of David, resurrected and renewed in a new heavens and a new earth where righteousness dwells and joy prevails, in the sight of all nations.

4. Therefore, if we and our communities are to be gospel messengers, we must passionately honor these priorities in our own contexts, and, as Remnant people, celebrate, catalyze, and advance these priorities in the life of wider Israel.

5. We should also celebrate any advance of any of these priorities within wider Israel. It is strangely provincial for us to imagine that such advances only "count" if taking place within the context of explicit Yeshua-faith or in response to our initiatives.

6. And so, in this fashion and toward such ends," all Israel will be saved." Does this mean every single Jew? Not likely. Rather, Paul is answering the question, "What is going to happen to the Jews as a whole?" And for Paul, the end of the story is good news for the Jews.

Related Implications

1. And what of Jewish people who refuse the message? That of course is a serious matter, as has always been the case whenever our people have rejected or been unresponsive to the saving acts of God. But it is interesting that the apostles, in their preaching to Jews, never pass a verdict that their rejecting hearers are going to hell. Rather they *warn* them to be careful concerning the possible consequences of such hardness of

heart. Giving warnings and delivering verdicts is not the same thing. Again, God alone is judge.

2. Under this paradigm, we need to view ourselves not as missionaries but as prophets. Missionaries come from outside a community with a foreign message: prophets come from within the community, calling the people back to communal standards of faithfulness to God. However, our outreach will fail if it is only a sales pitch. We must ourselves exemplify the faithfulness to which we are calling others, living for those things which Messiah is bringing to pass—the regathering, unification, spiritual repentance-renewal, and Torah obedience of all Israel.

3. Such outreach will involve the following:

    a. Developing modalities (communal expressions) where Yeshua-faith and the power of the Spirit are lived realities making our pursuit of these goals magnetically attractive yet indefinably *new* to Jewish onlookers.

    b. Seeing such outreach as recruiting and involving other Jews in the passionate pursuit of the entire Messianic agenda mapped out in Ezekiel 37:21–28.[68] We must always see Jewish people as part of a covenantal people, with covenantal responsibilities to which they are called to vigorously return as a manifestation of their Yeshua faith and repentance.

    c. Cooperating with and commending Jews of all kinds in their pursuit of whichever of these priorities they are committed to. We are not in competition with other Jews. We should seek out opportunities for cooperation. In such contexts too, our Yeshua-faith and the influence of the Spirit will be made known.

    d. Operating within such a model, even if Jewish people do not receive our witness of Yeshua, they will know that we are committed to the well-being of the Jewish people and that our the good news we proclaim, if true, is truly good news for all Israel.

EPILOGUE

Not too long ago I received a phone call from a friend, illustrating the burden of this chapter. She is an outspoken Messianic Jew in Los Angeles, and

---

68. I explore these matters in detail for the Messianic Jewish community in *Son of David* and for the church in *Christians and Jews Together.*

an effective messenger of her faith. She had been invited to visit the *sukkah* of an Orthodox rabbi active in the area who had been trying to win her back to Orthodox Judaism, while she had, in turn, been sharing with him her own journey to Yeshua faith. In the course of this in-the-*sukkah* onversation he saw that she was "a lost cause" from his point of view. At that point she mentioned Hashivenu, a think tank of which I am president, and which embodies the values underlying this chapter. She encouraged him to visit our website. She also mentioned me. It turned out he knew of me, but how?

About two years previously, the moderator of the General Assembly of the Presbyterian Church (USA) visited Los Angeles to speak at a local church on the issue of the Presbyterian church divesting from all companies that did business with Israel in any manner, as a demonstration of sympathy for West Bank Palestinians who were viewed as being oppressed by Israel. Advance publicity indicated that his perspective was bad news for the Jews. I wrote a letter to two rabbis in town, one an Orthodox rabbi who had shown himself willing to go outside the box, and the other a Reform rabbi with a strong social justice record. In my letter I proposed that the people of my congregation, under my leadership, joined with members of the wider Jewish community, would picket the Presbyterian church where this leader would be speaking, or the local Presbyterian Church (USA) headquarters, to protest their position on divestment.

I never heard back. But the truth came out in the *sukkah*. As mentioned, my friend's rabbi friend knew of me. And the reason he did was that "all the rabbis in town had discussed my letter, and had decided it was too loaded an issue to picket with a bunch of Messianic Jews."

What shall we say about this? Should we say, "That just goes to show you. The rabbis will never accept us and only want to convert us back and protect their people from us." Should we say that the letter was a wasted effort and a total loss? To say such things would be a grave mistake. It just will not do for the remnant of Israel to fold up its skirts and scuttle back into it own enclaves, or seek solace in the lap of the church!

I would say that it is wonderful that all the rabbis in Los Angeles know that the people at my messianic congregation cared about Jewish concerns and were prepared to take a stand for the issues that matter to the wider Jewish world. I suggest that Messianic Jews should form associations and congregations that actively incarnate the glorious future God has for all Israel: gathered, united, repentant, renewed, faithful to his statutes and ordinances, around Yeshua, the reigning Son of David. Those who do not yet agree with us should see us standing for the things that matter to them.

Is this not good news for all Israel?

8

Bilateral Ecclesiology and Postsupersessionist Missiology as Inseparable Jewels

With reason, many consider Mark Kinzer to be the premier theologian in the Messianic Jewish movement. Some imagine him to be displaying hubris in attempting to write *the* theology of Messianic Judaism, but Kinzer would be quick to protest that this is not his intent. Rather he seeks to address core issues either unrecognized or inadequately handled by others. Above all, he is introducing a new paradigm.

In his magnum opus, *Postmissionary Messianic Judaism: Redefining Christian Engagement With the Jewish People,*[1] he defines, explores, and defends that paradigm, bilateral ecclesiology. His presentation is brilliant, well-articulated, and true as far as it goes. However, some chafe, sensing he fails to go far enough because he hardly touches upon the missiological dimension. This chapter contends that one really can't have one without the other because ecclesiology and missiology are inseparably mutually interdependent. Because Kinzer's concerns are primarily ecclesiological he fails to treat missiological concerns with commensurate weight. I seek to at least partially redress this imbalance in this chapter, supplementing Kinzer while defending him against unjust attack.

If ecclesiology is the study of the nature of the people of God, then we may briefly define missiology as interdisciplinary study and reflection upon all things pertaining to the *ekklesia* extending, expressing, and replicating

---

1. Kinzer, *Postmissionary Messianic Judaism.*

itself in the world in service to the mission of God. One simply cannot have the *ekklesia* apart from such extension, expression, and replication, because without these, the *ekklesia* dies. Without mission, this self-extension, expression, and replication of itself in the world, the *ekklesia* inevitably dies much as the Shakers did when they elected to be a celibate group. Without reproduction, there is no continuity for the *ekklesia*. Therefore, this chapter is devoted to making explicit the missiology latent in Kinzer's paradigm, a postsupersessionist missiology compatible with his bilateral ecclesiology.

I begin by defining bilateral ecclesiology and naming some of its benefits. I then turn to examining one of Kinzer's theological bedfellows, Karl Barth, whose positions, when attributed to Kinzer, get him in trouble with his critics. I turn next to examining precursors whose praxis reflected elements central to Kinzer's model. I end by sketching features of a postsupersessionist missiology compatible with Kinzer's bilateral ecclesiology and the Converging Destinies paradigm.[2]

BILATERAL ECCLESIOLOGY: KINZER'S JEWEL

Kinzer's bilateral ecclesiology deserves to be widely known, widely discussed, and greatly respected as one of the most intriguing ecclesiological developments of recent decades. This paradigm states this:

> The *ekklesia* consists of a unified community that is essentially twofold, containing a Jewish sub-community that links it to the national life and history of the people of Israel, and a multinational sub-community that extends Israel's heritage among the peoples of the earth without annulling their distinctive cultural identities. Thus, the bilateral constitution of the *ekklesia* enables it to fulfill a universal vocation while maintaining solidarity with Israel.[3]

Kinzer sees the community of Jewish Yeshua-believers living in solidarity with Israel to be the living communal link whereby the church from among the nations is joined to the commonwealth of Israel. He further defines his model by outlining five ecclesiological principles inherent in it:

2. Although to be sure ecclesiology and missiology involve all the people of God in all aspects of their life, my focus will be on that missiology appropriate to bilateral ecclesiology, the role of the Messianic Jewish remnant, its missional responsibilities to the wider Jewish community, and the implications of this missiology for Christian relationship with the messianic Jewish remnant and engagement with the Jewish people.

3. Kinzer, "Postmissionary Messianic Judaism, Three Years Later," 175. Kinzer gives extensive biblical evidence in support of this model, and references the work of Markus Barth (in is study on Ephesians), and Karl Barth in Part II.2 of his *Church Dogmatics*.

The ecclesiological vision presented in this book calls into question the traditional Christian missionary posture toward the Jewish people. Our ecclesiology can be summarized in five basic principles: (1) the perpetual validity of God's covenant with the Jewish people; (2) the perpetual validity of the Jewish way of life rooted in the Torah, as the enduring sign and instrument of that covenant; (3) the validity of Jewish religious tradition as the historical embodiment of the Jewish way of life rooted in the Torah; (4) the bilateral constitution of the *ekklesia*, consisting of distinct but united Jewish and Gentile expressions of Yeshua-faith; (5) the ecumenical imperative of the *ekklesia*, which entails bringing the redeemed nations of the world into solidarity with the people of Israel in anticipation of Israel's— and the world's—final redemption. In short, we have argued for a bilateral ecclesiology in solidarity with Israel that affirms Israel's covenant, Torah, and religious tradition. According to this pattern, the Jewish *ekklesia* serves the wider Jewish community by constituting its eschatological firstfruits, sanctifying the whole and revealing the eschatological meaning of Jewish identity and destiny. It also serves the wider Jewish community by linking the redeemed of the nations to Israel's corporate life and spiritual heritage, thereby enabling Israel to fulfill its mission as a light to the nations. This ecclesiology stands in stark contrast to the Christian church's missionary posture toward the Jewish people, especially in the post-Constantinian era. In that setting, the Christian church approached the Jewish people from outside, as an external community opposed to Jewish national existence and the Jewish way of life. In effect, it treated the Jewish people the way the early Yeshua movement treated the idolatrous Gentiles—only with greater contempt.[4]

His book provides extensive biblical evidence for this paradigm, exploring its origins, justifications, and implications, confirming his findings by referencing respected textual and theological scholars.

Some Benefits of Bilateral Ecclesiology

For a variety of reasons, bilateral ecclesiology is a beneficial paradigm. First, it clearly upholds the election and dignity of Israel. In this postsupersessionist paradigm the church from among the nations becomes part of theological Israel without replacing the Jewish people.[5] Besides giving

4. Kinzer, *Postmissionary Messianic Judaism*, 264.

5. George Lindbeck reaches similar conclusions suggesting that if God's covenant

proper emphasis to Israel's continuing role in the *missio dei*, Kinzer affirms its foundational role. The church and Israel are not simply linked. Rather, the church is joined to Israel and not vice versa. He rightly contends that Israel must remain Israel, with the church from among the nations joined through Yeshua faith to Jews of like faith who are covenantally bound to the dictates of Torah. Kinzer insists that the apostles regarded Torah-based covenantal living as intrinsic to Jewish selfhood. Richard Bauckham concurs, stating "the vast majority of Jewish Christians in the NT period continued to observe the whole law, taking for granted that they were still obligated to do so."[6] This is a second benefit of bilateral ecclesiology, how it contradicts the widespread assumption that with the death of Christ, Israel's identity markers simply expired or became purely voluntary.

The third benefit of Kinzer's paradigm is that it affirms unity in diversity, manifest in an ongoing distinction (not separation) between two sub-communities, one from among the nations, and the other from among the seed of Jacob, with whom it lives in solidarity. Unity, not uniformity: precisely right.

A fourth benefit of Kinzer's model is its affinity with the complementarian ethos explored by R. Kendall Soulen who insists that the Jewish and Gentile components of the *ekklesia* need one another in order to properly understand their respective roles and to reach their respective destinies. Each sub-community serves the other as God's appointed means of blessing by living true to its own calling. Soulen goes yet further, holding that the people of Israel are divinely intended to be God's means of blessing to the Gentiles, and the Gentiles, especially the church from among the Gentiles, a blessing to the Jews. Far from undermining the unity of the *ekklesia*, bilateral ecclesiology highlights the intrinsic character of this unity. Indeed, the unity of the *ekklesia* would not be a sign of the kingdom if distinctions between the partners were leveled or ignored, because the presence of the kingdom is revealed as two communities that by design remain inherently distinct, and that formerly lived in appositional hostility, now live together in *shalom*, in vibrant reconciliation.[7]

---

with Israel is not revoked, and if the church does not replace Jewish Israel then both the Jews and the church can safely be Israel, albeit in different senses. "If the Church is nonsupersessionist Israel, then it can see its election as a subset of Jewish Israel's election, thus affirming both." Although it would take discipline for a church steeped in a history of supersessionism to learn to speak of itself as Israel without usurping the dignity that remains to the children of Jacob, this appears to be a solicitous formulation ("Postmodern Hermeneutics and Jewish Christian Dialogue," 163).

6. Bauckham, *James*, 147.

7. Kinzer cites Luke Johnson on the how the relationship between Jews and Gentiles in the One New Man is related to that of husbands and wives. "The relationship

The Flaw in Kinzer's Jewel

Although Kinzer's jewel shines brightly, it exhibits one major flaw, his failure to clearly define and explore a postsupersessionist missiology compatible with his bilateral ecclesiology. Because his new paradigm challenges prevailing assumptions, this omission presents a volatile flash point for critics seeking to portray him in a negative light. Most are still weighing Kinzer's paradigm, and new paradigms by their very newness invite resistance among defenders of the status quo and those with unformed opinions who are yet susceptible to "stay away from him" warnings. In such a climate, Kinzer would have done better to reassure the missiologically anxious. This is especially so in a book using the term "postmissionary" in its title. Detractors are quick to assume not only that he means anti-missionary Messianic Judaism, but also that he means to say non-missional Messianic Judaism. While he defends himself against the first charge, he fails to adequately address the second.

Kinzer's Ideological Bedfellow: Karl Barth

It is not only his failure to explicitly address missiological concerns that concerns Kinzer's critics. He is also open to attack because of one of the bedfellows he chooses, whose positions seem strange or dangerous to Kinzer's conservative critics.[8] This bedfellow is Karl Barth, who presciently intuited much that Kinzer explores.[9]

Barth treats the topic of Israel and the church under the heading "The Election of God." For Barth, all begins and ends in Jesus Christ. In a brilliant

---

between husband and wife, therefore, symbolizes the mystery of unity in plurality and makes it present within the community. This completes the Pauline perception of "neither Jew nor Greek, neither male nor female.' . . . Man and woman submit to each other in respect and love and service, finding unity and peace not in a false identification but in a pluralistic unity. So should Jew and Greek celebrate their unity in service to each other, so that God's purpose might be fulfilled, 'to unite all things in him, things in heaven and things on earth' (1:10)" (Johnson, *The Writings of the New Testament*, 378–79; quoted in Kinzer, *Postmissionary Messianic Judaism,* 170).

8. Karl Barth is certainly not the only theologian or textual scholar to whom Kinzer links his perspective. He finds sturdy support from others like David Noel Freedman, Markus Barth, Luke Timothy Johnson, and Jakob Jervell, among others. Karl Barth is singled out here because his views as quoted supply cannon fodder to Kinzer's critics, although Kinzer differs with Barth on these very matters of controversy.

9. Among other theologians he references, Kinzer's quotation from David Noel Freedman is especially striking for its prophetic insight. He conjectured just the kind of paradigm Kinzer outlines decades before Kinzer. See Freedman, "An Essay on Jewish Christianity," 246–47.

variation on the Reformed doctrine of double predestination, he presents Christ as both elected and condemned by God, taking upon himself the condemnation due Israel and the church, while being the one in whose resurrection all are raised to newness of life. Kinzer quotes Barth's further explanation of the unity and destiny of the Israel/church people of God, a broader conception of the *ekklesia*. It is here that some problems arise:

> [The *ekklesia*] exists according to God's eternal decree as the people of Israel (in the whole range of its history in past and future, ante and post *Christum natum*), and at the same time as the Church of Jews and Gentiles (from its revelation at Pentecost to its fulfillment by the second coming of Christ). In this, its twofold (Old Testament and New Testament) form of existence, there is reflected and repeated the twofold determination of Jesus Christ himself. The community, too, is as Israel and as the Church indissolubly one. It, too, as the one is ineffaceably these two, Israel and the Church.[10]

One searches in vain here for any incentive or room for missional action directed toward the Jewish people either by the church or by the Yeshua-believing Jewish remnant. Eberhard Busch strikingly summarizes Barth's thrust: "One difference between the two forms is that Israel is a 'people,' of which one usually becomes a member through birth, whereas one becomes a member of the church by being called."[11] If so, then why and where is there incentive and room for missional activity among the Jewish people either intracommunally by Messianic Jews, or intercommunally, by the church?

Furthermore, although Kinzer no doubt realizes how volatile the following Barthian position would be to his conservative readers, he does not choose to clarify its interpretation and limits:

> Barth sees the Jewish people as a whole, whether Yeshua-believing or non-Yeshua-believing, as bound inseparably to its Messiah. As part of the community of God, it is also part of Messiah's body. When Israel does not believe in Yeshua, it resists its own election. However, it cannot cancel that election nor cut itself free from its Messiah. Barth even asserts that Israel is now sanctified through its physical connection to Yeshua as his "kinsmen."[12]

10. Barth, *Church Dogmatics* II.2, 162–63, quoted in Kinzer, *Postmissionary Messianic Judaism*, 175.

11. Busch, "The Covenant of Grace Fulfilled in Christ as the Foundation of the Indissoluble Solidarity of the Church with Israel," 490.

12. Kinzer, *Postmissionary Messianic Judaism*, 176.

On the one hand these are exciting words highlighting truths the church is prone to miss concerning the unity of Israel and her bond with her Messiah even in the absence of explicit Yeshua-faith. I find these words exciting and refreshing. We can agree that "when Israel does not believe in Yeshua, it resists its own election." We can agree too that "it cannot cancel that election."[13] However, to go on to say that Israel cannot cut itself off from its Messiah and that it is "now sanctified through its physical connection to Yeshua as his 'kinsmen'" seems to leave little justification or need for any outreach to the Jewish people by those endeavoring to commend Yeshua faith to them. If this is not what Kinzer means by what he says, he errs by not making that clear. Perhaps he intends a "both/and" construct. However, that is not evident.[14] Because Barth's position sets off so many alarm bells, Kinzer's failure to articulate his own missiological convictions looms large.

Kinzer on His Ecclesiological and Missiological Affinities with Historical Precursors

We turn now to examining historical precursors whose praxis exemplified some features of Kinzer's construct. Is Kinzer's model enhanced by the association? Yes, but not in all respects nor in every case.

Joseph Rabinowitz (1837–1899)

Raised in the hasidic milieu, and later an adherent of the *Haskalah* movement (the Jewish Enlightenment), Joseph Rabinowitz came to believe in Yeshua as Messiah while on a journey to consider settling in Israel. After returning to Bessarabia (modern Moldova) he founded a congregation of Jewish Yeshua-believers, the Israelites of the New Covenant. He wanted them to be "a body of loyal Jews who were to live within the confines of the

---

13. Rom 11:29.

14. Kinzer helps his cause a bit when he says that "the terminology used by Barth here is noteworthy. He does not focus on Jewish Yeshua-believers as individuals, but instead focuses on their corporate identity" (Kinzer, *Postmissionary Messianic Judaism*, 176). One could guess that Kinzer is saying here that neither he nor Barth are excluding the propriety of outreach to individuals. But must we settle for mere inference? Do we not crave more? Yes we do! We crave a clarification writ large and explored explicitly, because his apparent reticence to make pronouncements on these matters is easily construed as negativity about extending Yeshua-faith in the Jewish world. Kinzer takes pains to state that his postmissionary Messianic Judaism is not anti-missionary Messianic Judaism. He needs also to take pains to reassure us that his is not post-missional Messianic Judaism.

Jewish people." What he meant by this was that "the Israelites of the New Covenant should practice circumcision, honor the Sabbath, and keep the Passover and other Jewish holidays."[15] Kinzer shows how Rabinowitz held to two categories of Torah obligation, a lesser, national obligation, and a greater, religious/moral obligation. Only transgression of the latter was to be considered sin. It is possible that he developed this two-tiered model to assuage the concerns of Christian advisors like Franz Delitzsch who, while supportive of his work, were at best skittish about treating circumcision, the seventh-day Sabbath, and the keeping of Jewish holy days as obligatory for Jewish Yeshua-believers. These ways of thinking may also be traced to his *Haskalah* roots, a perspective that valued moral commandments over ritual commands. *Haskalah* convictions also lay behind Rabinowitz's rejection of rabbinic tradition. Delitzsch proved to be far more positive about rabbinic sources than was Rabinowitz and sought unsuccessfully to ameliorate his antipathy.

Kinzer evaluates Rabinowiz by his five ecclesiological principles, examining the extent to which Rabinowitz's views and practice coincide with his own. He finds substantial agreement in all but the fifth principle:

> How does the Rabinowitz program match up with our five ecclesiological principles? First, Rabinowitz emphatically affirms Israel's enduring covenant and election. Second, he likewise affirms the enduring importance of Jewish practice, though his attitude toward the obligatory quality of that practice remains ambiguous. Third, he denies the value and validity of rabbinic tradition. Fourth, he takes the initial steps toward the formation of a bilateral ecclesiology. Fifth, though he demonstrates a radical solidarity with the Jewish people, his ecclesiology still reflects a missionary orientation in its disregard for historical Jewish religious experience and its focus on Israel entering the (universal) church (without a corresponding emphasis on the church joining Israel).[16]

Ignatz Lichtenstein (1824–1909)

Rabinowitz was a man before his time, a precursor of at least some aspects of the bilateral model. His contemporary, Hungarian Rabbi Ignatz Lichtenstein, commonly called Isak/Isaac Lichtenstein, in some respects anticipated

---

15. Kinzer, *Postmissionary Messianic Judaism*, 273–74. See also Kjaer-Hansen, *Joseph Rabinowitz and the Messianic Movement*, 82.

16. Kinzer, *Postmissionary Messianic Judaism*, 277–78.

aspects of Kinzer's paradigm even more fully than did Rabinowitz. He followed three principles bearing mention here: he refused to be baptized (but is reported to have baptized himself in Yeshua's name in a Jewish *mikveh*, a ritual bath), he continued to live a fully Jewish life in accordance with the dictates of Oral Torah, and he refused any attachment to any missionizing agency that sought to bring Jews into churches. He not only believed in living a Jewish life, he also refused cooperation with any agency that directed Jews to do otherwise. He therefore affirmed a more radical solidarity with Israel, strong in adhering to Kinzer's fifth ecclesiological principle, where Rabinowitz was weak.

Philip Paul Levertoff (1878–1954)/Lev Gillet (1893–1980)

Paul Levertoff was a descendant of the first Lubavitcher Rebbe, and a precocious graduate of the formidable Volozhin Yeshiva. Coming to Yeshua faith, he became an Anglican priest, a worker with two British missions, and a renowned educator at Franz Delitsch's Institutum Judaicum in Leipzig. Lev Gillet, an Orthodox priest who knew him, illumines Levertoff's thought in his own work, *Communion in Messiah*. According to this source, "[Levertoff held] the ideal of a Jewish Christian community, which he conceive[d] as 'a Jewish branch of the Catholic Church in a congenial Jewish traditional environment, where the essentials of Christian Faith and worship are expressed, as much as possible, in Jewish terms.'"[17] Toward this end, despite having at his disposal materials already prepared by the London Jews' Society, including a Hebrew translation of the *Book of Common Prayer*, Levertoff published a liturgy of his own, *Meal of the Holy King*, now no longer extant.[18] When he was a pastor in Shoreditch, he sought to gather a community of "those Jews who are not ashamed of the Gospel of Christ and of their Jewish origin . . . to unite as a Faith in terms of the rich background of devotional and mystical Jewish traditions."[19] In his Jewish services, Levertoff read from the Torah while wearing a *tallit* and *kippah* (prayer shawl and skull cap), an extraordinary measure for an Anglican clergyman of his day. It is clear that Levertoff was in all of these activities attempting to bridge both worlds of which he was a distinguished part. However, since he was above all else a scholar rather than organizer, and a functionary of a denominational structure with

17. Gillet, *Communion in the Messiah*, 203.

18. For extensive information about Levertoff and information about *Meal of the Holy King*, see Quiñones, "Paul Phillip Levertoff."

19. Levertoff, *The Possibility of a Hebrew-Christian Church*, quoted in Quiñones, "Paul Phillip Levertoff," 28.

well-established norms and boundaries, there were strict limits as to what he could accomplish and how far he imagined himself going.

His view of a Yeshua-believing Jewish communal reality as a branch of the Catholic church falls short of Kinzer's model, which harmonizes with Ephesians 2, seeing the church as joined to Israel, and not vice versa.

Kinzer's discussion of Lev Gillet's views is instructive for exploring the interface between ecclesiology and missiology. Some aspects of Gillet's thought which Kinzer highlights as compatible with his own include:

1. Yeshua was a Torah-observant Jew in the Pharisaic mold.

2. Paul's battles were not about Torah per se but over the issue of whether Gentiles should be compelled to obey Torah.

3. New Testament faith is wholly compatible with later rabbinical sources.

4. The Jewish people, like the Church, are a *corpus mysticum*, a mystical body,[20] and "perform a redeeming work in the *diaspora*."[21]

5. The sufferings of this obedient covenantal Israel are to be related to the Suffering Servant of whom Isaiah spoke.

6. "For Gillet, Christian thinking about the Jewish people and Judaism must be primarily ecclesiological rather than missiological. He does not view the Jewish people as an external field for church mission, but as intimately bound to the church's inner reality."[22]

It is especially in this last point that Kinzer, by association, opens himself up to criticism. Indeed, this position is the very axis upon which my current

---

20. Medievalist Ernst Kantorowicz, writing in *The King's Two Bodies,* says that the concept of the body of Christ evolved into a notion of two bodies during the Middle Ages. "The Pauline term originally designating the Christian Church [the Body of Christ] now began to designate the consecrated host [now called the *corpus naturale];* contrariwise, the notion *corpus mysticum,* hitherto used to describe the host, was gradually transferred—after 1150—to the Church as the organized body of Christian society united in the Sacrament of the Altar. In short, the expression 'mystical body,' which originally had a liturgical or sacramental meaning, took on a connotation of sociological context. It was finally in that relatively new sociological sense that Boniface VIII defined the Church as 'one *mystical* boy the head of which is Christ'" (*The King's Two Bodies,* 196). This term, *corpus mysticum,* which refers to the social body of the church, is viewed to be a collective social organization with an enduring, mystical essence. And it is this term Gillet applies to obedient Israel as well, so that she too is viewed to be a collective social organization with an enduring, mystical essence. No religious Jew would deny that to be so, even if eschewing the terminology.

21. Gillet, *Communion,* 157.

22. Items enumerated in this list from Kinzer, *Postmissionary Messianic Judaism,* 280–83.

chapter rests—the pursuit of ecclesiology to the neglect of missiology. Gillet sees Israel as so intimately connected with the church's "inner reality" as to make mission to the Jewish people superfluous and even ill-conceived.

We may detect in loyal churchmen like Lev Gillet, and in sensitive and diffident theologians like Mark Kinzer, a reticence or in some cases, a disinclination, to speak of missional action directed toward the Jewish people. But is it missional action itself which ought to be precluded, or is it not rather any missional action that derogates the Jewish people, their calling, and their way of life, mission that in some manner disrupts or disregards Jewish covenantal and communal cohesion? Surely it is the latter, and although I believe Kinzer would agree, his failure to adequately articulate and emphasize that agreement is a flaw in Kinzer's jewel.

Is Kinzer's Position Sparse, or Just His Presentation?

In his eighth and ninth chapters Kinzer deals explicitly with matters of mission in characteristically muted and diffident terms. We may detect here some tones reassuring to the missiologically anxious.

He portrays apostolic practice as including mission to the wider Jewish world, reminding us that "the apostles were Jews addressing other Jews, announcing that Israel's Messiah had come and that Israel's destiny was soon to be realized—if the community of Israel would only welcome its Messiah. Accepting this message entailed a new Jewish affiliation, but not one that required a rupture with the wider Jewish community or its generally accepted norms."[23] Here he affirms the propriety of Jewish Yeshua believers reaching out with the message of Yeshua, while at the same time preserving the warp and weft of Jewish communal life, a dominant concern for Kinzer, and myself as well.

In the journal *Kesher*, commenting on the term "postmissionary" in the title of his book, Kinzer responds to his critics by clarifying his views on the imperative of mission to the Jewish people. Here he also bears witness to his own recognition that bearing witness, or mission, is intrinsic to the life of the people of God—the unity of ecclesiology and missiology which I am underscoring in this chapter.

> My intention was not to suggest that Messianic Jews should set aside the obligation to bear witness to Messiah Yeshua, in both word and deed. In a strictly theological sense, neither Israel nor the Christian church can cease to be "missionary" without losing its own identity. God has established a relationship with

23. Ibid., 264.

a people, and that people has a mission in the world to reveal
God and God's ways to all creation. Believing that the "fullness
of God dwells bodily" in Yeshua (Col 2:9), Messianic Jews cannot divorce their witness to God from their witness to Yeshua.
Therefore, our "inner mission" to our fellow Jews must include
at its heart our expressed conviction that Yeshua is the Son of
God and Israel's Messiah.[24]

Many of Kinzer's critics would be surprised by this statement, and I would
guess that very few are aware of it. That he had to make it in a rejoinder to
critics of his book proves that the book fails to be missiologically explicit,
which I term the flaw in Kinzer's jewel.

In the paragraph following the one just quoted, Kinzer articulates an
approach to outreach which I also advocate. This missiology, compatible
with a bilateral ecclesiology, commends Jewish Yeshua faith in tandem with
underscoring the priority of Jewish covenant faithfulness. Kinzer says it
well:

I do think that this "inner mission" must entail a radical recon-
figuration of the traditional evangelical missionary model. . . . If
we truly affirm the irrevocable covenant with Israel, the centrality of Israel within the divine plan, and the enduring obligation
of Torah faithfulness for all Jews, then our "mission" among
contemporary Jews, who often lack faith in God, commitment
to the preservation of the Jewish people, and the practice of a
Torah-based way of life, must involve more than a call to believe
in Yeshua for forgiveness of sins and eternal life. . . . *Postmissionary* implies that our mission as Messianic Jews involves bearing witness to Yeshua as one who perfectly embodies covenant
faithfulness and who summons Jews back to a renewed life of
Torah observance. In effect, our mission—as servants and representatives of Yeshua—is to help awaken Israel as a whole to
its own mission: to be a kingdom of priests and a holy nation.[25]

All that is within me cries *bravo* and *amen* to such a missional vision which
I also champion. This is a postsupersessionist missiology compatible with
a bilateral ecclesiology. And of course, this stands in sharpest contrast to
mission to the Jews as normally conceive and conducted.

Kinzer remains controversial, chiefly in Messianic Jewish circles, for
two reasons, one misconstrued and the other not. First, some wrongly assume that he is opposed to missional efforts among the Jewish people. His

24. Kinzer, "Rejoinder to Responses to Post-Missionary Messianic Judaism."
25. Ibid.

own words reveal this to not be the case. Second, Kinzer is controversial because he calls Jews back to covenantal commitments Christendom long ago declared null and void—the priority of faithfulness to Torah and Jewish communal cohesion.

TOWARD A ROBUST POSTSUPERSESSIONIST MISSIOLOGY COMPATIBLE WITH BILATERAL ECCLESIOLOGY AND THE CONVERGING DESTINIES PARADIGM

Kinzer's bilateral ecclesiology is robust and rich, broad and deep, well-defined and well-defended. But as we have seen, it needs to be complemented with a commensurate missiology, robust, explicit, and lived out. The current volume is meant to serve as a first step in exploring such a postsupersessionist missiology, one compatible with a bilateral ecclesiology and the Converging Destinies paradigm. In what remains I examine six characteristics of such a missiology.

A Postsupersessionist Missiology is Part of a Wider Missiological Reality

We may most briefly define mission as "the bilateral ekklesia extending and expressing itself in the world as an agent of blessing, judgment, and redemption in service to the mission of God." Here is a more detailed definition:

> Mission is the Triune God's extending and expressing Godself within and through the created order in blessing, judgment and redemption so as to call forth a people for God's own Name from among Israel and the nations, reconciling them to each other, and enlisting them in individual, familial, and communal obedience of faith for the sake of His name in all aspects of relationship with the social, spiritual, and material aspects of the created order. This bi-lateral ekklesia is sent by the Triune God to increase God's glory through mirroring God's self-extension and self-expression in its own self-extension and self-expression, and in calling others from among Israel and the nations into the life here described and into participation in local communities of the faithful, looking forward to and hastening the consummation of all things in the new heavens and the new earth, free from the curse of sin and death, where righteousness dwells, and all things visible and invisible live together in loving synergistic celebratory harmony to the glory of God, world without end.

Without this kind of self-extension and expression, one does not have the *ekklesia* at all, but only an institutional or communal entity claiming a name it does not livingly bear. The Body of Messiah/Body of Christ is a community that shows its vigor through its resemblance to its living head in all aspects of life and relationship, an always-in-process community growing toward the measure of the stature of the fullness of Messiah. This is the self-expression of the body. But it must grow not only through maturation but also through a self-extending self-replication among all people groups. Such growth is not merely a matter of pragmatic institutional survival. Rather it is a matter of obedience and a sign of health—or the lack thereof.

Missiological deficit cannot be remedied by simply adding some idealized program of evangelism to the agendas of both the church from among the nations and the Messianic Jewish movement. This will not do. Mission is not an agenda nor a bundle of listable activities. Mission should not be equated solely with evangelism and techniques for its implementation. The mission of the *ekklesia* must instead reflect and respond to the entire mission of God in all the ways by which God extends and expresses Godself within and through the created order, in blessing, justice, and redemption. Our mission is incarnational. We are called to be individual, familial, and communal extensions and expressions of the presence and person of God, embodying him and his kingdom concerns in all the contexts we inhabit and encounter. This is an incarnational perspective. True, this entails evangelism, but also humanitarian aid, social justice, ecological responsibility, for Jews, living and transmitting a legacy of Torah obedience, and so much more.

There are only three postures we may take toward God's mission: we may be its object, its servant, or its impediment. If one agrees that of these three, it is the first two which are to be embraced, then we must always be asking and answering, "How has God's mission reached us, and what does God require we be and do to rightly serve and reflect God's mission in the world?"

According to his subtitle, Kinzer's book is about "redefining Christian engagement with the Jewish people." But perhaps this subtitle needs tweaking. He seems rather to focus on ontology, redefining Christian *relationship* with the Jewish people. Ecclesial engagement betokens action, going forth to meet the other, in a word, mission. True, we must acknowledge that mission to the Jewish people is a sensitive area obstructed and littered with remembrances of historical stigma and slander, negation and coercion, oppression and abuse. Kinzer ably recaps much of this sorry history, something crucial to do if newness is to be found. In view of this sordid past, and ecumenical and societal pressures to therefore forego any Christian mission activity toward the Jewish people, should the project therefore simply be abandoned and avoided?

No, this is a road that must not be taken. One cannot abandon or negate outreach to the Jewish people and yet claim a healthy bilateral ecclesiology. Despite all the horrors of past, present, or even future, such an ecclesiology must be inseparably linked to a robust postsupersessionist missiology. Due to the covenantal character and calling of the Jewish people, this mission is best implemented by Jews living out the obedience of Jewish faith for the same of his name. Outreach to the Jewish people was and remains foundational to the *ekklesia*'s communal being. And it is as the *ekklesia* engages in appropriate missional practice that its essence is clarified and made explicit.

A Postsupersessionist Missiology is Implicit in the Role of the Remnant

Kinzer ties his ecclesiology into the role of the remnant in two ways. First, he speaks of the remnant role of the Jewish component of the *ekklesia* as serving as the firstfruits of Israel's eschatological destiny, sanctifying the whole while revealing both the destiny and meaning of Jewish identity.[26] This "sanctifying" of the whole is unsettling to some of Kinzer's critics. However, the Apostle Paul takes pains to make the same point in Romans 11:16, using sanctification language (*hagia*, "holy"), and employing two reinforcing metaphors to illustrate his intended meaning: the holiness of the lump offered as firstfruits sanctifying the whole batch, and the holiness of the root sanctifying the branches. Kinzer's language is most careful and biblical, and when he evokes the "firstfruits" spreading to the harvest and the sanctity of the root spreading to the whole, he is incontrovertibly Pauline.[27]

What creates dissonance for some is the prevailing cultural penchant for hearing and interpreting the text individualistically, rather than communally. Kinzer (and Paul) are speaking of the destiny of Israel and the function of the remnant with respect to the whole of Israel, to the nations, and the destiny of the cosmos. He is speaking of communal rather than personal destinies. Both Paul and Kinzer hold that individuals should always honor the commitments entailed in covenants in which they are included, or face the consequences.

A second way Kinzer ties his ecclesiology into the role of the remnant is through referring to Israel's mission to be a light to the nations as fulfilled in the Yeshua-believing remnant's faithfulness to its Jewish commitments,

26. Kinzer, *Postmissionary Messianic Judaism*, 264.
27. Ibid.

thus forming a living communal link for "the redeemed of the nations to Israel's corporate life and spiritual heritage."[28] Because we have become habituated to thinking of the Yeshua believing remnant of Israel as being *extracted* from wider Israel rather than being and remaining *within* it, Kinzer's position arrests us. Contrary to supersessionist models, this remnant is not a replacement Israel. Instead it is comprised of Yeshua-believing Jews living in covenantal solidarity with their own people. It is only as and because this remnant lives in solidarity with Israel's calling that it can serve as a light to the nations. My preferred way of stating this obligation is that the Messianic Jewish remnant is meant to live as a sign, demonstration, and catalyst of God's consummating purposes for Israel.

Postsupersessionist Missiology Reflects Apostolic Priorities

In outlining the ontology of the early church, Kinzer appropriately and frequently quotes from Jakob Jervell, who earlier and better than most saw clearly the bilateral nature of the first-century *ekklesia*. Jervell's analysis of the Book of Acts also highlights the ongoing core of the church's identity and missional practice—mission to the Jews. We need to pay attention.

Jervell discusses Luke's portrait of a first-century church that was both ontologically/ecclesiologically Jewish and praxiologically/missiologically Jewish. He reports how even the rejection of the gospel in one synagogue led to its being preached in the next. He sees Luke taking pains to highlight how even in scenes where the gospel is rejected by Jews, a number of Jews come to Yeshua faith in synagogues that accept Gentiles (Acts 13:43; 18:7–8). "In 18:7–8 even the chief ruler of the synagogue becomes a believer, that is, after the scene in which Paul leaves the synagogue."[29] In that context, even when Paul preaches outside the synagogue, Jews hear and receive his message. There is not one, single, definite transition from mission among Jews to mission among Gentiles in the Book of Acts. Cornelius needs to be seen as a god-fearer rather than a rank Gentile. The preaching in Acts is so presented as to show that mission among Gentiles is connected with the mission among Jews. "It is taken for granted that there is no mission solely for Gentiles [divorced from a foundational mission among Jews]."[30]

It is common in our day for missionaries to the Jews to advocate for the *inclusion* of Jews in the mission of the church. Luke turns this on its head, insisting that the gospel remains fundamentally a gift and call to Israel and

28. Ibid.

29. Jervell, *The Unknown Paul*, 16.

30. Ibid.

through Israel to the nations. From beginning to end, Acts exhibits neither embarrassment nor flagging in zeal concerning mission to the Jews. Jervell insists that in Acts, mission to the Jews is not an add-on. If anything, it is mission to the Gentiles which is presented as an add-on. The church in Acts is a "primarily of Jews and for the Jews, in Palestine and in the various parts of the Roman empire. There is in Acts as a whole not one Gentile Christian missionary, because the mission of the Church is throughout Acts a mission to the Jews."[31]

The structure of Acts does not present the church as destined to be a Gentile concern, leaving behind its Jewish origins. "For Luke, the future is still uncertain. No history of salvation is evident, manifest, and easily read."[32] We misread Luke when we read his text through the lens of Christendom's later assumptions that the mission to the Jews was but a rocket booster destined to be jettisoned when Gentile mission reached orbit. Commonly this is done by emphasizing how from the beginning God was concerned with the salvation of the nations, with his work among the Jews being regarded as a means to that end.

From Peter's sermon on the Day of Pentecost (Acts 2) to Paul's conversation with the elders of the synagogue in Rome (Acts 28) nearly forty years later, the apostles proactively shared the message of Yeshua with Jewish audiences. This zeal for mission as expansion directed toward Israel is absent in Barth's construct. His is an ecclesiology stripped of missional action and motivation. However, there is a both/and solution to this dilemma of omission. In common with bilateral ecclesiology, we may and I believe should say with Barth that the people of God is comprised of both Israel and the church, and Jervell heartily agrees. But both Jervell and the Apostolic Witness highlight the priority of the Messianic Jewish remnant and the church calling the people of Israel to repentance toward God and faith in Yeshua the Messiah "that times of refreshing may come from the presence of the Lord, and that he may send the Messiah appointed for (them), Yeshua, whom heaven must receive until the time for restoring all the things about which God spoke by the mouth of his holy prophets long ago.[33] Until

31. Ibid, 17.

32. Ibid, 20.

33. See Acts 3:19–21. In this regard, it seems helpful consider evangelistic activity among the Jewish people not under the category of soteriology but rather of doxology and pneumatology. Our focus should be not on seeing the Jewish people as fundamentally "lost" or "unsaved," but as elect, but called to glorify the God of Sinai through glorifying Yeshua, thereby opening to themselves the spiritual wellsprings released in his resurrection and exaltation. I say this so as to inform attitudes and mentality toward the Jewish people in order to correct and challenge the missional church's habitual negative assessment and affect toward them which suppresses Scripture's positive assessment of

then, the *ekklesia* remains foundationally a Jewish institution, through the remnant living in the midst of, and for sake of Israel, and only therefore and thereby also God's means of blessing for the nations.

Postsupersessionist Missiology Is a Partnership in Obedience

We have already seen that a postsupersessionist missiology is part of a wider missiological reality, that it must grow out of and be related to the *missio dei* and to the kinds of missional concerns that drive and discipline the *ekklesia* as a whole. The Messianic Jewish movement needs to avoid pursuing these goals in social isolation from the wider *ekklesia*, thus violating the *bilateral* nature of the people of God, "a unified community that is essentially two-fold, containing a Jewish sub-community that links it to the national life and history of the people of Israel, and a multinational sub-community that extends Israel's heritage among the peoples of the earth without annulling their distinctive cultural identities."[34] That unity must be more than theoretical, rhetorical, and theological. It must be existential.

This missional unity in diversity can be best understood in relation to Paul's teaching on the fullness of Israel and the fullness of the nations (Rom 11). The church helps expedite the fullness of the nations through obeying the Great Commission to go to all nations: this is her mission. The Messianic Jewish remnant of Israel is to expedite the fullness of Israel through obeying what I term the Greater Commission, which Paul terms "greater (riches)" than the salvation of the nations.[35] Seen from this perspective, both portions of the *ekklesia* have their proper missions: the church from among the nations, mission to the nations; the messianic Jewish remnant, mission to wider Israel. However, were we to leave things this way, we would be fostering the isolationism we seek to avoid. This is why both the church from among the nations and the remnant of Israel each have a paramission: to come alongside one another to encourage and to assist the other half of the *ekklesia* in fulfilling its missional calling.

This relationship can perhaps best be understood as a "partnership in obedience." A good partnership models just the kind of unity in diversity we are seeking. Partners are individuals, with distinct giftings, personalities, and foci. Yet they serve a common goal, and, in a good partnership, are complementary to each other. The same is true of the relationship between the church from among the nations and the messianic Jewish component

---

the seed of Jacob and God's vouchsafed faithfulness toward them.

34. Kinzer, *Israel's Messiah and the People of God*, 178.

35. Rom 11:16.

of the *ekklesia*. They are distinct, yet they are meant to cooperate toward achieving a common goal. And in Pauline terms, this common goal is "life from the dead," the general resurrection, that is, the consummation of all things, which can only take place as the fullness of the nations and the fullness of Israel are each accomplished. Therefore, neither the Messianic Jewish remnant nor the church from among the nations can afford to be indifferent or passive about one another's associated fullness. Distinct though they may and must be, they must pull together to reach the goal, partners in obedience.[36]

Postsupersessionist Missiology Is a Relational Imperative

Missional imperatives are often crafted in statistical terms, in eschatological terms, or in pragmatic terms. But what of relational terms? My experience in the Messianic Jewish movement indicates that this personal dimension is largely unexplored.

In the memoirs of Mother Teresa of Calcutta one finds that the driving motive behind her ministry to the poorest of the poor was Yeshua's words on the cross, "I thirst." She directed that these words be placed beside the crucifixes at all her centers worldwide. She was impelled by an all-consuming desire to slake what she perceived to be his thirst for the souls of men and women, for whom, in love, he suffered and died. The Messianic Jewish remnant is called to embrace something quite similar.

Although we in the Messianic Jewish movement could certainly make Mother Teresa's motive our own, in his cry of loving anguish. "O Jerusalem, Jerusalem, how often . . . ."[37] we find an in-culture and explicit impetus for missional action toward our own people: Yeshua's longing to gather Israel to himself "as a hen gathers her brood." Although, with Kinzer, I affirm Yeshua as being already in the midst of Israel, even when unacknowledged, Yeshua's words make clear that something vital is lost and that Yeshua suffers anguish when his people Israel fail to welcome him as the Blessed One who comes in the name of the Lord. Something is lost for them, something is lost for him, and we must feel the loss ourselves.

Can we who name the name of Yeshua in faith and love justify being ambivalent or lax in responding to his tears and anguish over that people whom especially loves, as expressed in his cry, "O Jerusalem, Jerusalem. . . .

36. I explore the Great Commission and the Greater Commission, the fullness of the nations and the fullness of Israel at greater length in my monograph, *Christians and Jews Together*, and explore the role of the Messianic Jewish remnant with respect to the wider Jewish community in *Son of David*.

37. Matt 13:34; Luke 13:34.

How often would I have gathered your children together as a hen gathers her brood under her wings, and you would not?" No, our concerns will resonate with his, and his longing will be ours to see that this people might say with fullness of heart, "Blessed is He who comes in the Name of the Lord."

Postsupersessionist Missiology is Compatible With the Converging Destinies Paradigm

Bilateral ecclesiology and the Converging Destinies paradigm display a high regard for the covenantal calling of Israel as heirs and custodians of a holy way of life whereby they might collectively honor God. The Converging Destinies paradigm gives this conviction a certain eschatologically molded shape, voicing the conviction that in the end both the Christian and Jewish worlds will be affirmed and also chastened by the God who assesses all of us. This knowledge of a common accountability should foster a certain humility. At the same time, the Converging Destinies paradigm encourages partisans from both communities to hold firm to their own convictions. Even though we all see through a glass darkly, we do see: and we are accountable for what we see, and for being unashamed in taking a stand for it. While rewarding boldness of conviction, this paradigm precludes triumphalism. We see, but through a glass darkly, we know, but we know in part, we prophesy, but we prophesy in part. And we shall give an account of ourselves to a God who will both affirm and chasten us in the presence of the other.

This being true, each community should see each encounter with the other as a preview of that day, as a time for heightened listening to the voice of God, learning from one another, and testing our convictions in the Divine Presence.

CONCLUSION

In this chapter I examined Mark Kinzer's bilateral ecclesiology, outlining some of its strengths. I then considered the paradigm's linkage with Karl Barth's theologizing, as well as with the praxis of four nineteenth-/twentieth-century leaders who in various aspects anticipated Kinzer's model. I considered whether Kinzer's missiological convictions were weak, or whether it was his presentation of those convictions that needed shoring up, opting for the latter. I then outlined five characteristics intrinsic to a robust postsupersessionist missiology compatible with such a bilateral ecclesiology, and resonating with a Converging Destinies paradigm, seeking to make up deficits in Kinzer's presentation, while adding convictions of my own.

Although Kinzer's subtitle was "Redefining Christian Engagement With the Jewish People," I argued that he dealt rather with Christian *relationship* with the Jewish people, leaving quite a bit unsaid about missional engagement with this people. In *Postmissionary Messianic Judaism,* Kinzer did a splendid job deconstructing prevailing models of missional engagement with the Jewish people, demonstrating them to be linked to unviable, outdated paradigms grounded in supersessionist assumptions. While he provided a basis for a new kind of missional engagement with the Jewish people, he failed to directly explore what this engagement entails, leaving his readers to their own not always charitable conjectures.

Finally, I linked this missiology and bilateral ecclesiology with the Converging Destinies paradigm, showing how this facilitates communal self-reflection and deferential yet humble and vulnerable interaction for Christians and Jews.

9

Seeds, Weeds, and Walking the High Wire

The Role of the Messianic Jewish Remnant

IN RECENT YEARS, THE leadership of the Union of Messianic Jewish Congregations has been anxious to maintain or rather, to attain, unity among its member congregations. We have been wrestling over what that unity is. How broad are its boundaries, and where is its center? What are the essentials, and what are the non-essentials? What should be included and what omitted in the unity that gives the Union its character? Some are crying out for a return to the old paths, but wrangle over just which old paths we're talking about. Others distrust old paths, seeking to forge new avenues toward a reconceptualized future.

How can we and how shall we move forward when so much momentum is being dissipated through lateral conflict? What vision of unity will guide us toward the goals God has ordained for us?

Because we are part of the Messianic Jewish remnant, the only unity appropriate to our Union is one aligned with God's greater purposes for Israel. As he intends for Israel to be one nation, one people,[1] so God intends for our Union to be unified. But that unity will not be a unity of consensus. It cannot be simply a unity of compromise or of mutual toleration. It should not be a unity of peaceable feelings and fond embraces. It cannot be a unity of avoiding substantive issues, nor a unity of autocratic domination. Rather, the unity that God intends for Israel and for our Union is a unity of cov-

---

1. 2 Sam 7:23; 1 Chr 16:20; Jer 37:39; 50:4; Hos 1:11; 37:22.

enant obedience. When we become a people of a poor and humble spirit, trembling with the knowledge of having been commanded by God—then we will unify, stumbling and stampeding over each other in the rush to comply with the rule of heaven.

Of course, this can only happen with the Spirit's help. One of the ways he helps us is through widening our understanding. I am seeking to be his agent toward that purpose through building a case for a covenant obedience rooted vision of Israel's holy past and her holy consummation. As our Union learns to walk this pathway of covenant obedience we will fulfill our calling as the Messianic Jewish remnant of Israel.

My argument grows from two seeds—germinating ideas shaping our vision and role in the kingdom of God. I will also name four weeds to be uprooted if we would achieve that vision and build the kingdom. Finally, I will speak of the high wire, that narrow pathway of obedience to which we are called, and the factors we must keep in balance if we are to move forward and avoid falling into irrelevance and ineffectiveness, instead reaching our goal to the thunderous applause of a great cloud of witnesses.

Today we will take steps toward apprehending that vision. But first, we must travel to England to meet a mentor.

THE TIMES THEY ARE A-CHANGING

In his eighty-eight years, he proved himself genius, linguist, evangelist, saint, missionary statesman, and writer known more for the strength of his ideas than the length of his words. Returning to his native England after four decades of mission service in India, he found the West changed and himself a stranger. Old ways of thinking about the gospel and telling it to others didn't work any more. He quickly realized that if he was going to have any chance at winning the post-Christian, post-Enlightenment West to the cause to which he had devoted his life, he was going to have to find new, new, ways to tell the old, old, story. No sooner had he unpacked his bags than he began hammering away on his manual typewriter, crafting cogent analyses and strategies addressing the crisis.

Although he had arrived in England behind the times, he was soon decidedly ahead of them. He attracted a coterie of disciples, some of them improbable. That he was a Presbyterian didn't stop a prominent Roman Catholic theologian from referring to him as "his father in God" and speaking warmly of his missionary work, missionary thinking, and published works. When others expressed astonishment to the priest for so naming a Protestant, he responded, "Who else is there?"[2]

We too need to sit at the feet of Lesslie Newbigin. If we don't, we may find ourselves as out of step with our times as he was with his when he returned from India to England. Especially, we need to hear Newbigin's word that mission lives and moves and has its being only when it is "an action in which the Holy Spirit does new things, and brings into being new obedience."[3] The words leap off the page, demanding our response. What new things is the Holy Spirit doing today among the descendants of Jacob? And what new obedience is he agonizing to bring to birth from our Messianic Movement, two thousand years after Messiah came to shake us awake and point us toward the kingdom?

Newbigin spoke in terms of the post-Enlightenment, post-Christian West. Mark Kinzer speaks of a postmissionary Messianic Judaism. Standing at the intersection of changing times, changing minds, and changing paradigms, the term shouts at us, demanding that we reconceive and redefine our mission task. In a world where so much is changing, if we want to lead others toward the kingdom, we had better get reoriented.[4]

Part of that reorientation is adopting a postmissionary paradigm. This paradigm, explored at length in Mark Kinzer's *Postmissionary Messianic Judaism*, may be summarized as follows.

1. God is honored by Jewish Torah obedience. This applies no less to Messianic Jews than to the wider Jewish community.

2. Such Torah-faithful Messianic Jews form the living link whereby the from among the nations is joined to the Commonwealth of Israel, and serve the church by helping her reconceive of her identity and vocation as rooted in that of Israel.

---

2. Data from Beeby, "Obituary; The Right Rev Lesslie Newbigin."

3. Newbigin, *The Open Secret*, 139.

4. I mark five signs as evidence that we are living in changing times: (1) the rebirth of Israel; (2) the liberation of Jerusalem; (3) the regathering of the Jews to Israel especially from "the lands of the north," the former Soviet Union (Jer 23:7–8); (4) spiritual renewal among the Jewish people, including the Jesus Revolution of the late 1960s and early 1970s, the large proportion of Jews from the former Soviet Union who have come to Yeshua-faith in recent years, and recent statistics of an upsurge in Israelis coming to Yeshua faith; and (5) a notable upsurge in Messianic Jewish discussion of Torah-based covenant faithfulness, something not even on the radar screen as little as twenty years ago. These indicators coordinate with prophetic descriptions of spiritual developments among the Jewish people in the latter days to demonstrate that we are indeed in times of transition, changing times.

3. Understanding her identity and vocation in this context, the church will celebrate and support Jewish covenant faithfulness, seeing Yeshua-faith in the power of the Holy Spirit as its perfect embodiment, and will partner with Torah-faithful Messianic Jews as one *ekklesia*.

4. Messianic Jewish inreach to the wider Jewish community involves revealing the presence of Yeshua amidst Jewish life rather than importing him as an outsider or exporting Jewish Yeshua-believers to other communities.

5. Such inreach proclaims the name of Jesus, not the neediness of Jews.

6. The honor of God is enhanced, and his reign established, when his people honor Messiah whom he sent.

7. This paradigm enables concerned Christians to be both deeply faithful to Christ and deeply respectful of the living Jewish tradition and the Jewish community.

The last three points of this summary address issues of inreach to the wider Jewish community.[5] This chapter will develop the nature and implications of a postmissionary approach to inreach.

We need a postmissionary paradigm because Newbigin was right. Old ways of understanding the task and communicating the gospel aren't working any more. Having been warned to wait expectantly for the day of God, and to work to hasten its coming,[6] we must focus our best energies on rethinking and redefining our role if we are to unify, energize, and redirect our movement toward advance. In times of transition, failing to advance means falling behind.

Turning from a martial metaphor, let us turn now to more agrarian terms. What seeds need to be planted in us and by us if we are to fulfill our remnant responsibility?

---

5. I use the term "inreach" for what many people call "outreach" in order to emphasize that we are seeking to influence our own people, reaching in to our own community with the message we have.

6. 2 Pet 3:11–13. The New Living Translation adds additional verve to this text: "Since everything around us is going to melt away, what holy, godly lives you should be living! You should look forward to that day and hurry it along—the day when God will set the heavens on fire and the elements will melt away in the flames. But we are looking forward to the new heavens and new earth he has promised, a world where everyone is right with God."

SEEDS

Yeshua taught, "The Kingdom of Heaven is like a mustard seed."[7] In every generation, God gives his servants mustard seed ideas with divine power to transform the landscape.

David Stern points us toward one mustard seed in his translation of Messianic Jews (Hebrews) 11:22: "By trusting, Yosef, near the end of his life, *remembered about the Exodus of the people of Isra'el* and gave instructions about what to do with his bones." Reflect for a moment. Joseph lived long before Moses, before any Hebrews were enslaved, centuries before the exodus. How is it, then, that he "remembered about the Exodus?" This can only mean that he remembered what God had prophesied to his ancestor Abraham about the exodus, centuries earlier:

> Know this for certain: your descendants will be foreigners in a land that is not theirs. They will be slaves and held in oppression there four hundred years. But I will also judge that nation, the one that makes them slaves. Afterwards, they will leave with many possessions. As for you, you will join your ancestors in peace and be buried at a good old age. Only in the fourth generation will your descendants come back here, because only then will the Emori be ripe for punishment.[8]

On the basis of the prophetic word, Joseph remembered in advance the destiny of his people, coordinating plans and actions around a confident vision of things to come. We too must anticipate and facilitate the foreordained destiny of Jacob's children by devising and accomplishing strategic plans suited to a prophesied consummation.

7. Matt 13:31–32.
8. Gen 15:13–16 (CJB).

Ours is a *kairos* moment,[9] a doorway of opportunity. Missiologists call this *"adventus"*—a time of divine in-breaking.[10] We need to hear Paul addressing these words to us: "You know at what point of history we stand; so it is high time for you to rouse yourselves from sleep; for the final deliverance is nearer than when we first came to trust."[11]

Do we know at what point of history we stand? How can we act for the progress of the kingdom if we don't discern the times in which we live? Like arrows finding their target, the apostle's words strike home to our hearts: It *is* high time for us to rouse ourselves from sleep. If you sense that you are an early adopter, readily responding as if to the wake-up nudge of the Spirit, I invite you to awaken many others to the challenges facing all of us in changing times.

9 In 1987, Eric Charles White wrote:

Kairos is an ancient Greek word that means "the right moment" or "the opportune." The two meanings of the word apparently come from two different sources. In archery, it refers to an opening, or "opportunity" or, more precisely, a long tunnel-like aperture through which the archer's arrow has to pass. Successful passage of a kairos requires, therefore, that the archer's arrow be fired not only accurately but with enough power for it to penetrate. The second meaning of kairos traces to the art of weaving. There it is "the critical time" when the weaver must draw the yarn trough a gap that momentarily opens in the warp of the cloth being woven. Putting the two meanings together, one might understand kairos to refer to a passing instant when an opening appears which must be driven through with force if success is to be achieved (*Kaironomia*, 13).

In theology and in missiology, kairos is used describe the qualitative aspect of time, as opposed to chronos, which refers to the quantitative aspect of time. In the B'rith Chadasha, kairos means "the appointed time in the purpose of God", the time when God acts (e.g. Mark 1:15, the kairos is fulfilled).

10. Charles Van Engen comments:

Mission is also both missio futurorum and missio adventus. Missio futurorum has to do with the predictable results of God's mission as it takes place in human history. Thus missio futurorum extrapolates into the future the natural human results of the missions of the churches in the midst of world history.

But the story of mission is incomplete if it stops there. We must also include missio adventus. Adventus is the inbreaking of God, of Jesus Christ in the incarnation, of the Holy Spirit at Pentecost, of the Holy Spirit in and through the church. Missio adventus is, then, God's mission as it brings unexpected surprises, radical changes, new directions, almost unbelievable transformation in the midst of human life: personal, social, and structural. God works in the world through both missio futurorum and adventus. And in sorting out the theological issues of mission theology the mission theologian needs constantly to be asking about their difference and their interrelation" (*Mission on the Way*, 28).

11. Rom 13:11 (CJB).

For centuries, Jewish mission agencies have sponsored prophecy conferences and based their admonitions and appeals on prophetic scenarios. Messianic Judaism must go beyond such prophetic formulations, fascinations, and furors, instead shaping proleptic communities and institutions embodying and serving Israel's destiny.

Serving this destiny requires that we understand three key terms: *prolepsis, zikkaron,* and *anamnesis.* These name two reference points that plot out the pathway of faithfulness to our calling.

Prolepsis

"Prolepsis" is a Greek term that has passed into English usage because there is no suitable English equivalent. It refers to "the representation or assumption of a future act or development as being presently existing or accomplished."[12] Prolepsis names the future as dynamically present to shape and empower present thinking and conduct.

We must become a proleptic movement.[13] As a community of covenant responsibility, God is calling us to focus on an idealized Jewish future theologically and canonically developed in Scripture, clarified in communal discussion, and enshrined in our sacred calendar, liturgy, and ritual life. This idealized future is our destiny. It must live within us, and we must live for it. Because the Holy One holds us responsible to be signs, demonstrations, and catalysts of this proleptic future, we must become a community in whom the future has arrived. This is our first mustard seed idea. Its significance will become clearer as we discuss its companion.

Zikkaron/Anamnesis

Our second mustard seed comes from the other end of the same pod. It focuses on our relationship to the past rather than our relationship to the future.

The Hashivenu motto, "Bring us back to you, Hashem, and we shall return; renew our days as of old,"[14] was the seed of the Hashivenu vision. Proponents of the Hashivenu perspective have long known that contemporary

---

12. Webster's Third New International Dictionary.

13. As will become evident later in this paper, our role as the Messianic Jewish remnant of Israel demands that we embody a proleptic perspective.

14. Lam 5:21.

Messianic Jewish renewal requires that we reconnect with the holy Jewish past.

For a few years I have been maturing in my understanding of what this means. Now I see how this seminal idea is rooted in the biblical understanding of remembrance, as expressed in such terms as the Older Testamental *zikkaron*, and its Newer Testamental equivalent, anamnesis. I see as well that we will never comprehend who we are called to be and what we are called to do until we understand what the Bible means by "memory"—*zikkaron*, or anamnesis.

In 1962, Brevard Childs wrote *Memory and Tradition in Israel*,[15] a monograph on the nuances of how the Older Testament uses words from the *zkr* word group, words relating to remembrance. Childs helps us understand how, in God's design, the past is present among us, holding us accountable, transforming us, and propelling us forward.

The Holy Past Is Present as Catalytic Memory: Obedience

"Present Israel stands in an analogous situation with the people of the Exodus. Israel is still being tested [as to whether we will demonstrate by our obedience that we remember the saving acts of God and our covenantal obligations]."[16] Typically, we are commanded to do "this" because God did "that." A failure to obey is a failure to remember both what God has done, and a failure to respond as he demands. *Zikkaron*-memory is more than mere recalling. Such memory demands honoring God's redemptive mercies by embracing covenant obligations.[17]

Childs reminds us, "As in the past, Israel's history continues to be God's forcing his people to decide between life and death." We choose life by obedience, death by disobedience. "Memory plays a central role in making Israel constantly aware of the nature of God's benevolent acts as well as of her own covenantal pledge."[18] The keyword here is "pledge." Israel cannot fulfill its destiny nor honor its legacy apart from honoring this pledge. And if we are part of the Messianic Jewish remnant *of Israel*, this must be is true for our Union as well.

---

15. Childs, *Memory and Tradition in Israel*.

16. Ibid., 50–51.

17. This is especially highlighted in Deuteronomy.

18. Childs, *Memory and Tradition in Israel*, 51.

The Holy Past Is Present as Catalytic Memory: Our Holy Calendar

Childs reminds us that honoring our holy calendar is crucial to remembering the saving acts of God. And it is illegitimate to bypass our responsibility to honor these events and their attendant covenant obligations through recourse to personal choice or the liberty of the Spirit. When our calendar confronts us with God's saving acts and our history with him, the Spirit gives us liberty to do only one of two things: we may honor this holy occasion through our obedience, or desecrate it through our neglect. No third option is possible.

Giving an example, he states, "The festival of unleavened bread serves as a reminder to future generations of Yahweh's law. . . . Israel does not remember festivals, but observes them in order to remember [the saving acts of God and their attendant obligations]."[19] The purpose of honoring our holy calendar through ritual observance goes far beyond maintaining a sense of Jewish identity, or differentiating our identity from that of the church. The purpose of ritual observance is to honor God through honoring our covenant pledge, the binding oath of the children of Jacob.[20]

The Holy Past Is Present as Catalytic Memory: Once-for-All Yet Once Again

These redemptive events of the Older Testament shared a genuine chronology. They appeared in history at a given moment, which entry can be dated. There is a once-for-all character to these events in the sense that they never repeated themselves in the same fashion. Yet this does not exhaust the biblical concept. These determinative events are by no means static; they function merely as a beginning.

The Messianic Movement cannot and must not devolve into a religious equivalent of "The Society for Creative Anachronism," which is "an international organization dedicated to researching and re-creating the arts and skills of pre-seventeenth-century Europe."[21] We are not called to return to past glories. We must have a *living* relationship with the holy Jewish past shaped by who and where we are now in the flow of history. As Childs reminds us, "Each successive generation rewrites the past in terms of her own experience with the God who meets his people through the tradition. . . . These successive layers cannot be seen as subjective accretions covering the

19. Ibid., 55.

20. Exod 19:8; 24:7; Deut 29.

21. Found on the Internet at http://www.sca.org.

'real event.' The remembered event [in the now] is equally a valid witness to Israel's encounter with God as the first witness."[22]

We see new facets of the past as we grapple with the Holy One in the present, using the template of the past as a framework for self-understanding. When we encounter the story of the Exodus, we grapple with the God who redeemed us just as truly as did the Exodus generation. Our response now to the record of his saving mercies is as real and as consequential as was theirs, and the consequences of careless disregard, no less significant. We are as culpable for ingratitude as were they. "*Today*, if you hear his voice, harden not your hearts."[23]

The Holy Past Is Present as Catalytic Memory—with Judicial Power

The past is present in the event that we remember now, and our response to that memory is our response to the event itself and to the saving acts of God. "Each generation of Israel, living in a concrete situation within history, was challenged by God to obedient response through the medium of her tradition. Not a mere subjective reflection, but in the biblical category, a real event as a moment of redemptive time from the past initiated a genuine encounter in the present."[24] The events of Israel's redemption were such significant realizations in history of divine redemptive intervention that together with the rituals, rites, and commandments they entail, they have the authority to assess each successive generation of Israel, including ours. Our response to these events, rites, rituals, and obligations *is* our response to God. And we are accountable. Even though we may wish to avoid this accountability, this cannot be done.

The Haggadah, echoing the Talmud, agrees. It reminds us, "In every generation a man is bound to regard himself as though he personally had gone forth from Egypt."[25] Torah tells us of Passover, "This will be a day for you to remember [*v'haya hayom hazzeh lachem l'zikkaron*]."[26] The LXX translates *zikkaron* as "anamnesis." It is also the term used in the Newer Covenant underlying the phrase, "Do this in remembrance of me."[27]

22. Childs, *Memory and Tradition in Israel*, 89.

23. Heb 3:15, emphasis added. See 3:7–19; Ps 95:7.

24. Childs, *Memory and Tradition in Israel*, 83–84.

25. M. Pesachim 116b.

26. Exod 12:14.

27. 1 Cor 11:14.

The holy past is no mere collection of data to be recalled, but a continuing reality to be honored or desecrated. As a *zikkaron*, a holy memorial, the redemption from Egypt is so authoritatively present with us at the seder, that a cavalier attitude toward the seder marks as "The Wicked Son," unworthy of redemption anyone who fails to accord it due respect. In *zikkaron* or *anamnesis*, the holy past is present with power, assessing our response.

This is a new perspective for some of us and surely for most of our movement. It makes us wriggle with discomfort because it contravenes our axiomatic commitment to autonomy and voluntarism. We reflexively think ourselves to only be responsible when we choose to be so. The Bible, and our tradition disagrees; hence the discomfort.

That anamnesis has intrusive and unavoidable authority to judge our response is proven in Paul's discussion of the Lord's Table. In First Corinthians 11, he states that those who fail to discern the reality present among them in the *zikkaron*/anamnesis, who drink the Lord's cup and eat the bread in an unworthy manner, desecrate the body and blood of the Lord and eat and drink judgment upon themselves. He makes this point unambiguous when be states "This is why many among you are weak and sick, and some have died" (1 Cor 11:23–31).

Because of this numinous power of *zikkaron*/anemesis, honoring the holy Jewish past and the holy Jewish future as re-presented in the liturgy, ritual, and calendar of our people must become a lived reality in our movement. Our only other option is to dishonor God and to trifle with his holy saving acts. I think it no exaggeration to say that failure to properly honor our holy past, present as *zikkaron*/anamnesis, is just as truly an act of desecration as was the failure of the Corinthians to honor body and blood of Messiah present in their midst in the bread and the wine.

WEEDS

Sowing and growing the seeds of *zikkaron*/anamnesis and prolepsis is no uncontested operation. There are always weeds.[28] I will name four.

---

28. The American Heritage Dictionary defines "weed" as "A plant considered undesirable, unattractive, or troublesome, especially one growing where it is not wanted, as in a garden." Apparently the distinction between a plant or flower and a weed is subjective and culturally determined. The weeds I mention in this chapter are judged weeds because of how they hinder the growth of the mustard plants I believe us called to plant and cultivate for the kingdom. However, just as one man's weed is another man's wild flower, so our mustard plants will be judged weeds by others. Sitting under the authority of Holy Scripture, may we all remember that only God can unerringly separate the wheat from the weeds (Matt 13:24–30).

The Weed of Antinomianism[29]

For more than thirty years, in Jewish Yeshua-believer circles, Arnold Fruchtenbaum has held a unique position as a tightly organized and highly focused Bible teacher. The spores of his perspective on Torah observance continue to sprout stubborn weeds throughout our big tent.[30]

Fruchtenbaum says that the authority of the Mosaic Law has been annulled with the death of Messiah.[31] He teaches that although there are those who may choose to obey some aspect, or even many aspects, of the Torah, as a badge of Jewish identity or means of identity preservation and intergenerational transmission, such actions must only be treated as matters of personal preference, and never regarded as either obligations or communal norms.[32] For Fruchtenbaum and the Dispensationalism he champions, Torah obedience no longer has mandatory force. The one exception he allows is for those commandments required by Newer Testament teaching, by what he terms "the Law of Christ."[33]

It is right that we respect Fruchtenbaum and others like him who have worked hard and served well. However, spores spread by his brand of Dispensational theology posit the nullification of the Torah of Moses as a mandated standard of Jewish practice, and substitute voluntarism, personal volition, and a certain perspective on New Covenant standards in the place formerly occupied by communal Jewish covenantal responsibility. We might even consider this a form of neo-Marcionism, under which the expired, defunct, and impotent Older Testamental statues, ordinances, and commandments of God are replaced by a more "enlightened" canon: the Law of Messiah.

If we are only under the Law of Messiah, in what ways, beyond simply familial nostalgia and genetic markers, are we, our calling, and our legacy, actually, rather than simply theologically, different from other Yeshua believers? This perspective converts our covenantal Jewish identity into a genetic

29. Antinomianism in the Messianic Jewish Movement refers to the denial that Torah-based covenant faithfulness is a divine mandate for Messianic Jews.

30. "The Big Tent" is a prevailing metaphor in the UMJC used to describe the tolerant and inclusive ethos which the executive committee seeks to nurture in the Union. This leads to a climate that tolerates more diversity than some would prefer.

31. "The Law is a unit comprised of 613 commandments, and all of it has been invalidated. There is no commandment that has continued beyond the cross of Christ. . . . It has completely ceased to function as an authority over individuals" (Fruchtenbaum, *Hebrew Christianity*, 86).

32. Fruchtenbaum, "Messianic Congregations May Exist Within the Body of Messiah as Long as They Don't Function Contrary to the New Testament," 124–27.

33. Ibid, 121–22.

claim nurtured by nostalgia and collections of memorabilia, sustained by periodic get-togethers with other Jews.

Adherents to such a perspective are exiles from ongoing Jewish life and community, consigned to remember Zion by the waters of a strange theological Babylon. But how can we sing the songs of Zion in such a foreign land, exiled from the life of Torah, our spiritual homeland, and from the community to which we are covenantally joined?

Living under the Newer Covenant Law of Messiah, while treating the life of Torah obedience as "nice if that's your style," substitutes the cut glass of nostalgia for the bright diamond of Jewish covenantal life and community. Abandoning Israel's call to covenant faithfulness dooms the Messianic Jewish remnant to irrelevance. Instead, we condemn our families, our congregations, and our entire movement to eventual assimilation, while nullifying our capacity to assist wider Israel in achieving and fulfilling its foreordained destiny.

The Weed of Anti-Judaism

Anti-Judaism, a second noxious weed, should not be confused with anti-Semitism. Speaking of the writings of the church fathers, Lee Martin McDonald makes the distinction: "What at times may appear in the Church Fathers to be a reference to race—that is, Jews being condemned as a people or nation because of their race, is most often a reference to their *religious* identity rather than their ethnic origins."[34] While I am not saying that the Messianic Jewish movement has inherited anti-Semitic assumptions from the Jewish missions culture and the church, I am saying that we are frequently knee deep in anti-Judaism.

Anti-Judaism rises full-grown in Justin Martyr's *Dialogue with Trypho the Jew*, where he states: "And along with Abraham we [Christians] shall inherit the holy land, when we shall receive the inheritance for an endless eternity, being children of Abraham through the like faith. . . . Accordingly, He promises to him a nation of similar faith, God fearing, righteous . . . but it is not you [Jews], *in whom is no faith*."[35]

Notice how he characterizes the Jews as a people "in whom is no faith." This weed, widespread in the Jewish mission world, has projected its spores into our big tent.[36]

---

34. McDonald, "Anti-Judaism in the Early Church Fathers," 215.

35. Material found online at http://www.theologicalstudies.citymax.com/articles/article/1546226/17516.htm, emphasis added.

36. The "Big Tent" is a metaphor used by the leadership of the UMJC to describe

About two years ago I received an inquiry from the then-director of the Toronto Jewish Mission. He was a very nice man, mannerly and courteous. He wrote me to take sharp issue with a statement on the Hashivenu website. Notice his presuppositions, and see if you don't hear Justin Martyr in the wings. But first, the offending comment from our website.

> When we say that Messianic Judaism is "a Judaism," we are also acknowledging the existence of other "Judaisms." We do not deny their existence, their legitimacy, or their value. We are not the sole valid expression of Judaism with all else a counterfeit. We recognize our kinship with other Judaisms and believe that we have much of profound importance to learn from them, as well as something vitally important to share with them.

The director responded as follows:

> How does one recognize the "legitimacy" and "value" of a religious movement that, at its core, denies the all-sufficient atoning work of Yeshua, the Son of G-d. Given rabbinic Judaism's two millennia rejection of Yeshua, in what way does Messianic Judaism have "kinship with" these expressions of Judaism?
>
> For example, how do I reconcile that view with the words of Yeshua? "He who is not with Me is against Me, and he who does not gather with Me scatters abroad" (Mt. 12:30).
>
> "You know neither Me nor My Father. If you had known Me, you would have known My Father also" (Jn. 8:19). How should I understand the following text in light of the core value statement above?
>
> "I marvel that you are turning away so soon from Him who called you in the grace of Christ, to a different gospel, which is not another; but there are some who trouble you and want to pervert the gospel of Christ. But even if we, or an angel from heaven, preach any other gospel to you than what we have preached to you, let him be accursed" (Gal. 1:6–8).
>
> Stuart, if modern Judaism (Orthodox, Conservative, Reform, et. al.) denies Yeshua, in what sense can one say that these expressions of Judaism hold equal legitimacy and value with Messianic Judaism which embraces Yeshua as the Son of G-d and as Messiah and Saviour? However much the various denominations within modern Judaism differ, at their core they are all opposed to Yeshua.[37]

the attempt to create and maintain in the Union a collegial diversity, allowing for and respecting differing interpretations of how pathways of Messianic Jewish faithfulness are to be understood and pursued.

37. Private e-mail correspondence from Reverend David Daniels to Stuart

Many in the Jewish mission world join this director insisting that those who claim to be faithful to Christ must unambiguously denounce rabbinic Judaism. Derek Leman bearded this lion in its own den when he critiqued his colleagues on this very point at the 2006 meeting of the Lausanne Consultation for Jewish Evangelism:

> Many in LCJE are still infected with anti-Judaism while at the same time being pro-Jewish. It is as if we imagine you can love Jews and oppose the religion that has preserved Jewish identity. It is Judaism that has held Jewish people together, even though many do not practice it. Judaism the religion is what led to the succession of Brit Milahs (sic) through the ages, entering Jewish boys into the covenant of God. It is Judaism that led Jews to marry other Jews and not assimilate into the surrounding cultures. It is Judaism that has caused Jewish people to remain distinct, keeping Sabbath and dietary law as God commanded in the Bible. Without Judaism there would clearly be no Jewish people.

Thus, when God tells us, "All Israel will be saved," we should ask, "Who is Israel?" If our generation is the one that receives the fulfillment of this promise, how will God recognize Israel? If it is a generation hundreds of years from now, how will God recognize Israel? The only answer consistent through history since the time Jesus wept over Jerusalem and Paul declared that all Israel would be saved is that these will be a people reflecting rabbinic Judaism. Rabbinic Judaism is God's ordained instrument to preserve Israel for the last days and for God's restoration.

Seen in that light, *rabbinic Judaism is not quite the enemy many of us have made it out to be.* Ought we not to work with God and not against him? Should our methods encourage Jews to abandon the distinctives of rabbinic Judaism?[38]

The views Derek Leman decries are widespread and deeply entrenched in the Jewish missions world, and are widespread even if not universal. In recent years, Mitch Glaser, president of Chosen People Ministries, has been going through his own shifting of paradigms. This has brought him closer to the Hashivenu perspective than either he or we would have deemed possible even a few years ago. Dr. Glaser spoke at length of his changing views at the same Lausanne Consultation where Derek Leman presented the material quoted above.

Dauermann, September 14, 2005. The letter and Reverend Daniels' discussion of it may be accessed at http://www.newcovenanthouse.org/feature20060104a.shtml.

38. Leman, "Judaism and New Testament Faith" (emphasis added).

The position Glaser now advocates is by no means identical to that expressed by myself or colleagues like Mark Kinzer, nor does it replicate Hashivenu's perspective point by point. Nevertheless, his new views are highly compatible with and sympathetic toward ours.

On the issue of ecclesiology, Glaser states, "We are one in Christ, but not the same. We may be *one new man* (or woman?), but that is only one part of the truth as we are still spiritually distinct—for God marked the distinction between Jews and gentiles."[39] These are matters not normally discussed in polite LCJE circles, and are even hot button issues in the UMJC.

In his paper, Glaser speaks to three broad issues: evangelism, identity, and community. Here is what he says of identity:

> With regard to Identity, let me start by saying that I am beginning to believe that what some of our critics are saying is true—that we actually often do turn Jewish people into non-Jews by introducing them to Christ. We sometimes think that merely *getting* Jewish people saved is what evangelism is all about and it is not. That is not biblical—it is biblical reductionism and on a fast track towards Gnosticism! There is more to human beings than the soul. As Jews, we are an earthly people, attached to family, community and vitally interested in *Tikkun Olam*—the healing of our world.[40]

Relating these convictions to the area of evangelism, Glaser goes further, stating:

> In fact, by viewing ourselves as Jews, or by recognizing that we hope the Jewish people who come to Jesus will remain Jews and live within the Jewish community, [we will be caused] to rethink the manner and methods of our evangelistic approach.
>
> Effective Jewish evangelism should produce *better* Jews—both in their love for God, their holy lifestyle and in their identity as Jews. Again, this type of thinking will impact our strategy for evangelism, change the way we present the Gospel to Jewish people and impact the manner of our discipleship efforts.
>
> Without realizing it, I believe, primarily through omission, we have encouraged Jewish believers in Jesus to live detached from the Jewish community and eventually to become aliens within our own community.[41]

39 Glaser, "Towards a New Model for Jewish Evangelism in the 21st Century."

40. Ibid., 15.

41. Ibid., 18.

This entire quotation is significant, and for me, gratifying. But notice especially his phrase, "aliens within our own community." For Glaser too, as for Hashivenu, "the Jewish people are us, not them." On the subject of community, Glaser's words to the LCJE constitute an act of contrition. And he is calling the mission community to repent as well.

Glaser addresses how rethinking our relationship to the Jewish community gives rise to new possibilities that were formerly categorically excluded.

> More and more I am convinced that Messianic Jews have told themselves they cannot be part of the Jewish community and that this has become somewhat of a self-fulfilling prophecy.
> . . . I do not intend to paint a rosy picture that even suggests that all is OK between missionaries to the Jews who are Jewish and with the mainline Jewish community. This is not true. But, I do believe that if we want, relationships can improve without our needing to compromise on our message and stand for Jesus within the Jewish community. However, we might think through how we take that stand. Especially if we live within the community and are not simply "evangelistic" visitors to the Jewish communities we hope to reach for Yeshua.[42]

I am tempted to continue quoting Glaser's monumental paper, having collected thirteen pages of quotations that excited me. I am excited not simply because of the changes evident in my long-term friend, nor simply because he is reflecting the ethos and principles of Hashivenu. I am most excited because his own transformation, that of his organization, and his call to the Jewish missions world to do likewise confirms what I have long felt, a foundational conviction underlying this chapter: that we are living in changing times. The Spirit of God is up to something parallel to issues we in Hashivenu have been championing since our founding.

Without diminishing in any degree our excitement over these developments, we must exercise restraint. We need to remember that Mitch is still in process, that his views while not identical to our own are stigmatized minority views in Jewish mission circles, where stigma often attaches to what challenges prevailing practice and opinion. In addition it is one thing to call for changes and another to succeed in their implementation. It is reasonable for Mitch to expect a backlash and retrenchment on the part of mission leaders and structures seeking to justify their own policies through denouncing new paradigms as "dangerous" or even "heretical." The majority viewpoint in Jewish mission circles is antithetical to the views Glaser

42. Ibid., 26.

reported. Echoes of this majority viewpoint persist even in Messianic Jewish congregational circles, creating a kind of drag that slows down our momentum toward necessary change.

The majority view is more weed than wheat. Having considered the weeds of antinomianism and anti-Judaism, we turn now to yet another.

The Weed of Anti-Rabbinism

Anti-rabbinism is opposition to "the rabbis" as a class. The way the term "the rabbis" is used in Messianic Jewish circles demonstrates a polemical disdain fit only to be uprooted and discarded. A quick search of the Jews for Jesus website using the search term "religion of the rabbis" turned up the following:

> When I talk about being a Jew, I'm talking about something that is different from the religion of the rabbis. I'll be quick to tell you that I do not follow the Jewish religion.
>
> You might be surprised that the Jewish Bible, the T'nach, does not mention rabbis. According to Scripture, the priesthood was to be in charge. What is now considered "traditional Judaism" began at the Council of Yavneh, when a group of rabbis met and made certain decisions in light of the destruction of the Temple and the growth of Christianity. What decisions they made, we can only surmise. But after Yavneh, rabbis were in control of the religion.[43]

Regardless of the degree to which one agrees or disagrees with the author's historical reconstruction, we find here an appalling categorical hostility toward Judaism, toward the rabbis, and their religion.[44] Can the rabbis be wrong? Certainly! Has the rabbinical establishment been almost entirely opposed to Jewish Yeshua-faith? Surely! But should we therefore distrust all rabbis and all rabbinic writings as is commonly the case in our thinking, discussion, and polemical rhetoric? Must we consider the rabbis and their teachings to be guilty until proven innocent? Should we consider all of them to be seducers and enemies of Yeshua-faith, to be avoided by all who would exercise due caution? Must we assume, as some in the mission culture have stated, that those seeking irenic relationships with rabbis do so

---

43. http://www.jewsforjesus.org/publications/newsletter/2004_03/message moishe. This posting has now been removed from the web, and I would say rightly so!

44. I demonstrate that this construction oversimplifies and misrepresents the events of which it speaks in the second chapter of my dissertation, *The Rabbi as a Surrogate Priest*, 159–91.

only to pander for approval, prepared to sell out the gospel as a means to that end? None of this works for me. In fact, I am nauseated by this particularly noxious weed.

Such antipathy to "the rabbis" extends beyond distrust to disdain. A typical mission publication states, "Unfortunately, most rabbis have accepted the role of an apologist for Judaism, rather than a spiritual authority who can aid in or inspire a true encounter with God."[45] Will you join me in finding this comment presumptuous? How do we know the motivations of "most rabbis?" Where do we sign up for a dose of such omniscience concerning the motivations of the majority of an entire class of people? I submit that we are hearing are echoes of Justin Martyr and the *adversos Judaeos* tradition.

We ought not comfort ourselves that these are someone else's statements. A tendency to axiomatically suspect and distance ourselves from the rabbis and their religion persists in our movement. On every level, I find this to be a wrong course of action.

Dr. Michael L. Brown is a Jewish believer in Jesus who, while not a member of the Messianic Jewish congregational movement, is much read in our circles. One of his blog postings includes ample evidence of the weeds of categorical anti-Judaism and anti-rabbinism persisting in and around our ranks, broadly considered.[46] He states that he has "come to the conclusion that rabbinic traditions have little or no place in our private lives or public services." Brown continues, "While it is one thing to follow the rabbinic calendar as a matter of convenience, it is another thing entirely to pray the prayers of the rabbis or utilize their varied religious expressions and methods." He asks, "How can we pray the prayers of men whose very faith presupposes that Yeshua is not the Messiah?"[47] These positions are not his alone. His views are very much present in our movement, and for some, influential.

I am spreading the word: the term *the rabbis* should not be used as an epithet of scorn. We need to recognize and repudiate the tradition of anti-Judaism and anti-rabbinism as weeds, not wheat. Uproot them. These attitudes are only fit to be thrown into the fire and burned.

---

45. http://www.jewsforjesus.org/publications/havurah/5_4/question.

46. Michael Brown is knowledgeable, well-educated, and bright. A much published author, he also contributes to a wide variety of online communities including the Huffington Post. He is what might be termed a post-Judaism Hebrew Christian.

47. http://blog.myspace.com/index.cfm?fuseaction=blog.view&friendID=86182827&blogID=189155954.

The Weed of Illusory, Culturally Neutral Biblicism

It is healthy for people to differ. However, when doing so, some will set forth their own position as biblical and those with which they differ as either unbiblical or merely cultural.[48] What such persons fail to recognize is that all parties in such debates perceive and interpret the Bible in keeping with their own cultural conditioning and communal frame of reference. Those challenging others to forsake a "rabbinic position" for their own, which they view to be "the biblical view," are actually asking that people accept a Calvary Chapel perspective, a Neo-Pentecostal perspective, a New Apostolic Reformation perspective, a Dispensational perspective, a Reformed perspective, etc., as an alternative. It is not the Bible against culture. Rather, it is almost invariably one culture, tradition, or party line against another.

Of course I am not arguing against the authority of Scripture, nor against the need to ground and test our views through reference to the Bible. I am not even arguing for the superiority of one position over another. But I am saying that people arguing for "the biblical perspective" are often really arguing from and for the perspective of some culture or subgroup to which they conform.

Whether our rabbi is Judah the Prince or Derek Prince, Lewis Sperry Chafer or John Calvin, we all have our rabbis, and our own Oral Torah. So let us be done with naïve and self-congratulatory one-upmanship. Let's call a moratorium on dismissing a tradition-oriented Messianic Judaism as cultural in contrast to a presumed cultureless Biblicism. Such does not exist. It never has and never will.

The careful reader will note that these seeds and weeds all have one thing in common. All relate to the path of obedience to which God has called the Jewish people, including ourselves. It is a weed-strewn path between

48. For example, Michael Brown, in his blog posting, and teaching ministry, contrasts Judaism with "biblical truth," and seems unaware or unprepared to acknowledge that his vision of true spirituality is a particular brand of Pentecostal revivalism. He acts as though what he advocates is simply biblical, spiritual and life-giving, as opposed to rabbinic Judaism and Messianic Judaism influenced by it, which he views to be categorically "man-made" and "fleshly." He says, "Let me state clearly that the very best rabbinic traditions are still man-made, and as far as man-made religion goes, Yeshua spoke with unmistakable clarity: 'That which is born of the flesh is flesh; that which is born of the Spirit is spirit. . . . And the flesh [i.e., human effort] profits nothing. It is the Spirit that gives life" (John 3:6; 6:63). If we are going to worship and serve God in the Spirit, flesh-born traditions can only get in the way'" (Brown, Ibid.). Does Dr. Brown imagine that the traditions of approach, practice, and emphasis with which he aligns himself are purely God-given and not at all man-made? Apparently so. The fact is, God can and does work through man-made traditions. Traditions may or may not be God-honoring, but all of them are man-made. There is no other kind.

faithful response to the *zikkaron*/anamnesis of a holy past, the legacy of faithful Israel, and faithful proleptic service to a holy future, Israel's destiny. The Messianic Jewish remnant can only be faithful by honoring that legacy with our obedience, and serving that destiny by proleptically conforming our lives and institutions to an anticipated consummation.

We turn now to considering that consummation and our remnant responsibility.

THE MESSIANIC JEWISH REMNANT

I identify the Messianic Jewish movement as part of the Messianic Jewish remnant of Israel.

It will help to first differentiate between two uses of the term. Dan Johnson demonstrates that Scripture presents two different modalities of remnant identity, one being survivors of a time of judgment, the other being the seed from which God's continuing purposes will be realized. He points out how the verb form used in Genesis 7:23, "only Noach was *left* [*vayisha'er akh noakh*], along with those who were with him in the ark," is related to the noun *sh'erit,* "remnant." This is the first appearance of the verb in Scripture. Just as Noach/Noah, his family, and the animals in the ark were a sign of God's continuing purpose for the earth, and instruments for its realization, so the eschatological remnant of Israel discussed in Romans 9–11 is meant to be a sign, demonstration, and catalyst of God's continuing purposes for the Jewish people.[49]

The survivors of judgment motif is evident in Romans 9:27: "And Isaiah cries out concerning Israel, 'Though the number of the children of Israel were like the sand of the sea, only a remnant of them will be saved.'" This in turn references Isaiah 10:22, a word of temporary judgment: "For though your people Israel were like the sand of the sea, only a remnant of them will return. Destruction is decreed, overflowing with righteousness."

The other use of "remnant," as a seed sign of hope, is apparent in Isaiah 11:10–16 (CJB).

> On that day the root of Yishai, which stands as a banner for the peoples—the Goyim will seek him out, and the place where he rests will be glorious. On that day Adonai will raise his hand again, a second time, to reclaim the remnant of his people who remain from Ashur, Egypt, Patros, Ethiopia, 'Eilam, Shin'ar, Hamat and the islands in the sea. He will hoist a banner for the Goyim, assemble the dispersed of Isra'el, and gather

49. Johnson, "The Structure and Meaning of Romans 11."

the scattered of Y'hudah from the four corners of the earth. Efrayim's jealousy will cease—those who harass Y'hudah will be cut off, Efrayim will stop envying Y'hudah, and Y'hudah will stop provoking Efrayim. They will swoop down on the flank of the P'lishtim to the west. Together they will pillage the people to the east—they will put out their hand over Edom and Mo'av, and the people of 'Amon will obey them. Adonai will dry up the gulf of the Egyptian Sea. He will shake his hand over the [Euphrates] River to bring a scorching wind, dividing it into seven streams and enabling people to cross dryshod. There will be a highway for the remnant of his people who are still left from Ashur, just as there was for Isra'el when he came out from the land of Egypt.

This seed nature of the remnant is also evident in Isaiah 37:31–33 (CJB).

Meanwhile, the remnant of the house of Y'hudah that has escaped will again take root downward and bear fruit upward; for a remnant will go out from Yerushalayim, those escaping will go out from Mount Tziyon. The zeal of Adonai-Tzva'ot will accomplish this. Therefore this is what Adonai says concerning the king of Ashur: "He will not come to this city or even shoot an arrow there; he will not confront it with a shield or erect earthworks against it."

Although here, as in Isaiah 11, the term *remnant* denotes survivors of judgment, the second theme of the remnant as a seed of hope is also evident. John Paul Heil demonstrates how Romans 9–11 focuses on this second usage of the term remnant, and how the Apostle uses the term as a sign of hope even in Romans 9:27–29, normally viewed as a judgment text.

Heil shows that standard translations of Romans 9:27–29 obscure the strong note of hope in Paul's language, and fail to heed intertextual voices. Contrary to those who see the text as a judgment text, Heil views Romans 9:27–29 as foreshadowing the climactic note of victory, "and so all Israel will be saved," in Romans 11:26. After meticulous exegesis, he offers this translation of Romans 9:27–29, revealing Paul's use of remnant as a sign of hope:

But Isaiah cries out on behalf of (not "concerning") Israel (= still unbelieving Israel, not those from the Jews (9:24) who believe in Christ): "If the number of the sons of Israel be (not 'were') as the sand of the sea (which they will be in accord with God's word of promise in Gen 16:13; 22:17; 28:14; 32:121), surely, at least (not 'only') a remnant will be saved! For definitely deciding a word (that Israel will be as numerous as the sand of the sea), the Lord will accomplish (it) on the earth" (Isa 10:22–23; 28:22b;

> Hos 2:1a). And as Isaiah had foretold (and still foretells), "If the Lord Sabaoth had not left for us (= the unbelieving majority of Israel) a seed (= a remnant who will believe and be saved), we would have become like Sodom and we would have been made like Gomorrah" (Isa 1:9).[50]

Heil highlights what is often missed, that the remnant is a sign of hope concerning the divine purpose *for the rest of Israel*. This remnant is not simply the residue left after a time of judgment, nor a sign that there are others who comprise the remnant as well, but rather, this remnant is the earnest of God's continuing purposes *for Israel as a whole*.

Following both Johnson and Heil, I use the term *remnant* to indicate that communal seed of hope that is meant to serve as a sign, demonstration, and catalyst of God's gracious purpose for all Israel. Serving as this sign, demonstration, and catalyst is the job description of the Messianic Jewish remnant.

We may differentiate between a variety of Jewish remnants. What might be termed the General Jewish remnant, fully known only to God, is his sum-total Jewish remnant in the earth, objects of his grace, and precious in his sight. This includes those who have gone before, and those who will come after us. The Messianic Jewish remnant is the body of Yeshua-believing Messianic Jews within that group seeking, however imperfectly, to live in continuity with Jewish life and community. Not all Jewish believers are part of the Messianic Jewish remnant in this sense, although all are part of the General Jewish remnant. I reserve the term "Messianic Jewish remnant" for those Jewish Yeshua-believers seeking to live in continuity with Jewish life and community.

Other Jewish Yeshua-believers, living assimilated Jewish lives in churches, are also part of the General Jewish remnant, with the exception of those Jewish people who seek to obscure or deny their Jewish identity. It seems unjust to consider those who disidentify with the Jewish people as part of the remnant of Israel. We ought not say that the Messianic Jewish remnant plus other Jewish Yeshua believers is the sum total of the General Jewish remnant. My caution is due to Yeshua's warnings that many who are first will be last, and the last first,[51] and to God's warning to Elijah as repeated by Paul, that the true extent of the remnant is greater than we can know.[52] Therefore, claiming remnant status does not entitle us to deny that

---

50. Heil, "From Remnant to Seed of Hope for Israel: Romans 9:26–29," 719–20 (parentheses in the original).

51. Matt 19:30, 20:16; Mark 10:31; Luke 13:30.

52. Rom 11:4; 1 Kgs 19:18.

status to others known only to God. To insist on doing so is to repeat Elijah's presumptuous error.

While some write more extensively on remnant theology, discussing matters such as the role of the remnant in the Millennium, the role of the 144,00, and related issues, these are not my concern here. My concern is a missiological one: to address the responsibilities of the Messianic Jewish remnant now, especially regarding our relationship with rest of the Jewish world.[53]

THE MESSIANIC JEWISH REMNANT AND OLDER EXPIRING PARADIGMS

Although most agree that the Jewish people will experience a spiritual renewal, a major eschatological revival, in the latter days, few have asked, "What shape will this renewal take?" To answer this question, we must ask another: "What are the consummating purposes for Israel of which the Messianic Jewish remnant is called to be a sign, demonstration, and catalyst?"

Before addressing both of these questions, first let us consider why current paradigms are not working and deserve to expire. Among these expiring paradigms evident especially in the Jewish missions world is one that conceives of outreach as primarily a matter of making the sale, or closing the deal. In our evangelicalized culture, we are too wedded to a sales model of outreach.[54] We make our pitch to the person we are witnessing to, who is called a "contact," a term borrowed from the world of sales. We know we have closed the "sale" when the "contact" prays to "accept the Messiah as their personal savior." Forgive me, but this sounds like a person buying a car and signing on the dotted line.

---

53. I am foregoing interacting with the excellent recent discussions of remnant theology such as those by Wright, *Jesus and the Victory of God*; Elliot, *The Survivors of Israel*; and Pitre, *Jesus, the Tribulation, and the End of the Exile*. My focus is both narrower and more general than these fine treatments, restricted to missiological concerns pertaining to the present role of the Messianic Jewish remnant, especially in view of the general picture of Jewish eschatological faithfulness and fulfillment I find in Scripture.

54. In referring to standard mission approaches, I use the term "outreach," because missions generally see themselves as extensions of the church's witness to the Jewish people, and accordingly use the term "outreach." In our postmissionary model, we use the term "inreach" to name our representation of Yeshua-faith to the wider Jewish world, because we see ourselves within that community. In discussing standard missional approaches I will use the term "outreach." In discussing what is coming to be called "The Emerging Messianic Jewish Paradigm" growing from Mark Kinzer's *Postmissionary Messianic Judaism,* I will revert to using the term most appropriate to our context and approach, that is, "inreach."

Another inadequate concept of outreach sees it primarily in terms of increasing the size of our congregational population. Outreach then becomes not so much a matter of sales, as a matter of advertising. Here again, the emphasis is on numbers, on statistics, on the bottom line.

Confrontational approaches are equally unsatisfactory. These seem to vitiate the very nature of the kingdom message, robbing it of its relational spirit. Such approaches are overly message-centered, usually treating relational matters as secondary, temporary, and purely utilitarian. I remember a woman telling me that she could always expect a phone call from "her missionary" on Thursday night, because Friday was the day when statistical reports had to be handed in to mission officials. This kind of utilitarian approach that cares about the message, while treating the recipients as a means to statistical ends, is far from satisfactory. We instinctively sense such approaches do violence to the deeply relational nature the kingdom of God.

These approaches all reduce the gospel to a propositional message suitable for bumper stickers. Mitch Glaser wisely critiques this widespread error:

> Some of us would perhaps define evangelism as communicating the Gospel message and stop there! Others, like myself, might suggest that that there are issues beyond the communication of the Gospel message—such as follow-up, ongoing discipleship and congregational planting which are also part of the evangelistic enterprise and that the separation between these critical activities is somewhat artificial. [Glaser later adds issues of identity and community as being likewise intrinsic to the evangelistic enterprise].[55]

In addition to rejecting sales-oriented, reductionist models, we must also reject approaches to Jewish evangelism that treat as axiomatic Judaism's supposed spiritual bankruptcy and inability to meet the spiritual needs of its adherents, and postulate the certain and universal perdition of all Jews except those who welcome the evangelist's message. Even on purely pragmatic grounds, predicating one's gospel "pitch" on selling one's "contact" on the inadequacy of his own religious heritage severely limits one's pool of "buyers." As for the "find heaven/avoid hell approach," although axiomatic in Jewish missions, one fails to find it represented in the preaching of the apostles. And claiming to know the full census of perdition entails a claim to omniscience not likely to find favor in the postmodern world, nor, I would guess, with the Holy One of Israel.

55. Glaser, "Towards a New Model for Jewish Evangelism in the 21st Century," 15, 14–29.

This gospel normally presented to Jewish people under the standard Jewish missions approach is anything but good news for the Jews. It assumes that the Jewish person receiving the witness is most likely the first person in fifty generations of his family to avoid hell.[56] How is such a message good news for the Jews? It is the worst possible news for the Jews, except when the persons receiving the witness are narcissists. Only a narcissist will experience delight in being saved, while suppressing awareness of the abysmal and certain eternal fate suffered by countless forbears and family members. This is not good news for the Jews, and not an approach likely to win many. In the main, the approach fails, and deservedly so.[57]

All of these approaches are substandard products of a marketing mentality. Very few are likely to purchase such a product, which is likely to expire on the shelf. In our post-Enlightenment, post-Christian, postmodern world, tomorrow's Messianic Judaism must replace these caricatures with a postmissionary paradigm.

CHANGING THE PARADIGM

Is there a better paradigm for effective Messianic Jewish "inreach" than those we have inherited from the Jewish missions culture? There most certainly is. Beginning with a succinct definition, we should define Messianic Jewish inreach as *the Messianic Jewish remnant being what it should be, and doing what it should do with respect to God's consummating purposes for the descendants of Jacob.*

What is it that we should be and do? Despite much remnant rhetoric in our circles, little if any attention has been paid to the responsibilities of the Messianic Jewish remnant. They may be outlined as follows:

1. The Messianic Jewish remnant must serve as a *sign* that God has a continuing purpose for the Jewish people.

2. The Messianic Jewish remnant must serve as a *demonstration* of that purpose—a proleptic preview.

3. The Messianic Jewish remnant must serve as a *catalyst* assisting greater Israel toward that divine purpose.[58]

---

56. Fifty generations is computed as 2,000 years at 40 years per generation.

57. I will later discuss other motivations for mission to the Jews which I view to be more biblical and appropriate. See the discussion of Johannes Verkuyl below.

58. This breakdown of the responsibilities of the remnant is based on Johnson, "The Structure and Meaning of Romans 11," discussed earlier in this chapter.

GOD'S CONSUMMATING PURPOSES FOR THE DESCENDANTS OF JACOB

What does Scripture say about God's consummating purposes for the descendants of Jacob?

Repeatedly and often, Scripture portrays God's ultimate purpose for Israel in terms of national repentance-renewal[59] evidenced in a return to Torah-based covenant faithfulness. Messiah's centrality to this scenario is not a Newer Covenant addition, but a datum established in the Older Testament.[60] Frequently, this return to covenant faithfulness is linked to a Jewish return to the Land. Three key texts best portray these interconnected eschatological expectations.

The first text is the thirtieth chapter of Deuteronomy. Notice the repeated linkage of spiritual repentance-renewal, return to the Land, and covenant obedience.

> When the time arrives that all these things have come upon you, both the blessing and the curse which I have presented to you; and you are there among the nations to which *Adonai* your God has driven you; then, at last, you will start thinking about what has happened to you; and you will return to Adonai your God and pay attention to what he has said, which will be exactly what I am ordering you to do today—you and your children, with all your heart and all your being. At that point, Adonai your God will reverse your exile and show you mercy; he will return and gather you from all the peoples to which *Adonai* your God scattered you. If one of yours was scattered to the far end of the sky, Adonai your God will gather you even from there; he will go there and get you. Adonai your God will bring you back into the land your ancestors possessed, and you will possess it; he will make you prosper there, and you will become even more numerous than your ancestors. Then Adonai your God will circumcise your hearts and the hearts of your children, so that you will love *Adonai* your God with all your heart and all your being, and thus you will live . . . you will return and pay attention to what Adonai says and obey all his mitzvot which I am giving you today. Then Adonai your God will give you more than enough in everything you set out to do—the fruit of your body, the fruit of your livestock, and the fruit of your land will all do

---

59. I have chosen here to use the compound noun "repentance-renewal" because the two always accompany each other, although the order varies. They are also inseparably conjoined in the texts under discussion.

60. See, among others, Jer 30:9; Ezek 34:23; 37:24–25; Hos 3:5.

well; for *Adonai* will once again rejoice to see you do well, just as he rejoiced in your ancestors. "not needed However, all this will happen only if you pay attention to what Adonai your God says, so that you obey his mitzvot and regulations which are written in this book of the Torah, if you turn to Adonai your God with all your heart and all your being.[61]

Another example is the very familiar and central Messianic Jewish text, Jeremiah 31:31–33, where Jewish spiritual renewal is evidenced by a return to Torah obedience.

"Here, the days are coming," says Adonai, "when I will make a new covenant with the house of Isra'el and with the house of Y'hudah. It will not be like the covenant I made with their fathers on the day I took them by their hand and brought them out of the land of Egypt; because they, for their part, violated my covenant, even though I, for my part, was a husband to them," says Adonai. "For this is the covenant I will make with the house of Isra'el after those days," says Adonai: "I will put my Torah within them and write it on their hearts; I will be their God, and they will be my people."

Perhaps the strongest prophetic text on this end-time renewal, return to the land, and return to covenant faithfulness, is found in Ezekiel 36, beginning at verse 24. This text reads like a checklist of Jewish eschatology.

Ezekiel 36:24—*"For I will take you from among the nations, and gather you out of all the countries, and will bring you into your own land."* (Regathering: Most Messianic Jews are prepared to say "Amen" to this: Hallelujah, we believe in the regathering of our people to the Land.) 36:25—*"And I will sprinkle clean water upon you, and ye shall be clean: from all your filthiness, and from all your idols, will I cleanse you."* (Renewal: We are likewise prepared to say "Amen" to this national spiritual renewal as well.) 36:26—*"A new heart also will I give you, and a new spirit will I put within you; and I will take away the stony heart out of your flesh, and I will give you a heart of flesh."* (We say "Hallelujah" to this as well: national regeneration . . . a new heart of flesh instead of a heart of stone.)

But then things get "difficult"—at least for some of us wedded to old and expiring paradigms: 36:27—*"And I will put my Spirit within you, and cause you to walk in my statutes, and ye shall keep mine ordinances, and do them."* (Here is where many apply their brakes. But is it not clear that this spiritual renewal, this return to the Land, is evidenced and accompanied by a return to the commandments God gave to our people? This is all signed,

61. Deut 30:1–6, 8–10.

sealed, and delivered through an *inclusio*, a verse ending this section which echoes what was said at the beginning of the section.) 36:28—*"And ye shall dwell in the land that I gave to your fathers; and ye shall be my people, and I will be your God."*

Nothing could be clearer: repentance/renewal, return to the Land, and return to covenant faithfulness are all joined in Scripture. Yeshua is central in this scenario, and not as a New Covenant add-on. The Older Testament itself establishes this inseparable centrality (see Jer 30:9; Ezek 34:23; 37:24–25; Hos 3:5). There is no end-time consummation for the Jewish people apart from Messiah. And there is no gospel appropriate to the Jewish people that separates Messiah from this end-time consummation. As the Messianic Jewish remnant, our message is not simply "Yeshua only." Our message is *this* Yeshua, the one through whom all of this is accomplished and who is glorified by these things coming to pass. Anything less is a truncated gospel that should not be foisted upon the Jewish people.[62]

THE LETTER TO THE ROMANS AND MESSIANIC JEWISH INREACH

In the Newer Testament, Romans 11 further explores aspects of this consummating purpose for the descendants of Jacob. Romans 9–11 ends in a doxology of astonishment. Paul is amazed at the outworking of God's consummating purposes. Who would have guessed that the people of Israel would turn down their Messiah when God sent him? And who would have guessed that idolatrous blood-drinking carousing pagans would come to a living relationship with the God of Israel without having to become Jews first? And who would have guessed that at the end of history, God would bring the Jewish people back to covenant faithfulness through this same Messiah, with the Jews being regathered and renewed, in the power of the

---

62. Acts 1:11 reminds us, "This Jesus, who was taken up from you into heaven, will come in the same way as you saw him go into heaven." I am of the firm conviction that many people are expecting a different Jesus than the one who left us in the ascension because our concept of Jesus has been tailored, modified, and added on to. For example, how many people expect a circumcised Jew to return on the clouds of heaven? Although he rose in a resurrection body, it was his transfigured human body, and he is and remains "the Lion of the Tribe of Judah," and the king of the Jews. And how many expect a Jesus who is coming to complete the fulfillment of promises made long ago to the Jewish people? Many in the church consider those promises to have been abandoned or transmuted into spiritual blessings for the church. I have no doubt that there will be many surprises when the "this Jesus" of Acts 1:11 returns to people who have shifted their expectations away from the specificities of God of the one who was born of the Virgin Mary.

Spirit, and through the very same Messiah through whom pagan nations turned to this same God, while for their part, not having been required to embrace Jewish life? How astounding! How miraculous! How unexpectedly and uniquely the work of God!

Is it not clear that this is what is astonishing the Apostle? Or do we imagine that the best God can pull off at the end of history, when "all Israel will be saved," is that vast numbers of Jews will become Baptists, Pentecostals, or Presbyterians?

To just ask the question is to answer it.

We must remember that in Romans 9–11, Paul is contrasting Israel and the other nations as aggregates. He is not speaking of Gentile and Jewish individuals, but of these respective groups, the dyad found throughout Scripture: Israel and the nations.

God's final act toward the Jews will be directed toward us as a people—he will bring the Jewish people to covenant faithfulness and to repentance/renewal through the one "despised by the nation."[63]

At the end of history God will clarify two realities, despite the widespread denial that has historically prevailed. Yeshua, whom Isaiah refers to as "the one despised by the nation," the one "despised and rejected by men," will be demonstrated to be everlastingly God's beloved one, and Israel, the nation so long despised by the nations, will be demonstrated to be God's beloved, his chosen people.

Therefore the inreach responsibility of the Messianic Jewish Remnant includes the following:

1. Our inreach is accomplished as we serve as a sign that God has a continuing purpose for the Jews, a consummating purpose of renewed covenant faithfulness in obedience to Torah in the power of the Spirit through Yeshua the Messiah.

2. Our inreach is accomplished as we demonstrate communally that we are a demonstration of that purpose—a proleptic preview of that covenant faithfulness which will one day be true of all Israel: a return to the Land, and to Torah-living in the power of the Holy Spirit, to the honor of Yeshua the Messiah

3. Our inreach is accomplished as we catalyze and assist greater Israel toward this consummating purpose.

---

63. Isa 49:7; Zech 12:10; Isa 53:3.

Implications of the Remnant Model for Messianic Jewish Inreach

If this analysis of Scripture is true, what might the results be for how we pursue inreach?

First, inreach would no longer be adversarial and confrontational. We would commend all religious Jewish efforts toward Torah-based covenant faithfulness. We would seek to assist and would applaud all efforts by religious Jews to honor God in the context of Torah.[64]

Second, we ourselves would form communities committed to this kind of Torah-based covenant faithfulness, for we could not be faithful to our remnant responsibility unless we served as a sign, demonstration, and catalyst of this kind of faithfulness. True, our Torah faithfulness would have its own unique aspects due to the impact of Yeshua and the Apostolic Writings on our halacha, our honoring of Yeshua, and our experience of the Spirit. Yet, we would live in continuity with historic Jewish practice and precedent, and would seek to be exemplars and prototypes of a covenantal renewal anticipated and coveted by other Jews, to which the Holy Spirit would draw many.

Third, our mission to the wider Jewish world would be to advocate faith in Yeshua and the power of the Spirit as the divine means toward their own greater covenant faithfulness. This moves inreach beyond simply individual soul salvation. We would be walking the same road as the rest of religious Israel, seeking to take the wider Jewish religious world further in the direction in which they are already heading—in the power of the Spirit and through Yeshua the Messiah.

Fourth, in addition to affirming and yet further catalyzing and challenging religious Jews, our ministry to secularized Jews would be very strong, calling them back to the God of our ancestors and the ways of our ancestors, back to Jewish community through Yeshua the Messiah in the power of the Spirit.

---

64. Some wrongly imagine that the perspective being advocated here envisions making all Messianic Jews into Orthodox Jews. Hardly! What is advocated is a covenantally faithful observant Messianic Judaism. Not all observant Jews are Orthodox, nor are all who call themselves Orthodox Jews observant. In view of our loyalty to the teachings of Yeshua and the apostolic writings, as we awaken to the responsibility to be covenantally faithful, and thus observant, our community will have to work hard exploring issues of continuity and discontinuity concerning our practice and that of the wider Jewish community. This will require of us responsible and ongoing halachic discussion honoring our continuity with Jewish tradition and our unique perspective as Messianic Jews. The Torah of God is no straitjacket, and I would be ecstatic to live as part of a broad community serving as a foretaste, a sign, a demonstration, and a catalyst of that observant Messianic Judaism that is our prophetic destiny and missional responsibility. May it come speedily and soon!

Fifth, at first some, and the later, hopefully many, church people would applaud us for being fully Jewish in practice and in community rather seeking to woo us into being more like themselves. They would realize that moving deeper into Jewish life is our destiny and remnant responsibility.

Sixth, we would return to a communal concept of inreach rather than an individualistic one.[65] Our communities, living in covenant faithfulness, would be missonal magnets as was the case for the earliest Yeshua-believing Jerusalem congregation that proved so attractive to the surrounding Jewish world. We would be a proleptic sign, demonstration, and catalyst of Israel's future, a foretaste of things to come.[66]

Why Is It Crucial That We Adopt a Postmissionary Messianic Jewish Inreach Paradigm?

This paradigm of Messianic Jewish inreach should not be viewed as one option among many, but as the wave of the future shaping our present and continuing agenda. I offer the following reasons for the superiority of this paradigm over others we have known:

1. It better aligns Messianic Jewish inreach with the revealed purposes of God for the Jewish people. It is fully consonant with our responsibilities toward our holy past and our holy future—*zikkaron*/anamnesis and *prolepsis*.

2. It is a necessary corrective to the kind of truncated and supersessionistic gospel that separates Yeshua and his work from his central role in the consummation of God's promises to Israel. Yeshua is not simply the Savior of individual souls, not even of individual Jewish souls, nor simply the Lord of the church. He is the Son of David, through whom Israel's return to the Land, spiritual repentance-renewal, and restoration to covenant faithfulness is guaranteed and accomplished. We ought not to think of Yeshua apart from this eschatological agenda.

---

65. Glaser also calls for a return to communal witness, stating: "There are two ways a Messianic community evangelizes—through the efforts of those natural evangelists who are part of the community and also through more programmed efforts. Both gifted evangelists and programs are important. However, my assertion is that all efforts, spontaneous and planned will become more effective in a community context" ("Towards a New Model for Jewish Evangelism in the 21st Century," 24).

66. This is not to say that we ought to embrace a realized eschatology. Until Yeshua returns, we know in part, and prophesy in part, and have only a foretaste of the powers of the Age to Come. Still, we *are* called to be a foretaste of that future consummation.

This is the agenda that we are called to serve, and that constitutes a major component of the armature of Messianic Jewish discipleship.

3. It is an antidote to culturally determined and limited sales-oriented approaches to the task such as closing the sale, confronting the avoidant, filling the pews, and find heaven/avoid hell predicated on the bankruptcy of Jewish spirituality.

4. It instantly neutralizes the adversarial posture that we have inherited from generations past that ill-serves the greater purposes of God and undermines ongoing communication with our Jewish people.

5. It articulates a call to the Jewish people to a return to covenant faithfulness that we must heed ourselves.

6. It challenges us to expand and reevaluate the role of the Holy Spirit's presence in our congregations, "And I will put my Spirit within you, and cause you to walk in my statutes and be careful to observe my ordinances" (Ezek 36:27). Contrary to those whose reflex is to polarize the life of the Spirit and commandment-keeping, this paradigm calls for a return to that biblical perspective which sees the life of the Spirit and commandment-keeping as coordinate.

7. It provides a firm theological foundation for vigorously supporting and participating in aliyah for others and ourselves. Under this paradigm, we would see aliyah, and support of our people in the Land, as a necessary aspect of the consummation of all things. We would see our support of aliyah as hastening the end through accommodating ourselves to the foreordained shape of that consummation.

8. It provides better, transcendent motivations for our inreach. Our gospel for the Jews would be more positive than that formerly preached, which has been predicated on the universal perdition of Jews who fail to accept the evangelist's message and on the spiritual impotence of the Jewish way of life. Instead, our gospel message would be this: "*The Messiah has come, and he is coming again. His name is Yeshua. Through him, all of God's promises to Israel and the nations are being fulfilled.*"

Until now, proponents of the standard Jewish Missions model have resisted this kind of message. They imagine that the motivation and momentum of outreach to the Jewish people dies if we disengage the missional engine from a "find heaven/avoid hell" paradigm rooted in the superiority of Christianity to a bankrupt Judaism. They contend that a postmissionary Messianic Judaism is *anti*-missionary and spells the end of faithful mission/outreach to the Jewish people. But they are wrong. This approach is not less but more: more solid, more effective, more faithful to Scripture, and more missional.

The great missiologist Johannes Verkuyl lends support to these bold assertions. Among six motivations for mission he names, the first three are, the doxological motive—in our terms, *kiddush Hashem* (the sanctification of God's Name), the eschatological motive— in our terms, *acharit hayamim* (the end of days), involving pursuit of that fullness suitable to the consummation, and obedience to the Divine command—in our terms, *avodat Hashem* (service/obedience to God). These are the very motivations Yeshua taught us when he said, "Hallowed be Thy Name" (*kiddush Hashem*), "Thy kingdom come" (*acharit hayamim*—the eschatological motive), and "Thy will be done" (*avodat Hashem*—service/obedience to God).[67] These motivations are not less but more than those commonly driving the Jewish mission enterprise, and form the firm foundation for an eschatological postmissionary Messianic Jewish inreach suited to the times while hastening the consummation of all things.

(9) It addresses the greatest obstacle to effectiveness in Messianic Jewish inreach: the widespread assimilation of Jewish Yeshua-believers. Even the secularized Jewish community has a right to assume that when Messiah comes, he will make Jewish people into better Jews. When Jewish Yeshua-believers assimilate and become indifferent to Jewish life and community, the Jewish community has a right to say: "Don't be ridiculous! Put your Bibles away and don't waste your time trying to convince us! What kind of a Messiah is this that makes goyim out of Jews?" Game. Set. Match. But our own return to Jewish covenant faithfulness, which is the will of God for the Messianic Jewish remnant and for all Israel, has the added benefit of rendering this objection null and void.

Some protest that most Jews today are not religiously observant, and that we ought therefore to abandon such a vision of Torah-true Messianic Judaism in favor of one more marketable to today's secularized Jews. The answer to this objection is manifold.[68] First, we are not engaged in sales, but in prophetic faithfulness. We are not simply called to sell what will sell but to speak in his Name. Second, we ought not forget that the Jesus Revolution of the late 1960s and early 1970s came during the era of "sex, drugs, and rock and roll," a time manifestly ill-suited to a young people's revival. And yet, that is what we had.

---

67. Verkuyl, *Contemporary Missiology*, 164–67.

68. Kinzer handily addresses this issue, summarizing his exegesis of texts from Matthew, Luke-Acts, and Paul, in his "Rejoinder to Responses to Postmissionary Messianic Judaism," responding to a critique on this point by Mitch Glaser.

Therefore, in accordance with the promise of the prophetic word and the Spirit's prior activity, how can we not anticipate and seek to be a sign, demonstration, and catalyst of a renewal of covenant faithfulness among our people Israel hastening the consummation of all things? Is it not clear that we are being called to sacrificial commitment to this kind of vision, grounded as it is in the Scriptures?

Keywords, Key Concepts, and Key Practices

How can we make this paradigm stand up and walk in the various contexts in which we live? The following keywords, concepts, and practices will help make this happen.

1. In our relationship to the wider Jewish world, we must begin to see ourselves not as a missionary movement but as a prophetic movement. Missionaries are people from another context, prophets are people from within one's own context. We must see ourselves as a prophetic movement calling our own people as well as ourselves to ongoing repentance/renewal, to return to the Land, and to return to that covenant faithfulness which yet remains the only proper indicator of our reverence for our holy past (*zikkaron*/anamnesis) and our service to Israel's holy future. Being a prophetic movement must become one of our key concepts.

2. In our relationship to the wider Jewish world, we must seek out every opportunity to partner together in matters of common concern. We must shuck off the polemical garments which we have outgrown, and, as a proleptic community, begin to model wherever and however we can that unity which will one day be manifest, when Hashem will make us "one nation in the land, on the mountains of Isra'el; and one king will be king for all of them. . . . My servant David will be king over them."[69] *Partnership* must become one of our keywords.

3. In our relationship with the church from among the nations and its missionary mandate, we must begin to see our role in these times of eschatological change as "paramission." We ought to support our brothers and sisters in the church as they seek to bring about the fullness of the gentiles, in service to the Great Commission. But Paul refers in Romans 11 to another fullness, the fullness of Israel, and speaks

69. Ezek 37:21ff.

of this fullness as "greater riches" than the fullness of the nations.[70] As the Messianic Jewish remnant in times of eschatological transition, our primary missional call is to this Greater Commission, not to the exclusion of our support of our brothers and sisters in the church in their primary call, the Great Commission. And they for their part, should support us in fulfilling our primary missional call. It is true that this approach has not existed until now. However, it is right and necessary that roles should shift considering signs that God's focus is shifting toward pursuing the fullness of Israel. Again, the keyword here is paramission. By all means, let us work side by side, fulfilling our complementary callings, hastening that day when Israel and the nations will all proclaim Yeshua their King to the honor of God the Father. And in that day, the LORD will be one, and his name one. *Paramission* is another key word.

4. We must learn to accept process and commit to it. It is one thing to have a compelling vision of a goal toward which one is heading. It is quite another to initiate and sustain proper processes to facilitate the journey. Some of us are impatient. Certainly I am. If we are to succeed, we will need wise and trusted leaders who understand and respect process, who will outline and even detail how we might best get where we are headed. Such parties will help us exercise proper patience and discretion in traveling on, while building and preserving rather than dissipating momentum.

5. We must work out the political implications of this vision. If we change our paradigm, we will alter our every line of association and affiliation. Some current organizations, groups, or individuals will be enthusiastic, some will not know what to think, and others will mobilize against us. If we are serious about partnering with the Jewish community in matters of common cause, and about redefining our relationship with the church from among the nations, we will need to form new alliances, new organizational and affiliational structures, both informal and formal. As we do so, we will encounter fierce opposition and frequently, misrepresentation and polemical attacks. We must prepare to face these things: they will surely come upon us, and seldom at a time of our choosing. We will need new and renewed institutions, compatible with this vision and the lines of association it embodies.

6. If we sense that this description of our remnant calling and our positioning between *zikkaron*/anamnesis and consummation is a calling

---

70. Rom 11:12.

from God and not just an intriguing idea, we must devote ourselves to prayer of all kinds, most certainly including communal liturgical prayer. God has summoned us to be servants of a high and holy calling. Therefore, we should devote ourselves to prayer as individuals, working groups, minyanim of various kinds, and as a union, finding strength and guidance for our service.

7. We must commit to an ongoing process of diligent study and teaching on the nature and implications of this paradigm, relating it to Scripture. One of the reasons I am growing in my commitment to this vision is that the Bible makes more sense to me from this perspective. More pieces fit in place, and the overall picture grows clearer. We will need to devote ourselves and lead others into a renewed engagement with Scripture that these insights might be tested, refined, and hopefully, deepened into firm convictions. And we must diligently study and teach from liturgical and traditional sources useful in informing and shaping our covenant faithfulness.

8. If this is a holy calling, and if the measure of our service to God as the Messianic Jewish remnant is how we honor our holy past and serve our holy future, then we must become a community that walks in reverence toward God—a people "of a poor and humble spirit, who tremble at his word" in conformity to the demands of this model.

9. We must commit to listening to one another in order to discern the will of God. If what I have written here is substantially true and a calling from God, then listening to others, to their views, their fears, their objections, and their accusations, will not be threatening. I am sensing that it is our responsibility to open up dialogue on these matters within and around our community, and the time to do so is near, at the very gates. The purpose of such listening to one another is not to simply canonize diversity but rather to discern the will of God.

10. We will need to develop halachic guidelines suited to our holy calling and not dictated by our preferences, convenience, or communal political issues. These guidelines must express the freedom of the Spirit, but embody the obedience of faith for the sake of his name. The key word here is obedience to a standard to which we are called, not simply one self-chosen.

WALKING THE HIGH WIRE

Picture us as a movement walking a high wire strung between the poles of a holy past and a holy future.[71] This is our path of covenant faithfulness. If either end of the high wire disconnects, we tumble into unfaithfulness, irrelevance and disconnection from the path God called us to. Both poles must be firmly in place. To be anchored only to anamnesis, remembering a holy past, consigns us to irrelevant but seductive restorationism. To be anchored only to prolepsis, to embodying a holy future, consigns us to irrelevant undisciplined apocalypticism. Both ends of the high wire must be anchored and the tension maintained.

However, we do not walk this high wire alone. Obedient Israel is on the high wire with us, and has been there for a long time. We would do well to learn from their experience up there. We should look and listen, relying upon the wisdom of tradition to tell us how to keep the wire taut, connected rightly to both poles, how fast to move, and how to maintain our balance. And to the extent that the church understands and respects the path of faithfulness to which we are called, they too assist us, cheering us on, and perhaps by warning us about leaning to much in this direction or that.

It is helpful to summarize the thrust of this paper in the following terms: Messianic Jewish covenantal and missional faithfulness is lived out in the interplay between honoring an idealized Jewish past (our legacy), and an idealized Jewish future (our destiny), in the inter- and intra-communal present, which is the ever-shifting intersection of that future and that past.

When I speak of the inter-communal and intra-communal present, I mean that these commitments must be fleshed out in our own community and in our relationship with other communities; the wider Jewish world, the church world, Jewish mission agencies, the wider Messianic Jewish context, and the general culture. This is no merely theoretical construct. The context of our divine service is the world(s) in which we live.

Keeping Our Balance on the High Wire

High wire walkers routinely carry long poles, held perpendicular to their bodies. These poles, weighted at the ends, help high wire walkers adjust their center of gravity, thus helping them maintain their balance. We too will need to maintain our balance as we walk the high wire of the present,

---

71. I didn't have the heart, or perhaps the nerve, to introduce another arcane term besides *anamnesis* and *prolepsis*, but the technical term for tight-rope walking is *funambulism*. Save that one for your next Scrabble game!

strung between honoring a holy past and serving a holy future. The question arises, what are some factors to keep in balance in order to not lose our footing in our high wire walk toward the consummation?

1. Finding the balancing point between Older Testament and Newer Testament perspectives—Issues of continuity/discontinuity.

2. Being able and willing to hear others shouting good directions to us as we walk the high wire.

3. Being able to recognize, screen out, and not lose our balance due to distracting voices and obstacles thrown in our path by others, maliciously or otherwise.

4. Being adept at navigating gusts and contrary winds of viewpoint and perspective.

5. Pursuing covenant faithfulness in ways that breathe and are warmly human, eschewing both rigidity and laxity.

6. Being humble, yet confident—without both one cannot walk the high wire.

7. Being team players—we need to be the Flying Wallendas and not solo acts. If we don't work together we will fall, separately at first, but eventually all of us together.

8. Learning to keep our eyes on the goal.

9. Learning to not be over-reactive in any manner.

10. Achieving a balance between being decisive and courageous—too much caution on the high wire is the most dangerous thing of all.

11. Making room for both leaders and laity, women and men, Jews and gentiles to make the contributions God has called them to make in our movement.

12. Finding the balancing point between pastoral sensitivity to the gentiles who have given their lives to our movement and avoiding being diverted, losing our way and compromising that faithfulness to which God is calling us as reflected in a particular kind of Jewish community formation.

13. Finding the balancing point between a sense of urgency and a respect for process.

14. Finding the balancing point between the demands of our filial relationship with the church and the prior calling of our familial relationship with Israel.

15. Finding the balancing point between aiding the church in its pursuit of the Great Commission and not sacrificing our prior Messianic Jewish remnant responsibility to serve the Greater Commission.

16. Finding the balancing point between being peace-makers and being prophetic.

17. Finding our center of gravity being both filled with the Spirit and covenantally faithful.

If We Don't Change Our Paradigm—Then What?

Joel Barker is an independent scholar and "futurist" who popularized the term "paradigm shift" in his book, *Paradigms: The Business of Discovering the Future*.[72] Using compelling illustrations, he demonstrates why understanding paradigms and how they work is a life or death issue whether we are marketing products, promulgating concepts, or building the kingdom of God. Any and all desiring to play their parts in molding the future of the church, of the Messianic Jewish Movement and of the world need to heed his able counsel. When paradigms change, the world changes, and the labors of those who do not change with the paradigm suddenly become irrelevant.

Barker illustrates this from the experience of the Swiss watchmaking industry. He tells how a change in paradigms revolutionized the industry almost overnight, leaving advocates of the older paradigm suddenly and irrevocably irrelevant, and ultimately, out of work.

In 1968, the Swiss sold 65 percent of the watches manufactured worldwide and controlled well over 80 percent of watchmaking profits. They dominated watchmaking for generations by making the best mainsprings, gears, jewels, and cases. For generations it was axiomatic that if you wanted a fine watch, you wanted a Swiss watch. By 1980, their market share collapsed to less than 10 percent, and in two years, 50,000 of the 62,000 watchmakers lost their jobs. What happened?

What happened was that the Swiss slept through a paradigm shift— and when they woke up, their world had changed, while they hadn't. Almost overnight they became irrelevant. The wave of the future—the quartz crystal watch— had descended upon them. The Swiss were unprepared. The wave became a tsunami decimating their share in an industry they had dominated for generations.

72. Barker, *Paradigms*.

It is astounding that Swiss scientists invented the electronic quartz movement in 1967 at their Research Institute in Neuchâtel, Switzerland. However, the Swiss manufacturers and decision-makers dismissed the idea. "Everyone knows that watches are made with gears and springs! You call yourselves scientists and you don't know that?" They laughed the idea off the stage of industrial opinion.

They did think the idea at least a cute novelty. That is why, without protecting the patent, they displayed the technology as a gimmick at the World Watch Congress that year. Some Japanese observers from a company called Seiko walked by, and having the imagination and flexibility the Swiss lacked, picked up the idea and ran with it, running away with the watch-making market as well.

Bob Dylan was right: "The times they *are* a-changing." If we don't want to become as irrelevant as a Swiss watchmaker in the 1970s, we will need not only to change with the times, but also become change agents. Scripture agrees, challenging us to be like "the descendants of Yissachar who understood the times and knew what Israel ought to do" (1 Chron 12:32). If we as members and leaders of the Messianic Jewish Remnant will not understand the times and becoming God's change agents hastening Israel's rendezvous with its foreordained destiny, who will? And if not now, when?

Epilogue
Can Two Walk Together Unless They Be Agreed?

A FEW INITIATIVES BEAR mention, prayer, and appropriate participation as we arise to apply the lessons of this book, serving together the converging destinies of the Jewish and Christian communities in the mission of God. These initiatives are noted below in random order.[1]

The first is the Helsinki Consultation, "an international fellowship of Jewish scholars and theologians who acknowledge Jesus as Israel's Messiah and who live as members of diverse ecclesial bodies. Named after the city where their first meeting was convened, the Consultation includes Messianic Jews and Jews from Catholic, Protestant, and Orthodox churches."[2] While the Messianic Jewish congregational movement is predominantly Protestant and evangelical in its ethos, the Helsinki Consultation is mainly concerned with the historic churches, seeking to define and promote a proper place for Jews to live as Jews within these contexts, and providing an arena for developing a united voice articulating and promoting common concerns. In short, members of the Consultation hold that "the Church must find a way to support Jews in its midst in sustaining a distinct Jewish identity."

Mark Kinzer and others of the members are involved in the Messianic Jewish Movement, which pursues its aims through establishing congregations. The Consultation realizes this may be neither advisable nor possible in Catholic, Orthodox, and Protestant church contexts. Still there is much to be gained and learned through representatives of these varied contexts listening to and learning from each other. The Consultation meets once yearly, when papers are presented on coordinate themes, with a joint statement prepared each year to report on their findings and discussion. Founding members of the Consultation are Mark S. Kinzer, Antoine Levy, David M.

---

1. Mark Kinzer plays a key role in almost all of these initiatives, for which due credit is due him.

2. All quoted material about the Helsinki Consultation accessed October 19, 2015, http://helsinkiconsultation.squarespace.com/helsinki-consultation/.

Neuhaus, Lisa Loden, Svetlana Panich, Vladimir Pikman, Boris Balter, and Richard Harvey.

Mark Kinzer is a prime mover in another initiative so delicate as to have neither a name nor public profile. It involves interaction and inquiry between a select group of Messianic Jewish scholars and scholars from the wider Jewish world. Beginning with informal conversations behind closed doors, the group has slowly coalesced, carefully building bridges of trust and channels of information where the bridge has been out for nearly two millennia. These relational efforts have produced various and precious first fruits such as public lectures by Mark Nanos and Michael Wyschogrod sponsored by Messianic Jewish Theological Institute, a lecture by Daniel Boyarin at Messianic Congregation Ruach Israel in Needham, Massachusetts, and more recently scholarly interactions at the annual meetings of the NAPH (National Association of Professors of Hebrew) held contiguously with the annual meetings of the Society of Biblical Literature.

The first of these NAPH meeting concerning Messianic Jewish themes was held November 2014, with Zev Garber, Yaakov Ariel, and Isaac Oliver participating. The session was spurred by the publication of *Introduction to Messianic Judaism* (Zondervan, 2013), edited by David Rudolph and Joel Willits. At this session, Mark Kinzer spoke on "The Renewed Perspective: Post-Supersessionism: A Hermeneutical Course Correction 1700 Years in the Making." Isaac Oliver of Bradley University spoke on "Twenty-First Century Messianic Judaism: Evangelical and Post-Evangelical Trajectories," and Yaakov Ariel of University of North Carolina at Chapel Hill, on "Messianic Jews and the Early Jewish Followers of Jesus." Zev Garber of Los Angeles Valley College spoke on "An Intellectual and Theological Coming of Age: Messianic Judaism at the Turn of the 21st Century," while the session concluded with a discussion of the book by Rudolph and Willits, both of whom were present.[3]

The following year, 2015, the NAPH Annual Meeting included a session titled "Post-Missionary Messianic Judaism (Brazos, 2005) Ten Years Later: Assessing the Value and Viability of Mark Kinzer's Proposal for the Role of Jewish Followers of Jesus in the Jewish-Christian Relationship." That such interaction would take place between academics in the wider Jewish world and academics from the Messianic Jewish world is remarkable, and was inconceivable even twenty-five years ago. That these have happened is

---

3. Another session touching on related issues is planned for the next meeting of the NAPH, to be conducted November 2015, still future as of this writing, but a past event by the time this book is published. Besides Messianic Jews like Mark Kinzer and David Rudolph, the meeting will include Zev Garber and Peter Ochs. David Novak was to attend but had a scheduling conflict.

a credit to the quality of scholarship being generated by Messianic Jews like Kinzer and Rudolph, their alliances with Christian scholars like Joel Willits, and the principled courage demonstrated by Jewish scholars willing to reconsider long-stigmatized issues.

Another initiative worth noting is Toward Jerusalem Council II. According to their website,

> Toward Jerusalem Council II is an initiative of repentance and reconciliation between the Jewish and Gentile segments of the Church. The vision is that one day there will be a second Council of Jerusalem that will be, in an important respect, the inverse of the first Council described in Acts 15. Whereas the first Council was made up of Jewish believers in Yeshua (Jesus), who decided not to impose on the Gentiles the requirements of the Jewish law, so the second Council would be made up of Gentile church leaders, who would recognize and welcome the Jewish believers in Yeshua without requiring them to abandon their Jewish identity and practice.[4]

The initiative is directed by a fourteen-member International Leadership Council broadly representative of international movements and churches, historic and modern, that confess Yeshua (Jesus) as Lord and Savior.[5]

When speaking of Roman Catholics and Jews, one must consider initiatives where representatives of the Church have interacted with both representatives of the wider Jewish community and with representatives of the Messianic Jewish world. One such initiative is the Roman Catholic-Messianic Jewish Dialogue Group, which began in 2000. While there is overlap in players between this group and both the Helsinki Consultation and Toward Jerusalem Council II, the three initiatives are nevertheless quite distinct in identity and purpose.

At the request of the Vatican, in 1970 the Jewish community established the International Jewish Committee on Interreligious Consultations (IJCIC) to serve as the Jewish community's official liaison with the Holy See. Relations between the Jewish world and the Vatican have been on the upswing since the papacy of Pope John Paul II, through the brief papacy of Benedict XVI, and now in the papacy of Pope Francis, who had

---

4. All quoted material is taken from the Toward Jerusalem II website, accessed October 19, 2015, http://tjcii.org/about-us/.

5. The International Leadership Council of Toward Jerusalem II includes Benjamin Berger, Martin Bühlmann, the Reverend Canon Brian Cox, John Dawson, Johannes Fichtenbauer, Father Peter Hocken, Dr. Daniel Juster, Fr. Vasile Mihoc, Avi Mizrachi, Marcel Rebiai, Rabbi Marty Waldman, and Wayne Wilks Jr. The emeritus members are Don Finto and Pastor Olen Griffing.

long-standing irenic relationships with Jewish community leaders in Bue-
nos Aires when he served there as cardinal.[6]

While the Jewish community is greatly reassured by the Church's progress during the fifty years since the promulgation of *Nostra Aetate* (No. 4),
many in the Messianic Jewish world are concerned about the Church's shift
in position in a document issued December 10, 2015, by the Commission
for Religious Relations with the Jews, marking the fiftieth anniversary of
Nostra Aetate. In paragraph 40, the document states, "the Catholic Church
neither conducts nor supports any specific institutional mission work directed toward Jews," before temporizing this statement by stating, "While
there is a principled rejection of an institutional Jewish mission, Christians
are nonetheless called to bear witness to their faith in Jesus Christ also to
Jews, although they should do so in a humble and sensitive manner, acknowledging that Jews are bearers of God's Word, and particularly in view of
the great tragedy of the Shoah."[7] What is being said then is that the Church
encourages evangelism by the laity, but offers no institutional embodiment
or support of mission to the Jews.

As a Jew who believes in Yeshua/Jesus as Messiah, while I can well
defend how the imperative of preserving Jewish communal and covenantal
continuity mitigates against the Church pursuing programs and policies for
Jews converting to Roman Catholicism, like many other Messianic Jews,
I also insist on the propriety and priority of Jews being introduced to the
one whom I term "the more Jewish Jesus." While being Messiah, the more
Jewish Jesus also affirms Jewish community structures, Jewish communal
continuity, Jewish values, and Jewish customs. Such a figure is no enemy
of the Jewish people nor of Jewish communal continuity, nor should he be
considered an unwelcome stranger. No one should be embarrassed about
being his representative to inquiring Jewish people.

Another group fostering dialogue between Messianic Jews and
Christian academics was the Church Working Group that met at Southern
Methodist University, now on hiatus due to inadequate funding. The group
was co-chaired by Mark Kinzer and Professor William Abraham, included
Kendall Soulen, Fr. Jean-Miguel Garrigues, Bruce Marshall, and Tommy
Givens, and met three times: in 2011, 2012, and 2013, funded by SMU.
Mark Kinzer looks forward to this group resuming its work when further
funding becomes available.

6. Peter Jesserer, "Pope Francis: Breaking New Ground in Jewish-Catholic Relations," *National Catholic Register*, November 8, 2013, accessed December 17, 2015,
https://www.ncregister.com/daily-news/pope-francis-breaking-new-ground-in-
jewish-catholic-relations/.

7. *The Gifts and Calling of God Are Irrevocable*, paragraph 40.

All of the foregoing initiatives are rather "high end," involving well-qualified and well-established leaders and academics. We might liken these initiatives to the day of *mattan Torah,* the giving of the Law at Sinai. Surely, what was happening at the top of the mountain was momentous, for there Moses received God's eternal Law. But what happened at the bottom of the mount was also crucial, and had Aaron and Hur done a better job of managing affairs, Jewish history would have been much the better for it! The lesson is clear. It is not enough that fine scholars and leaders should do their crucial work at the top of the mount. Leaders at the bottom of the mountain, in contact with the people, must also exert themselves to help their communities embrace new paradigms instead of reverting to the familiar idols of the past. Failing to embrace new paradigms will only mean consigning ourselves to more years of wandering, delaying that converging destiny of synerjoy which is the inheritance to which the true and living God summons us all. Let us rise up and go, all of us helping each other along the way, attentive to the Voice that summons us all.

Bibliography

Asch, Sholem. *One Destiny: An Epistle to the Christians*. New York: G. P. Putnam and Sons, 1945.

Baker, Alan, ed. *Israel's Rights as a Nation-State in International Diplomacy*. Jerusalem: Center for Public Affairs—World Jewish Congress, 2011.

Bamberger, Bernard J. *Proselytism in the Talmudic Period*. New York: KTAV, 1939.

Bard, Michael G. "Myths and Facts Online." Jewish Virtual Library, http://www.jewishvirtuallibrary.org/jsource/myths3/MFUN.html.

Barker, Joel Arthur. *Paradigms: The Business of Discovering the Future*. Reprint. New York: HarperCollins Canada/Collins Business, 1993.

Barth, Karl. *Church Dogmatics* II.2. Edinburgh: T&T Clark, 1957.

Barth, Markus. *The People of God*. JSNT Supplement Series 5. Sheffield: JSOT, 1983.

Bauckham, Richard. *James: Wisdom of James, Disciple of Jesus the Sage*. New Testament Readings. New York: Routledge, 1999.

Beasley-Murray, George Raymond. *The Book of Revelation*. London: Marshall, Morgan and Scott, 1974.

Becker, Adam H., and Annette Yoshiko Reed, eds. *The Ways That Never Parted: Jews and Christians in Late Antiquity and the Early Middle Ages*. Texts and Studies in Ancient Judaism 95. Minneapolis: Fortress, 2007.

Beeby, H. Dan. "Obituary; The Right Rev Lesslie Newbigin." *The Independent*, London, February 4, 1998.

Bezalel, Judah Loew ben. *Sefer Gevurot Hashem*. Hebrew Edition. PublishYourSefer.com, 2007.

Birnbaum, Philip. *Ha-Siddur Hashalem Daily Prayer Book*. New York: Hebrew, 1977.

Blaising, Craig A. "The Future of Israel as a Theological Question." *Journal of the Evangelical Theological Society* 44 (2001) 435–50.

———. "Premillennialism." In *Three Views on the Millennium and Beyond*, edited by Darrell L. Bock, 157–227. Grand Rapids: Zondervan, 1999.

Blaising, Craig A., and Darrell L. Bock. *Progressive Dispensationalism*. Grand Rapids: Baker, 1999.

Bock, Darrell L. "The Reign of the Lord Christ." In *Dispensationalism, Israel and the Church*, edited by Craig A. Blaising and Darrel L. Bock, 37–67. Grand Rapids: Zondervan, 1996.

Bokser, Ben Zion. "Witness and Mission in Judaism." In *Issues in the Jewish-Christian Dialogue: Jewish Perspectives on Covenant, Mission and Witness*, edited by Helga Croner and Leon Klenicki, 89–107. New York: Paulist, 1979.

Bosch, David J. *Transforming Mission: Paradigm Shifts in Theology of Mission*. Maryknoll, NY: Orbis, 1991.

Boyarin, Daniel. *Border Lines: the Invention of Heresy and the Emergence of Christianity and Judaism*. Stanford, CA: Stanford University Press, 2004.

Boys, Mary C. "Does the Catholic Church Have a Mission 'with' Jews or 'to' Jews?" *Modern Christian-Jewish Dialogue* 3.1 (2008). http://escholarship.bc.edu/scjr/vol3/iss1/5/.

Brill, Alan. *Judaism and Other Religions: Models of Understanding*. New York: Palgrave Macmillan, 2010.

———. "Judaism and Other Religions: An Orthodox Perspective." A paper commissioned by the World Jewish Congress for the "World Symposium of Catholic Cardinals and Jewish Leaders," January 19–20, 2004, in New York City. Available online, Boston College, Center for Christian-Jewish Learning, Christian-Jewish Relations Library, https://www.bc.edu/content/dam/files/research_sites/cjl/texts/cjrelations/resources/articles/Brill.htm.

Brockway, Allan. "General Trends: Assemblies of the World Council of Churches." In *The Theology of the Churches and the Jewish People: Statements by the World Council of Churches and its Member Churches*, edited by Allan Brockway et al., 123–39. Geneva: WCC Publications, 1988.

Brown, Michael L. "The Place of Rabbinic Tradition in Messianic Judaism." 1988 UMJC Conference Theology Forum. Posted on AskDrBrown website, November 18, 2012. https://askdrbrown.org/portfolio/the-place-of-rabbinic-tradition-in-messianic-judaism/.

Busch, Eberhard. "The Covenant of Grace Fulfilled in Christ as the Foundation of the Indissoluble Solidarity of the Church with Israel: Barth's Position on the Jews During the Hitler Era." *Scottish Journal of Theology* 52 (1999) 476–503.

Cameron, Averil. "Jews and Heretics—A Category Error?" In *The Ways that Never Parted*, edited by Adam H. Becker and Annette Yoshiko Reed, Texts and Studies in Ancient Judaism 95, 345–60. Tübingen: Mohr Siebeck, 2003.

Campbell, Joseph. *Myths of Light: Eastern Metaphors of the Eternal* (The Collected Works of Joseph Campbell). Reprint. Novato, CA: New World Library, 2012.

Carson, Donald A. *Exegetical Fallacies*. 2nd ed. Grand Rapids: Baker, 1996.

Cassuto, Umberto. *Commentary on the Book of Exodus*. Translated by Israel Abrams. Jerusalem: Magnes, 1967.

Catholic News Service Documentary Service. No 13. *Origins*. Washington, September 5, 1991.

Childs, Brevard S. *Memory and Tradition in Israel*. London: SCM, 1962.

———. *The Book of Exodus*. Philadelphia: Westminster, 1974.

"Christian-Jewish Dialogue Beyond Canberra '91." Geneva: Central Committee of the World Council of Churches. Online: http://jcrelations.net/Christian-Jewish_Dialogue_Beyond_Canberra.2585.0.html?id=1495.

"The Church and Her Witness." Section Four of *The Church and the Jewish People*. Geneva: The Commission on Faith and Order of the World Council of Churches, 1967. http://www.bc.edu/dam/files/research_sites/cjl/texts/cjrelations/resources/documents/protestant/WCC1967.htm.

"The Churches and the Jewish People: Toward a New Understanding." Sigtuna, Sweden: Consultation on the Church and the Jewish People, May 11, 1988, Article A (Preamble). Online: http://www.jcrelations.net/The_Churches_and_the_Jewish_People__Toward_a_New_Understanding.1512.0.html.

Cohen, Shaye J. D. "Conversion to Judaism in Historical Perspective: From Biblical Israel to Post-Biblical Judaism." *Conservative Judaism* 36.4 (Summer 1983) 31–45.

Cohn, Leopold. *The Story of a Modern Missionary to an Ancient People*. New York: American Board of Missions to the Jews, 1908. http://baptistbiblebelievers.com/BookList/STORYOFAMODERNMISSIONARYTOANANCIENTPEOPLE/tabid/454/Default.aspx.

Commission for Religious Relations with the Jews. *Notes on the Correct Way to Present the Jews and Judaism in Preaching and Catechesis in the Roman Catholic Church.* Vatican, Holy See, 1985. http://www.vatican.va/roman_curia/pontifical_councils/chrstuni/relations-jews-docs/rc_pc_chrstuni_doc_19820306_jews-judaism_en.html.

———. *'The Gifts And The Calling of God Are Irrevocable' (Rom 11:29): A Reflection On Theological Questions Pertaining to Catholic-Jewish Relations on the Occasion of the Fiftieth Anniversary of 'Nostra Aetate' (No. 4)*. Ccjr.us, December 10, 2015. http://www.ccjr.us/dialogika-resources/documents-and-statements/roman-catholic/vatican-curia/1357-crrj-2015dec10.

Cunningham, Philip A. "Introduction" to *Christ Jesus and the Jewish People Today: New Explorations of Theological Interrelationships*, edited by Philip A. Cunningham, Joseph Sievers, Mary C. Boys, and Hans Hermann Henrix, ix–xxxii. Grand Rapids: Eerdmans, 2011.

Delegates of the Union of Messianic Jewish Congregations. "Defining Messianic Judaism." http://www.umjc.org/core-values/defining-messianic-judaism/ .

———. "Union of Messianic Jewish Congregations." http://www.umjc.org/core-values/defining-messianic-judaism/.

D'Elia, John A. *A Place at the Table: George Eldon Ladd and the Rehabilitation of Evangelical Scholarship in America*. Oxford: Oxford University Press, 2008.

Dauermann, Stuart. *Christians and Jews Together*. Eugene, OR: Wipf and Stock, 2008.

———. *The Rabbi as a Surrogate Priest*. Eugene, OR: Pickwick, 2009.

———. "Seeds, Weeds, and Walking the High Wire: The Role of the Remnant—Embodying Israel's Destiny." Unpublished paper from the Hashivenu Forum. Hashivenu: Pasadena, CA, 2006.

———. *Son of David: Healing the Vision of the Messianic Jewish Movement*. Eugene, OR: Wipf and Stock, 2010.

Dauermann, Stuart, and Mark Kinzer. *The Emerging Messianic Jewish Paradigm*. Unpublished, 2005.

Dershowitz, Alan. *The Case for Israel*. Hoboken, NJ: John Wiley and Sons, 2004.

Dickens, Charles. *Hard Times*, chapter 2, "Murdering the Innocents." http://www.mtholyoke.edu/acad/intrel/hardtime.htm.

Dogmatic Constitution On The Church Lumen Gentium Solemnly Promulgated By His Holiness Pope Paul VI On November 21, 1964. http://www.vatican.va/archive/hist_councils/ii_vatican_council/documents/vat-ii_const_19641121_lumen-gentium_en.html.

Dorff, Elliot. "The Meaning of Covenant: A Contemporary Understanding." In *Issues in the Jewish Christian Dialogue: Jewish Perspectives on Covenant, Mission and Witness,* edited by Helga Croner and Leon Klenicki, 38–61. New York: Paulist, 1979.

Dupuy, Bernard. "What Meaning Has the Fact that Jesus was Jewish for the Christian?" In *Christians and Jews*, edited by Hans Kung and Walter Kasper, Concilium: Religion in the Seventies 98, 73–79. New York: Seabury, 1974.

Durham, John I. *Exodus*. Word Biblical Commentary 3. Waco, TX: Word, 1987.

Eichorn, David Max, ed. *Conversion to Judaism: A History and Analysis*. New York: KTAV, 1965.

Elliot, M. A. *The Survivors of Israel: A Reconsideration of the Theology of Pre-Christian Judaism*. Grand Rapids: Ee Hirschrdmans, 2000.

Ellison, Harry L. *Exodus*. Philadelphia, PA: Westminster. 1982.

Epstein, Isidore, ed. *The Babylonian Talmud*. London: Soncino, 1967.

Epstein, Lawrence J. "A Religious Argument for Welcoming Converts." *Judaism: A Quarterly Review* 40.2 (1991) 217–20.

Estrin, Daniel. "Rabbinic Text or Call to Terror?" *The Jewish Daily Forward*, online edition, January 20, 2010. http://forward.com/articles/123925/rabbinic-text-or-call-to-terror/.

Falk, Avner. *Anti-Semitism: A History and Psychoanalysis of Contemporary Hatred*. Westport, CT: Praeger, 2008.

Falk, Henry. *Jesus the Pharisee—a New Look at the Jewishness of Jesus*. Mahwah, NJ: Paulist, 1985.

Fischer, John. "Messianic Congregations Should Exist and Be Very Jewish: A Response to Arnold Fruchtenbaum." In *How Jewish is Christianity? Two Views on the Messianic Jewish Movement*, edited by Louis Goldberg, 129–39. Grand Rapids: Zondervan, 2003.

Fisher, Eugene J. "A Commentary on the Texts: Pope John Paul II's Pilgrimage of Reconciliation." In Pope John Paul II, *Spiritual Pilgrimage: Texts on Jews and Judaism 1979–1995*, edited by Eugene J. Fisher and Leon Klenicki, xx–xxxix. New York: Crossroad, 1995.

———. "Nostra Aetate." In *A Dictionary of Jewish-Christian Relations*, edited by Edward Kessler and Neil Wenborn, 320–21. Cambridge: Cambridge University Press, 2005.

Freedman, David N. "An Essay on Jewish Christianity" [1969]. Reprinted in *Divine Commitment and Human Obligation: Selected Writings of David Noel Freedman*, vol. 1: *Ancient Israelite History and Religion*. Grand Rapids: Eerdmans, 1997.

French, Ray, Charlotte Rayner, Gary Rees, and Sally Rumbles. *Organizational Behaviour*. Hoboken, NJ: Wiley, 2008.

Fretheim, Terence E. *Exodus*. Louisville: Westminster John Knox, 1991.

Frost, Robert. "Mountain Interval." New York: Henry Holt and Company, 1920; Bartleby.com, 1999. www.bartleby.com/119/.

Fruchtenbaum, Arnold G. *Hebrew Christianity: Its Theology, History, and Philosophy*. Seventh Printing. Tustin, CA: Ariel Ministries, 1995.

———. *Israelology: The Missing Link in Systematic Theology*. Rev ed. Tustin, CA: Ariel Ministries, 2001.

———. "Messianic Congregations May Exist Within the Body of Messiah as Long as They Don't Function Contrary to the New Testament." In *How Jewish is Christianity? Two Views on the Messianic Jewish Movement*, edited by Louis Goldberg, 109–28. Grand Rapids: Zondervan, 2003.

Frymer-Kensky, Tikva, et al., eds. *Christianity in Jewish Terms*. Boulder, CO: Westview, 2000.

Gaebelein, Arno C. "The Present Day Apostasy." In *The Coming Kingdom of Christ*. Chicago: The Moody Colportage Association, 1914.

Gaston, Lloyd. *Paul and the Torah*. Eugene, OR: Wipf & Stock, 2006, 92.

Gill, David, ed. *Gathered for Life: Official report, Sixth Assembly, World Council of Churches.* Geneva: WCC, 1983.

Gillet, Lev. *Communion in the Messiah: Studies in the Relationship between Judaism and Christianity.* London: Lutterworth, 1942.

Glaser, Mitch. "Personal Reflections on the 3rd Global Lausanne Consultation on World Evangelization, Cape Town, South Africa, October 17–24, 2010: Challenges and Disappointments." http://lcje.net/High%20Leigh/Monday,%20 August%208/13%20Personal%20Reflections%20on%The%203rd%Global%20 Lausannne%20Consultation%20on%20World%20Evangelization%20 Challenges%20andDisapppointments%20by%20Mitch%20Glaser.pddf.

———. "Towards a New Model for Jewish Evangelism in the 21st Century." A paper presented to the LCJE North America, April 2006.

Goldingay, John. *Theological Diversity and the Authority of the Old Testament.* Grand Rapids: Eerdmans, 1987.

Greenberg, Irving. *For the Sake of Heaven and Earth: The New Encounter Between Judaism and Christianity.* Philadelphia: The Jewish Publication Society, 2004.

Guder, Darrell L. *Be My Witnesses: The Church's Mission, Message, and Messengers.* Grand Rapids: Eerdmans, 1985.

Harink, Douglas. *Paul Among the Postliberals: Pauline Theology beyond Christendom and Modernity.* Grand Rapids: Brazos, 2003.

Hawthorne, Steven C. "The Story of His Glory." In *Perspectives on the World Christian Movement: A Reader,* edited by Ralph D. Winter and Steven C. Hawthorne. Pasadena CA: William Carey Library, 1999. PDF at www.waymakers.org/_files/ glory/StoryGlory.pdf.

Heil, John Paul. "From Remnant to Seed of Hope for Israel: Romans 9:26–29." *Catholic Biblical Quarterly* 64 (2002) 719–20.

Herberg, Will. "The 'Chosenness' of Israel and the Jew of Today." In *Arguments and Doctrines: A Reader of Jewish Thinking in the Aftermath of the Holocaust,* edited by Arthur Cohen, 270–83. New York: Harper & Row, 1970.

Hiebert, Paul. "Epistemological Foundations for Science and Theology." *Theological Students Fellowship Bulletin,* March 1985, 5–10.

———. "The Flaw of the Excluded Middle." *Missiology* 10, January 1982, 35–47.

———. "The Missiological Implications of an Epistemological Shift." *Theological Students Fellowship Bulletin* (May–June 1985) 12–18.

Hilborn, Rev. Dr. David, Head of Theology, Evangelical Alliance UK, Member, World Evangelical Alliance Theological Commission, reporting on the Porto Allegre Assembly of the WCC (2006). http://www.eauk.org/theology/wea/upload/ REPORT%20ON%20WCC%20ASSEMBLY.pdf.

Hirsch, Samson Raphael. *Nineteen Letters of Ben Uzziel.* Translated by Bernard Drachman. New York, 1942.

Holwerda, David E. *Jesus and Israel: One Covenant or Two?* Grand Rapids: Eerdmans, 1995.

Holy See. *Notes on the Correct Way to Present the Jews and Judaism in Preaching and Catechesis in the Roman Catholic Church.* Vatican, Commission For Religious Relations With The Jews, 1985, VI:1. http://www.vatican.va/roman_ curia/pontifical_councils/chrstuni/relations-jews-docs/rc_pc_chrstuni_ doc_19820306_jews-judaism_en.html.

Horn, Sam. "The Heart of Biblical Missions." Sharper Iron. http://www.sharperiron. org/2006/10/05/the-heart-of-biblical-missions/.

Horner, Barry E. *Future Israel: Why Christian Anti-Judaism Must Be Challenged.* Nashville: B & H Academic, 2007.

Isaac, Jules. *The Teaching of Contempt: Christian Roots of Anti-Semitism.* New York: Holt, Rinehart & Winston, 1964.

Jervell, Jacob. *The Unknown Paul: Essays on Luke-Acts and Early Christian History.* Minneapolis: Augsburg, 1984.

John Paul II. "Address to International Catholic-Jewish Liaison Committee on the Twentieth Anniversary of *Nostra Aetate* (October 28, 1985)." In *John Paul II on Jews and Judaism 1979–1986,* edited by Eugene J. Fisher and Leon Klenicki, 54–57. Washington, DC: Office of Publishing and Promotion Services United Catholic Conference, 1987.

————. "Address to the Jewish Community—West Germany (Nov 27. 1980)." In *Spiritual Pilgrimage: Texts on Jews and Judaism 1979–1995,* edited by Eugene J. Fisher and Leon Klenicki, 13–16. New York: Crossroad, 1995.

————. *Redemptor Hominis,* n.p. http://www.vatican.va/holy_father/john_paul_ii/encyclicals/documents/hf_jp-ii_enc_04031979_redemptor-hominis_en.html.

————. "To Delegates to the Meeting of Representatives of Episcopal Conferences and Other Experts in Catholic-Jewish Relations: Commission for Religious Relations with Judaism (3/6/82)." In *Spiritual Pilgrimage: Texts on Jews and Judaism 1979–1995,* edited by Eugene J. Fisher and Leon Klenicki, 17–20. New York: Crossroad, 1995.

Johnson, Dan G. "The Structure and Meaning of Romans 11." *Catholic Biblical Quarterly* 46.1 (1984) 91–103.

Johnson, Luke Timothy. *The Writings of the New Testament.* Philadelphia: Fortress, 1986.

Juster, Dan. "Do We Want the Jews to Disappear?" Tikkun International newsletter, January 2006. http://tikkunministries.org/newsletters/dj-jan06.php.

————. *Jewish Roots: A Foundation of Biblical Theology for Messianic Judaism.* Rockville, MD: Davar, 1986.

Kaminsky, Joel S. *Yet I Loved Jacob: Reclaiming the Biblical Concept of Election.* Nashville: Abingdon, 2007.

Kantorowicz, Ernst. *The King's Two Bodies: A Study in Medieval Political Theology.* Princeton, NJ: Princeton University Press, 1957.

Kauffman, Yehezkel. *Christianity and Judaism: Two Covenants.* Translated by C. W. Efroymson. Jerusalem: Magnes, 1988.

Kinzer, Mark S. *Israel's Messiah and the People of God: A Vision for Messianic Jewish Covenant Fidelity.* Edited by Jennifer M. Rosner. Eugene, OR: Cascade, 2011.

————. *Postmissionary Messianic Judaism: Redefining Christian Engagement with the Jewish People.* Grand Rapids: Brazos, 2005.

————. "Postmissionary Messianic Judaism, Three Years Later: Reflections on a Conversation Just Begun." Epilogue in Mark S. Kinzer, *Israel's Messiah and the People of God: A Vision for Messianic Jewish Covenant Fidelity,* 175–95. Eugene, OR: Wipf and Stock, 2011.

————. "Rejoinder to Responses to Post-Missionary Messianic Judaism." *Kesher: A Journal of Messianic Judaism* 20 (2006) 58–62. http://www.kesherjournal.com/Features/Rejoinder-to-Responses-to-Post-Missionary-Messianic-Judaism.

Kjaer-Hansen, Kai. *Joseph Rabinowitz and the Messianic Movement.* Grand Rapids: Eerdmans, 1995.

———. "What Do We Stand For? A Look at LCJE Statements 1980—2005." A paper presented at the Twenty-Fourth North American LCJE Meeting, San Antonio, Texas, April 16–18, 2007. http://www.lcje.net/Statements.html.

Klenicki, Leon. "On Christianity: Towards a Process of Historical and Spiritual Healing—Understanding the Other as a Person of God." In *Jews and Christians: Rivals or Partners for the Kingdom of God? In Search of an Alternative for the Theology of Substitution*, edited by Didier Pollefeyt, 62–94. Louvain: Peeters, 1997.

Klijn, A. F. J., and G. J. Reinink. *Patristic Evidence for Jewish-Christian Sects*. Leiden: Brill, 1973.

Kook, Zevi Yehudah. *Judaism and Christianity* [Hebrew]. Sifriyat Chava: Beit El, 2001.

Kravitz, Leonard. "The Covenant in Jewish Tradition: Historical Considerations." In *Issues in the Jewish Christian Dialogue: Jewish Perspectives on Covenant, Mission and Witness*, edited by Helga Croner and Leon Klenicki, 13–37. New York: Paulist, 1979.

Lakoff, George. *Don't Think of an Elephant! Know Your Values and Frame the Debate— The Essential Guide for Progressives*. White River Junction, VT: Chelsea Green, 2004.

Leman, Derek. "Judaism and New Testament Faith: Evaluating Mark Kinzer's Post-Missionary Messianic Judaism—A Chapter by Chapter Summary of Kinzer's Argument." A paper presented at the 2006 North American LCJE Conference. Pittsburgh, PA, April 2006.

Levenson, Jon. *Creation and the Persistence of Evil: The Jewish Drama of Divine Omnipotence*. San Francisco: Harper and Row, 1988.

Levertoff, Paul. *The Possibility of a Hebrew-Christian Church*. London: Conferences of Missionary Societies in Great Britain and Ireland, n.d.

Lindbeck, George. "Postmodern Hermeneutics and Jewish Christian Dialogue: A Case Study." In *Christianity in Jewish Terms*, edited by Tikva Frymer-Kensky et al., 106–13. Boulder, CO: Westview, 2000.

Lundström, Klas. "The Background and Emergence of the Lausanne Movement." Chapter 5 in *Gospel and Culture in the World Council of Churches and the Lausanne Movement with Particular Focus on the Period 1973–1996*, Studia Missionalia Svencana CIII, 181–204. Uppsala: Swedish Institute of Mission Research, 2006.

Lustiger, Cardinal Jean-Marie. *The Promise*. Grand Rapids: Eerdmans, 2007.

"The Manila Manifesto: An Elaboration of the Lausanne Covenant Fifteen Years Later (1989)." In *Making Christ Known: Historic Mission Documents from the Lausanne Movement, 1974–1989*, edited by John Stott, 242–43. Grand Rapids: Eerdmans, 1996.

McDonald, Martin Lee. "Anti-Judaism in the Early Church Fathers." In *Anti-Semitism and Early Christianity: Issues of Polemic and Faith*, edited by Craig A. Evans and Donald Hagner, 215–52. Minneapolis: Fortress, 1993.

Mendes, Henry Pereira. "Orthodox or Historical Judaism." In *The Dawn of Religious Pluralism: Voices from the World's Parliament of Religions, 1893*, edited with introductions by Richard Seager, 328–30. La Salle, IL: Open Court, 1993. Reprinted from Walter R. Hougton, ed., *Neely's History of the Parliament of Religions*, Chicago, 1894.

Mounce, Robert H. *The Book of Revelation*. Rev. ed. Grand Rapids: Eerdmans, 1998.

Newbigin, Lesslie. *The Gospel in a Pluralist Society*. Grand Rapids: Eerdmans, 1989.

———. *The Open Secret: An Introduction to the Theology of Mission.* Rev. ed. Grand Rapids: Eerdmans, 1995.

Novak, David. *The Election of Israel: The Idea of the Chosen People.* Cambridge: Cambridge University Press, 1995.

———. *Jewish-Christian Dialogue: A Jewish Justification.* New York: Oxford University Press, 1992.

———. "What to Seek and What to Avoid in Jewish-Christian Dialogue." In *Christianity in Jewish Terms*, edited by Tikva Frymer-Kensky et al., 1–6. Boulder, CO: Westview, 2000.

Osborne, Grant R. *The Hermeneutical Spiral: A Comprehensive Introduction to Biblical Interpretation.* Downers Grove, IL: InterVarsity, 1991.

Paton, David M., ed. *Breaking Barriers: Nairobi 1975.* London: SPCK, 1976.

Paul VI. *Lumen Gentium: Dogmatic Constitution on the Church.* Solemnly Promulgated by His Holiness Pope Paul VI on November 21, 1964. http://www.vatican.va/archive/hist_councils/ii_vatican_council/documents/vat-ii_const_19641121_lumen-gentium_en.html.

Pawlikowski, John T. "Antisemitism." In *A Dictionary of Jewish-Christian Relations*, edited by Edward Kessler and Neil Wenborn, 22–24. Cambridge: Cambridge University Press, 2005.

Peace, Richard. *Conversion in the New Testament: Paul and the Twelve.* Grand Rapids: Eerdmans, 1999.

Perlman, Susan. "Eschatology and Mission: A Jewish Missions Perspective." *International Bulletin of Missionary Research* 33.3 (July 2009) 115–18.

Peters, Joan. *From Time Immemorial: The Origins of the Arab-Jewish Conflict over Palestine.* New York: Harper & Row, 1984. Reprinted Chicago: JKAP, 2001.

Piper, John. *Let the Nations Be Glad! The Supremacy of God in Missions.* 2nd ed. Grand Rapids: Baker Academic, 2003.

Pitre, Brant. *Jesus, the Tribulation, and the End of the Exile: Restoration Eschatology and the Origin of the Atonement.* Grand Rapids: Baker Academic, 2006.

Prager, Dennis. "Judaism Seeks Converts: Part Two of Jews Must Seek Converts—or Become Irrelevant." *Ultimate Issues: A Quarterly Journal* 7.1 (January–March 1991) 3–4.

Quiñones, Jorge. "Paul Phillip Levertoff: Pioneering Hebrew-Christian Scholar and Leader." *Mishkan* 37 (2002) 21–34. http://files.meetup.com/598889/levertoff.pdf.

Rees, Neal. "Snatch Others from the Fire and Save Them: An Examination of Belief in Hell as a Motivating Factor in Missions." Unpublished paper, originally submitted as a term paper to William Carey International University, at http://web.archive.org/web/20050228025757/perso.wanadoo.es/neil/Hell.htm.

Rentenbach, Barb. *Synergy.* Bloomington, IN: Author House, 2009.

Robinson, Rich. "The Challenge of Our Messianic Movement, Part 2." *Havurah*, vol. 6, no, 3, July 31, 2003. https://www.jewsforjesus.org/publications/havurah/6_3/challenge2.

Rosenbloom, Joseph R. *Conversion to Judaism: From the Biblical Period to the Present.* Cincinnati, OH: Hebrew Union College Press, 1978.

Rudolph, David J. "Messianic Jews and Christian Theology: Restoring an Historical Voice to the Contemporary Discussion." *Pro Ecclesia* 14.1 (2005) 58–84.

Sacks, Jonathan. *The Dignity of Difference: How to Avoid the Clash of Civilizations.* London: Continuum, 2002; Rev. ed. London: Continuum, 2003.

Sarna, Nahum B. *Exodus.* Jewish Publication Society Torah Commentary. Philadelphia: Jewish Publication Society, 1991.

Schwartz, Seth. *Imperialism and Jewish Society from 200 B.C.E. to 640 C.E.* Princeton, NJ: Princeton University Press, 2001.

Seder Olam Rabbah Vezuta. Translated by Henry Falk, in *Jesus the Pharisee—a New Look at the Jewishness of Jesus.* Mahwah, NJ: Paulist, 1985.

Seltzer, Robert M. "Joining the Jewish People from Biblical to Modern Times." In *Pushing the Faith: Proselytism and Civility in a Pluralistic World*, edited by Martin E. Marty and Frederick Greenspahn, 41–63. New York: Crossroads, 1988.

Sigal, Phillip. "Early Christian and Rabbinic Liturgical Affinities: Exploring Liturgical Acculturation." *New Testament Studies* 30, no. 1 (1984) 63–90.

Soncino Talmud, Mac OS X version. Institute for Computers in Jewish Life and Davka Corporation, 2007.

Soulen, R. Kendall. *The God of Israel and Christian Theology.* Philadelphia: Fortress, 1996.

———. "The Grammar of the Christian Story." *The Institute*, vol. 10, Autumn 2000, http://www.icjs.org/news/vol10/soulenrevised.html.

———. "Supersessionism." In *A Dictionary of Jewish-Christian Relations*, edited by Edward Kessler and Neil Wenborn, 413. Cambridge: Cambridge University Press, 2005.

Stackhouse, John G., Jr., ed. *What Does It Mean to Be Saved? Broadening Evangelical Horizons About Salvation.* Grand Rapids: Baker Academic, 2002.

Stern, David L. *Jewish New Testament Commentary: A Companion Volume to the Jewish New Testament.* Clarksville, MD: Messianic Jewish Resources International, 1996.

———. "Torah." In *Messianic Jewish Manifesto*, 3rd ed., 125–58. Clarksville, MD: Messianic Jewish, 1997.

Stott, John R. W., ed. *Making Christ Known: Historic Mission Documents from the Lausanne Movement, 1974—1989.* Grand Rapids: Eerdmans, 1997.

Stott, John R. W. *The Message of Acts: The Spirit, the Church, and the World.* The Bible Speaks Today. Downers Grove, IL: InterVarsity, 1994.

Tiessen, Terrance L. *Who Can Be Saved? Reassessing Salvation in Christ and World Religions.* Downers Grove, IL: InterVarsity, 2004.

Toward Jerusalem Council II. "What is TJCII?" http://www.tjcii.org.

Van Engen, Charles. *Mission on the Way: Issues in Mission Theology.* Grand Rapids: Baker, 1996.

Van Rheenen, Gailyn. "Changing Motivations for Missions: From 'Fear of Hell' to 'the Glory of God.'" In *The Changing Face of World Missions: Engaging Contemporary Issues and Trends*, edited by Michael Pocock, Gailyn van Rheenen, and Douglas McConnell, 161–81. Grand Rapids: Baker Academic, 2005.

Verkuyl, Johannes. *Contemporary Missiology: An Introduction.* Grand Rapids: Eerdmans, 1978.

Vicedom, Georg. *The Mission of God: An Introduction to the Theology of Mission.* Translated by G. A. Thiele and D. Hilgendorf. St. Louis: Concordia, 1963.

Visser t' Hooft, Willem. *Memoirs.* 2nd ed. Geneva: WCC Publications, 1987.

Webster's Third New International Dictionary. Springfield, MA: Merriam-Webster, 1986.

"What Is SR? Gateways to Scriptural Reasoning." *Journal of Scriptural Reasoning* Forum website. http://etext.lib.virginia.edu/journals/jsrforum/gateways.html.

"What is TJCII?" http://www.tjcii.org/what-is-toward-jerusalem-council-ii.htm.

White, Eric Charles. *Kaironomia: On the Will-to-Invent*. Ithaca, NY: Cornell University Press, 1987.

Wilson, Todd A. "The Law of Christ and the Law of Moses: Reflections on a Recent Trend in Interpretation." *Current Issues in Biblical Research* 5 (2006) 123–44. http://cbi.sagepub.com/cgi/reprint/5/1/123.

Wright, Christopher J. H. *The Mission of God: Unlocking the Bible's Great Narrative.* Downers Grove, IL: IVP Academic, 2006.

———. "A Christian Approach to Old Testament Prophecy Concerning Israel." In *Jerusalem Past and Present in the Purposes of God,* edited by P. W. L. Walker, 1–19. Cambridge: Tyndale House, 1992.

Wright, N[icholas] T[homas]. *The Climax of the Covenant: Christ and the Law in Pauline Theology*. Minneapolis: Fortress, 1991.

———. "Jerusalem in the New Testament." In *Jerusalem Past and Present in the Purposes of God*, 53–77. Cambridge: Tyndale House, 1992.

———. *Jesus and the Victory of God*. Minneapolis: Augsburg/Fortress, 1997.

———. "The Messiah and the People of God: A Study in Pauline Theology with Particular Reference to the Argument of the Epistle to the Romans." DPhil diss., University of Oxford, 1980.

———. "Paul's Gospel and Caesar's Empire." In *Paul and Politics: Ekklesia, Israel, Imperium, Interpretation: Essays in Honor of Krister Stendahl,* edited by Richard A. Horsley, 160–83. Harrisburg, PA: 2000.

———. "Romans and the Theology of Paul." In *Pauline Theology*, vol. 3: *Romans,* edited by David M. Hay and E. Elizabeth Johnson, 30–67. Minneapolis: Fortress, 1995.

———. *What Saint Paul Really Said: Was Paul of Tarsus the Real Founder of Christianity?* Grand Rapids: Eerdmans, 1997.

Wyschogrod, Michael. *The Body of Faith: God and the People Israel.* Northvale, NJ: Aronson, 1996.

———. "Israel, the Church and Election." In *Abraham's Promise: Judaism and Jewish-Christian Relations,* edited by R. Kendall Soulen, 179–87. Grand Rapids: Eerdmans, 2004.

Yoder, John Howard. *The Jewish-Christian Schism Revisited.* Edited by Michael G. Cartwright and Peter Ochs. Grand Rapids: Eerdmans, 2003.

Index

CPSIA information can be obtained
at www.ICGtesting.com
Printed in the USA
FSHW011253290420
69746FS